The Word of Love

The Word of Love

Preaching in the Ministry of

STEPHEN ELKINS-WILLIAMS

THE WORD OF LOVE
PREACHING IN THE MINISTRY OF STEPHEN ELKINS-WILLIAMS

iUniverse books may be ordered through booksellers or by contacting:

iUniverse
1663 Liberty Drive
Bloomington, IN 47403
www.iuniverse.com
1-800-Authors (1-800-288-4677)

ISBN: 978-1-4917-7300-0 (sc)
ISBN: 978-1-4917-7345-1 (hc)
ISBN: 978-1-4917-7344-4 (e)

Print information available on the last page.

iUniverse rev. date: 08/06/2015

*This volume is lovingly dedicated
to the faithful people of the Chapel of the Cross,
past, present and future.*

Contents

For whosoever shall call upon the name of the Lord shall be saved. How then shall they call on him in whom they have not believed? and how shall they believe in him of whom they have not heard? and how shall they hear without a preacher? and how shall they preach, except they be sent? as it is written, How beautiful are the feet of them that preach the gospel of peace, and bring glad tidings of good things!

Romans 10:13-15, *King James Version*

There is in these sermons of the Reverend Stephen Elkins-Williams a deep wisdom clearly born of the creative mixture of human life really lived in and by the light and love of God. Archbishop Desmond Tutu speaks of this creative and miracle-generating relationship when, paraphrasing St. Augustine of Hippo, he says of the realization of God's dream in and for the world:

By himself, God won't,
By ourselves, we can't,
But together with God, we can!
These sermons could well be titled, *Together With God, We Can!*

The ancient doctrine of the Council of Chalcedon teaches the miracle that Jesus is the fruit of the perfect union and communion of the Divine and the human. So the miracle of a new and better world, the miracle of human life truly lived, finds its true genesis in that sometimes wonderful, sometimes elusive, but ever-real miracle of the divine and human working together in human life. *Together with God, we can!*

After a painful period in the life of the congregation, when funds were embezzled and spirits were low, Stephen preached a sermon facing the reality of sin, the complexity of motives, and the sheer power of the capacity of forgiveness to redeem the past by creating a new future. *Together with God, we can!*

In a sermon on taking the yoke of Christ (Matthew 11:29), preached on the 30th anniversary of his ordination as a priest and his 20th anniversary as rector of the Chapel of the Cross, he said "freedom as an absence of service and commitment is an illusion." True life is to be lived not for purposes of the self alone or primarily, but for the greater purposes of the God who is the author of life itself. *Together with God, we can!*

In another sermon, Stephen interpreted the teaching of Jesus this way: Those who follow in his way are "the salt of the earth" and "the light of the world," even when their lives fall far short of enhancing the world's flavor or illuminating God's dream. Quoting the wise words of another, he said in that sermon, "We call you, not what you presently are, but what we know you are becoming." As the saying goes, "God's not finished with us yet." For, as he says in another sermon, quoting Thomas Merton, "Souls are like wax waiting for the seal." Indeed, *together with God, we can!*

These are sermons in which the wisdom of God crosses the "crowded ways of life," as that old hymn says. "Easter is for the broken-hearted," Stephen says. There's no prosperity Gospel here, but rather the full-blooded Gospel of a real God involved in real human life, a real world of both beauty and ugliness, nobility and depravity, goodness and guns, grit and glory. Here, in these sermons, we catch a glimpse of the risen and living Jesus who, as Richard Holloway, the former Primus of the Episcopal Church of Scotland, once wrote, "*goes on breaking out of all the tombs into which we have consigned him.*" This is the God who, as Stephen's young daughter-in-law said to his son when he had to go on a perplexing journey, "I will go with you."

By himself, God won't,
By ourselves, we can't,
But together with God, we can!

The Rt. Rev. Michael B. Curry
XI Bishop of North Carolina
XXVII Presiding Bishop of the Episcopal Church

When the family of the Chapel of the Cross sets its collective mind, heart and hands to something, it's always done well, and I am most grateful for the very idea that the parish should publish some of my preaching.

I want to thank Ted Vaden and the celebration committee — Laurie Alexander, Alice Cotten, Katherine Kopp, Nancy McGuffin, Pat Phelan, David Ross and Kim Sullivan — for proofreading, key decisions and moral support; David Frazelle, Vicky Jamieson-Drake and Tammy Lee for their special help in the selections; Walker Mabe for her marketing direction and overall guidance; Phil Meyer for consultation on publishing; Eugene Dauchert for legal consultation; Travis Powers for a steady hand with information technology; Jerry Cotten, Ted Pratt, Lance Richardson and Jason Smith for the wonderful photography; Kate Anthony for her keen eye on the cover design; Kyle Highsmith for permission to use his stunning portrait of the church and chapel, and especially David Brown as the dedicated editor.

Stephen Elkins-Williams

One of the gifts of working in a large parish is that you get to hear a variety of sermons from your colleagues. I have been blessed to hear almost 22 years worth of Steve Elkins-Williams sermons and read all those preached since his institution as rector 30 years ago. If I happened to have missed a given Sunday in my 22 years here, I always found my way to the back of the chapel or church to pick up a printed copy (if there's one left), or made sure I pulled it up on the website to listen.

Many folks tell me they have done the same or taken the copies home and tucked them away in their Bibles where they have saved everything that matters to them. I have done it because when Steve preaches I always learn something that changes my understanding of God and/or the practice of faith. I have always attributed this to his capacity as one of the first teachers of the faith. All those years of Jesuit education shaped his soul so that we as Episcopalians are the beneficiaries of his many gifts!

Many of us sat riveted as he preached a sermon on forgiveness in the aftermath of the embezzlement by a trusted employee. Steve stood before the congregation and, in a moment of great vulnerability, said, "sometimes you just have to want to want to forgive first," noting how some situations are significant enough to make forgiveness a process. I cannot tell you how many times I have shared this concept with folks who have sat in my office struggling with similar issues.

I have learned from him the complexity and the accessibility of the doctrines represented in the major feast days of the Church, including the most difficult of the six, the Trinity. Because of the perplexing doctrine, a wise or cunning parishioner endowed a fund at the Chapel of the Cross so that the rector is required to preach on it every Trinity Sunday as a condition of his salary!

During his tenure Steve has done it exceptionally well, and one sermon in particular highlighted the Trinity as community, using differing examples from the Church Fathers. Each illustration showed the cooperation and community of all Persons of the Trinity, reminding us, as Augustine once said, "that explaining it may well be as challenging as pouring water from the ocean onto the sand in hopes of emptying the ocean!"

I have heard 21 Easter sermons, including "The Moving on Movers" which taught me about the value of everyday images to capture the listener's imagination for God. As most insightful preachers know, there is no richer landscape than that of ordinary life to craft an extraordinary message bearing God's intention for the people who have gathered in worship and to listen for the "word of the Lord."

What has been most meaningful for me is reading *all* of Steve's sermons, including those prior to my arrival in 1993. Turning the pages and hearing God's word spoken and heard felt as if I were a keeper of the Chapel of the Cross' salvation history. A mark of a good sermon is whether it is dated or stands the test of time for the community in which it was written. As you read these sermons you will find them speaking truth to you now as if they had been penned yesterday. The sermons are filled with wonderful stories, tapping deeply into the well of emotions, passions and feelings even as they represent the fullness of sacramental, personal and parish life.

Steve's Christmas sermon in 1988, showing the power of the incarnation as strength made perfect in weakness, left me in tears as I read it in 2015.

I have learned most powerfully from Steve when he moves into the pulpit during sacramental rites of passage, our incarnational moments, be they funerals, weddings or baptisms. His command of "the outward and visible signs of inward and spiritual grace as a sure and certain means of God's grace" is never more evident than when he is called on to preside during these moments when heaven and earth have stopped for those present as the Holy breaks into the ordinary, making it extraordinary in its meaningfulness. He preached at his son's wedding, a longtime parishioner's, and my own. He presided over the pulpit as he buried his in-laws, his former wardens, and a beloved Carolina basketball coach. He reminded us that the only death that matters is the one we die at our own baptism, as he baptized his first grandson. He also presided during significant moments of parish transition, be it our 150th anniversary or the dedication of our new buildings in 1993 and 2014.

Preaching is one of the most meaningful, challenging and humbling acts of ministry. We approach it with fear and trembling — and always great preparation — listening for what God would have us say to the faithful, seeking community of God gathered. Steve begins every sermon by saying "In the name of the Father and of the Son and of the Holy Spirit." And so, we begin this book with the same. In the fullness of that Trinitarian formula we are reminded, "The Word is always very near to us. It is in our hearts and minds and on our lips." The Word being nothing short of God's incarnate love and, by virtue of his grace, the written word of these sermons.

The Reverend Tambria Elizabeth Lee
Chapel Hill, North Carolina
July 6, 2015

I

More than We Can
Ask or Imagine:
The Life of the
Chapel of the Cross

My Grace Is Sufficient for You
The Sixth Sunday after Pentecost
July 7, 1985

Most of you know, I am sure, that the scripture readings which we hear each Sunday are not the arbitrary choice of the rector, but that they are part of a lectionary (shared by the Episcopal Church with a number of other Christian denominations) which assigns specific readings for each Sunday on a three-year cycle. At least I hope you know that. Otherwise you will think it quite pretentious of me to have chosen for my first Sunday as rector the Gospel passage about a prophet not being without honor except in his own country. Worse yet, you might be feeling quite defensive about the Old Testament reading which describes, in the first person, a prophet being sent to an impudent and stubborn people!

I promise you that I did not choose these readings, but that they are the ones assigned for Year B, Proper 9, "The Sunday closest to July 6," last read here on July 4, 1982. For those who are struck by such things, that happens to be the very Sunday upon which Betsy and I came, incognito, to the 10 o'clock service to see what Chapel of the Cross was like. At any rate, let me assure you that I do not consider you an impudent and stubborn people who refuse to hear (although I realize that there may be times in the future when that may be a tempting assessment); so I am not even opting for interpreting these readings as being providentially chosen for this Sunday.

I do, however, find a providential message for us in the Epistle; one which I would like us to reflect on together for a few moments on this Sunday when we, as rector and people, are beginning a new chapter in this parish's ministry. That message is God's words to Paul, which today God addresses to us, "My grace is sufficient for you, for my power is made perfect in weakness."

I, for one, need desperately to let those words sink deep into my soul. While I begin my tenure as rector with a great deal of enthusiasm and excitement, I also feel no small amount of anxiety and doubt about my

3

ability to handle such a responsibility. And while so many of you have expressed to me your confidence about the future of Chapel of the Cross, I know that there is some measure of anxiety among us about what the future holds and what changes may be in store.

So I think it quite providential indeed that we hear God say his sentence to us today: "My grace is sufficient for you, my power is made perfect in weakness." Let's look at that in two sections.

"My grace is sufficient for you" serves as both a reminder for us, and an assurance. It is a reminder to us that God, and not we ourselves, must be our focus. "Grace," God's grace, i.e., God's love, God's help, God's strength, God's power, is what we must rely on, not our own ability. Like Peter walking on the stormy waves, the second we look to ourselves for strength, we will sink. Our ministry at Chapel of the Cross will flourish to the extent that we rely on God's grace.

In fact, God must be so much the focus of our lives that we do not consider it "our" ministry in any possessive sense. It is certainly not "my" ministry as rector, nor in an important sense is it "your" ministry. What we must be engaged in together is God's ministry.

I am not speaking in the same way here as do some pretentious and insecure television preachers who characterize whatever they are doing at the moment as "God's ministry." I am talking about an acknowledgment that we are not here simply to "do our own thing," nor to make a name for ourselves, nor to create for ourselves an insulated, comfortable environment. We are here to carry on God's work.

It is God's ministry that we must be concerned about, the work that he would have us do. It is not our reputation or comfort or security which must be our focus, but God himself. "My grace is sufficient for you" reminds us, then, of that focus, but it also assures us in the midst of our anxieties that God is enough for us. No matter what we may be asked to take on, no matter what may come our way, God promises us that he will be enough for us. Nothing can overcome us, not new rectors, not changes in the Church, not difficult responsibilities, not our own impudence and stubbornness, not even death itself. "My grace is sufficient for you."

"For," God's words to Paul and now to us go on, "my power is made perfect in weakness." That is a bit harder pill to swallow. It butts so hard against the world's values, which we are all so steeped in. Who among us wants to be weak? We want to be strong, self-reliant, independent, competent, capable. To be weak that God may make me strong? That's for those who cannot make it on their own. To boast of our weaknesses as a parish that the power of Christ may rest upon us? That's for parishes with less resources than we.

For when I am weak, then I am strong? We have great difficulty accepting that truth into our lives with any degree of depth or integrity. And yet we are touching on the heart of the Christian message here, that which Jesus lived out in his birth, life, and especially his death and resurrection; that which Jesus taught over and over again: "Whoever would be great among you must be your servant," "Unless you become like little children, you shall not enter the kingdom of heaven," "The one who loses his life will save it."

Jesus is not extolling incompetence here. He is not urging us to be childish, nor witless, nor a passive, passionless burden upon others. What he is holding up to us is the simple truth that without God we can do nothing, that it is God who works in us and not we ourselves as we imagine, that we must die that Christ can live in us.

When we are weak, when we find ourselves stretched beyond our comfortable limits, when we allow God to lead us where we would rather not go, then is God's power made perfect in us. When we are weak, we are more pliable, less resistant, less stubborn and impudent, because we are forced to rely on God and not on ourselves. When we are weak, because of God's grace, then we are strong.

Let us, then, as rector and people embarking on a new segment of the ministry entrusted to us, allow these words to penetrate deep into our hearts. May the focus of our lives, both as individuals and as a parish, become increasingly centered on God and not on ourselves. May our vision, for our parish and what we are to be about, be shaped less by the world and more by God's Word, so that we strive not so much to be a successful parish as a faithful parish. And in the midst of our anxieties and worries about our capability and strength, let us draw on the words of God to Paul and today to us, "My grace is sufficient for you, for my power is made perfect in weakness." Amen.

Ezekiel 2: 1-7
II Corinthians 12:2-10
Mark 6:1-6

Continuing the Ministry and the Financial Struggle
The Twenty-Second Sunday after Pentecost
October 19, 1986

When I settled with the Every Member Canvass chairman some four or five months ago on October 19 as the Sunday on which I would preach on financial stewardship, I had no idea that this date marks the 138th anniversary of the consecration of our chapel. That choice has turned out to be a providential one; for, even though the 138th anniversary is not a particularly significant one (I imagine that we will "do it up big" on this date 12 years from now, in 1998), still it is an anniversary, a time to be renewed and to learn about one's roots.

And so I was led back to the written records of this parish, and I found there an inspirational story of a people of faith, of their struggle to establish this parish and to be faithful servants of God, and of how that struggle was inextricably bound up in a financial struggle as well.

Two incidents in that history particularly struck me: One concerned the very building of the chapel, and the other occurred on the 100th anniversary of its consecration, some 38 years ago.

In May of 1842, 26 people under the leadership of the Rev. William Mercer Green, a professor at the University, formed themselves into a "Congregation of Christian people to be known by the name of the Church of the Atonement, Chapel Hill, N.C." and agreed to "adopt and be governed by the constitution and canons of the Episcopal Church in these United States." A year later, the building of the church, which we now refer to as our chapel, was begun, and in a year's time it was three-fourths completed. But it was to remain unfinished for four more years because $1,200 was still needed. On May 24, 1846, Bishop Levi Silliman Ives officiated in the University Chapel in the morning and at a private house in the evening. He later wrote, "When I observed around me a large congregation crowded together in a most inconvenient manner in a private home, numbers for want of room having been forced away, and recollected that within two or three hundred yards there stood a beautiful Gothic edifice, which a few hundred dollars would open to the wants of the people, I felt mortified and humbled for our spiritual indifference."

But the money was finally raised, and on this day in 1848, Bishop Ives officiated at the consecration of the House of Worship, which he called the "Chapel of the Holy Cross," but which quickly became known as the Chapel of the Cross. "This act gives me particular satisfaction," he said, "as the completion of the hopes and prayers of a most valued brother (meaning Mr. Green), and also as a work promising in itself most essential advantages to the Diocese" (referring to the importance of what we now call campus ministry and its effect on the entire state). Some 100 years (and a few months) later, a great celebration was held here, marking that earlier occasion. Some of our present parishioners were part of that celebration. I have read the addresses given by the Rt. Rev. Edwin A. Penick, bishop at that time, and Dr. Archibald Henderson, who both gave thoughtful comments on the history of this place.

But I was most struck by the words of Professor William Wells, then senior warden, who looked to the future, and spoke on "The Needs of the Parish Today."

"This commemoration," he said, "is not merely a courteous acknowledgment to history. Today we make a rededication of the parish and of ourselves to the faith shown here. A tradition is significant not only because it has a past but also because it is alive: it breathes the air of succeeding generations and lives by virtue of their continuing accomplishments."

He went on to say:

"We are aware of the fear which benumbed the parish during the darkness of the Reconstruction period. Perhaps fear is the greatest obstacle the church has had to surmount except one — complacency. We pause today to look with satisfaction on the achievement of other generations. We must not accept it with complacence as our own. Rather, the tradition of this place requires us to receive that achievement as a signpost pointing into the future. The continual growth of the university community must be reflected in the increase of numbers of communicants; but numbers of themselves have never made a parish strong. The strength of a parish is best gauged by how many of those enrolled in the parish regard their memberships as active rather than honorary."

Professor Wells went on to imply that part of being an active member involved contributing significantly to the parish, because he then stated the need for $3,700 for the "renovation of the church buildings and equipment (which) is pressing."' And in fact the listing of the order of service shows that his address preceded the Offering. It is interesting to note that Professor Wells' connection between being an active member and contributing is explicitly stated in The Book of Common Prayer, in the Catechism (p. 856): "The duty of all Christians is to follow Christ; to come together week by week for corporate worship; and to work, pray, and give for the spread of the kingdom of God." After listing some specific needs of the renovation, Professor Wells ended his address by saying, "These are but a few of the material improvements we may seek; their achievement can in some measure symbolize the faith which gives to this memorial its significance."

These stories, this bit of our history, is enlightening and moving to me, as I hope it is to you. We stand in the line of that tradition. We are now the "congregation of Christian people" in this place, charged with carrying on Christ's ministry as those who have gone before us were, and we share in the same financial struggles, both as a parish and as individuals, as they did.

What has changed today is the scale of things: The numbers, both of people and dollars, have grown much larger. And the scope of our ministry has mushroomed: The outreach of this parish, which is still first and foremost to the University (which just celebrated its 193rd birthday last Sunday), has been widening to meet the needs of a burgeoning community and an increasingly complex world; the number and variety of worship services have increased dramatically; the education program has kept pace with the increase both of numbers of people and variety of needs; and the pastoral needs of our people have grown, not only proportionately with the increase of membership, but frequently qualitatively, because larger numbers often bring less sense of being cared for.

What has not changed today is the financial need that the parish found itself in in 1848 and in 1948 and now in 1986. A few facts about our situation today are these: Although we have run small operating surpluses the last three years, we did so only because of clergy vacancies. In 1985, our deficit would have been over $20,000 if a rector would have been in place for the entire year. This year we seem certain to have a deficit of that size. Despite having over 1,000 communicants, many of whom are single, we have far fewer than 500 pledges. Our average pledge (which is admittedly a very limited statistic since it does not take into account an individual's circumstances, although it does give us some sense of our financial stewardship health) is $657. Encouragingly, that is up over $100 from 1985, but it is still $150 lower than the diocesan average of over $800.

The "bottom line" in all these statistics is this: The financial backing of the parish is not keeping pace with its expanding ministry. My simple, and I hope clear, message to you is this: If you are a participant in this parish and are in any position to do so, I encourage you to give generously and even sacrificially to the Chapel of the Cross (and to commit to that in the form of a pledge for 1987 if at all possible). We need to give in that measure for two reasons.

The first is that the ministry which was begun in this place 138 years ago, and which has been handed on to us, needs and demands our utmost financial support. We cannot reach out to this University community and beyond, we cannot worship together, we cannot proclaim and teach the Good News of God in Christ, we cannot effectively care for and pastor one another without adequate facilities and program resources, without staff, without sufficient funds to respond to needs beyond the parish.

The second reason is that we as individuals and as a community need to give freely in order to grow in faith. "Where your treasure is, there will your heart be also." If we are invested only in ourselves, our hearts will be stunted. If we give a significant proportion of our resources for the spread of the kingdom of God, our hearts will be there as well. Professor Wells' last thought — that the material improvements made possible by people's giving might "symbolize the faith which gives to this memorial its significance" — aims at that very thought.

The needs of the ministry of this parish and the needs of parishioners to grow in faith are both significant motives for us to pledge as much as we possibly can for the spread of the kingdom of God through this parish. On the 138th anniversary of the consecration of the Chapel of the Cross, let us make ours the statement of Professor William Wells, senior warden at the time of our 100th anniversary, "Today we make a rededication of the parish and of ourselves to the faith shown here." Amen.

Our Stained Glass Windows: God's Word in Imagery
The Fifth Sunday after Pentecost
July 12, 1987

Today's Gospel reading reminds us of the importance of a story, of using imagery, to make God's word come alive. Jesus tells a parable about a sower who sowed seed, employing some vivid imagery of thorns and birds and rocky ground. In doing so, he helps us to "hear and understand," that we might bear fruit 30-fold, 60-fold, and 100-fold.

This morning, I thought some images would also be helpful to us in hearing and understanding God's word to us that we might bear fruit, and I have in mind our stained glass windows, which are steeped in scripture, which beautifully and dramatically reveal God's word. Since they have just this week finished being restored and cleaned, I thought this would be a good time for us to examine what is really there.

In reading through the various historical accounts and records of the parish, I have been amazed to find no references to our stained glass windows. Aside from one reference to the fact that they were made by Percy Bacon and Brother in London, England, in the early 1920s when the church was built, they are not commented on. We do not know how the decisions were made regarding which scenes would be included, for example. It is quite clear, however, from looking at them, that the images and the scenes were chosen with great care, and with a particular sense of the mission of this parish, called the Chapel of the Cross, located in the midst of a university campus.

Let us begin with the back window. (Feel free to turn around and look or not as I talk. Pews are not the easiest thing to manuever in!) The back window is dominated by the middle portion of the center panel, which holds Jesus and Mary and Joseph. The center panel is just slightly wider and the middle section definitely longer than the top or the bottom, focusing our attention there. The scene is the birth of Jesus, of course, but here, Jesus is not lying in a manger, but upright on Mary's lap, extending his arms in an "orans" or praying (or what my sons call "the Lord be with you") position. Whether you see in that gesture an embracing of the world or a prefigurement of the crucifixion, or both, it is clear that the emphasis of the window is away from the sentimentalizing of Christmas and toward the reality of God giving himself to the world.

Mary holds a prominent position in this window, holding Jesus, and also some lilies, symbol of purity. Joseph is standing in the background; not an unusual place for him. He holds a staff, which is quite traditional, and a lantern.

On either side of the center panel are parallel scenes of the shepherds (on the right) and the wise men (on the left). There are three of each, one kneeling in the foreground and two standing. They face in toward Jesus, focusing our attention and the theological emphasis there.

Jesus already wears a crown, symbol both of being a king and of the victory of "martydom." The lamb, in front of Jesus, given prominence by being put in the center panel, does not just accompany the shepherds, but speaks of "the Lamb of God, which takes away the sin of the world," pointing to the cross and, as we will see in a moment, connecting it with the front window.

Undergirding all this nativity event is the solid foundation of the law and the prophets. On the bottom you see five figures. The middle one, which is slightly wider, remember, and therefore emphasized, is Moses holding the tablets of the Ten Commandments — symbol of the law, the revelation of God. Jesus is seen in the New Testament as the new Moses, as the fullness of God's revelation of himself. At the Transfiguration, for example, Jesus goes up on the mountain (like Moses did) and his face shines, and he is seen talking to Moses.

On either side of Moses are four Old Testament prophets: Isaiah, Jeremiah, Ezekiel and Daniel, a grouping that appears elsewhere in religious stained glass. Each of them hold symbols in their hands, mostly scrolls and scepters. Isaiah holds tongs with a burning coal, and Ezekiel holds a model of the Temple of Jerusalem.

13

At any rate, these five represent the law and the prophets which culminate in Jesus. Recall, for example, the story of the risen Jesus talking to the two disciples on the road to Emmaus. "Beginning with Moses and all the prophets, he interpreted to them in all the scriptures, the things concerning himself." (Luke 24:27)

In the bottom right hand corner, the point of the window is made clearer for us in the words, "The Word was made flesh." That also appears on the top of the window, along with clusters of grapes, referred to often in scripture, and various angels. The ones with the red wings are, I suppose, seraphim, who are regarded as "burning with love of God," and the others above them are cherubim. Both are spoken of in the Old Testament as surrounding the heavenly throne of God and singing God's praises.

At the very top of the window is a star, the one which appeared over Bethlehem, and out of its rays emanate a golden cross, which fills its quatrefoil. That cross, along with the crown and the outstretched arms of Jesus, and the lamb, proclaim that the Nativity, and this window, are not complete in themselves, but point to the victory of the cross, which is depicted in the front window.

Again, here, the center scene is dominant. Jesus is shown on the cross, although not much of the cross can be seen. The focus is on Jesus himself, already having died, his arms raised rather than perpendicular, as if in victory. Around his feet appear the words, "Behold the Lamb of God, which taketh away the sin of the world," pointed to by the rear window. In the bottom right hand corner are Jesus' own words, "It is finished," by which he refers not only to his death, but to the completion of the work his Father gave him to do. Both quotes are from John's Gospel.

On either side of Jesus stand Mary (on the left) and "the disciple whom Jesus loved," traditionally identified as John. The Gospel of John places them at the foot of the cross, which along with the quotes makes this a very Johannine scene. It is also worth noting that Mary is the only figure, besides Jesus, to appear twice in our windows.

Above Jesus, at the top of the window, are the letters "IHS," which are really the Greek letters, "iota, eta, sigma," the first three letters of Jesus' name in Greek, "iesus." Those letters are surrounded by a golden crown of thorns, again suggesting Jesus' triumph on the cross. On either side of that, a bit hard to see, (in black letters over gold on white) are an alpha and an omega (a capital "A" and an upside down horseshoe), the first and the last letters of the Greek alphabet, recalling Jesus' statement about being the alpha and the omega, the beginning and the end. Just above Jesus' head are the letters "INRI," the initials of the words Pilate had nailed at the top of the cross: "Jesus Nazarenus, Rex Judaeorum" — "Jesus of Nazareth, King of the Jews."

The side windows to this climactic scene are most remarkable choices. As near as I can tell, they appear, if at all, only rarely in the history of stained glass or Christian art. Both portray powerful, but little known, stories from the Acts of the Apostles, itself a powerful, but too often little known, book of the New Testament.

Both stories tell how the Gospel was proclaimed to those who did not know Jesus, and they say something to us in this parish about our mission to proclaim the Good News in this university community.

On the right side is Paul, preaching to the Athenians, and on the left side is Peter, speaking to some Romans. Both appear as dominant figures in their windows, standing with arms raised in speaking gestures. Both are facing Jesus, focusing us toward the center window, and also revealing their faith and theological focus, which those who have their backs to Jesus do not yet share.

I encourage you to read both of these stories and to pray over them. The one shown on the right is Acts 17:16-34. Paul is in Athens and he finds himself provoked in his spirit by the prevalence of idols. He begins to argue with anyone who will listen to him; so some of the Athenians, who loved novelty, take him to the Areopagus to hear him. And that is our scene.

So Paul, standing in the middle of the Areopagus, said, "Men of Athens, I perceive that in every way you are very religious. For as I passed along, and observed the objects of your worship, I found also an altar with the inscription, 'To an unknown god.' (You see the pedestal there with the

Greek words, "Agnosko Theo" on it. And the words "to the unknown god" appear at the top of the window.) What therefore you worship as unknown, this I proclaim to you. The God who made the world and everything in it, being Lord of heaven and earth, does not live in shrines made by man, nor is he served by human hands, as though he needed anything since he himself gives to all men life and breath "on all the face of the earth, having determined allotted Aperiods and the boundaries of their habitation, that they should seek God, in the hope that they might feel after him and find him. Yet he is not far from each one of us, for in him we live and move and have our being; as even some of your poets have said. For we are indeed his offspring."

I find that a powerful story to be constantly before us in stained glass. It is certainly apropos for us with our geographical and historical ties with this university, where, like Athens, knowledge is held supreme, and there is seeking and feeling after knowledge of all kinds. This window proclaims, and impels us to proclaim, that all our seeking will lead us to God, who is the "Lord of heaven and earth," as it says in the bottom right hand corner.

The parallel window on the left is the depiction of a scene from Chapter 10 of Acts, which tells a quite profound story in three parts. The first part tells of a devout centurion named Cornelius in prayer.

"About the ninth hour of the day he saw clearly in a vision an angel of God coming in and saying to him, "Cornelius." And he stared at him in terror, and said, "What is it, Lord?" And he said to him, "Your prayers and your alms have ascended as a memorial before God." (In recounting this conversation later in the chapter, Cornelius quotes the angel as saying, "Thy prayer is heard," which are the words at the top of the window). And now send men to Joppa, and bring one Simon who is called Peter; he is lodging with Simon a tanner, whose house is by the seaside.

"While they were on their way, Peter was praying on the housetop of Simon's house. And he became hungry and desired something to eat; but while they were preparing it, he fell into a trance and saw the heaven opened, and something like a great sheet, let down by four corners upon the earth. In it were all kinds of animals and reptiles and birds of the air. And there came a voice to him, "Rise, Peter; kill and eat." But Peter said, "No Lord; for I have never eaten anything that is common or unclean." And the voice came to him again a second time, "What God has cleansed, you must not call common." This happened three times, and the thing was taken up at once to heaven.

"Then the men from Cornelius arrived and Peter went back with them to Caesarea, where Cornelius and his kinsmen and close friends were waiting. After finding out that Cornelius also had a vision (and this is our scene), Peter said to them: Truly I perceive that God shows no partiality (or in the King James translation, "God is no respecter of persons," which appears in the bottom right hand corner of the window); but in every nation any one who fears him and does what is right is acceptable to him. (In retrospect, what a powerful theological foundation for the integration that happened in the South some three or four decades after this window was made). You know the word which he sent to Israel, preaching good news of peace by Jesus Christ (he is Lord of all), the word which was proclaimed throughout all Judea, beginning from Galilee after the baptism which John preached: how God anointed Jesus of Nazareth with the Holy Spirit and with power; how he went about doing good and healing all that were oppressed by the devil, for God was with him. And we are witnesses to all that he did both in the country of the Jews and in Jerusalem. They put him to death by hanging him on a tree; but God raised him on the third day and made him manifest; not to all the people but to us who were chosen by God as witnesses, who ate and drank with him after he rose from the dead. And he commanded us to preach to the people; and to testify that he is the one ordained by God to be judge of the living and the dead. To him all the prophets bear witness that every one who believes in him receives forgiveness of sins through his name."

There you have our stained glass windows. From the depiction of the prophets, to that of the Word made flesh, the victory of the cross, and the stories we have just heard, they are a proclamation of the God who loves us, who died for us, who offers salvation to all, who is no respecter of persons, and who need not be unknown. To him be all honor and glory, world without end. Amen.

One Call, One Lord, One Faith, One Baptism
150th Anniversary Celebration
May 16, 1992

I [Paul], a prisoner for the Lord, beg you to lead a life worthy of the calling to which you have been called, with all lowliness and meekness, with patience, forbearing one another in love, eager to maintain the unity of the Spirit in the bond of peace.

"... to maintain the unity of the Spirit..." All too frequently, life's events and conditions conspire against us to prevent our recognizing our unity in the Spirit. Our personal struggles, which seem to us unique, our pain and hurt, our failures and disappointments, all separate us from one another and convince us of the illusion of our isolation. Age gaps, gender gaps, racial gaps, economic gaps, generation gaps perpetuate this illusion and conceal from us the glorious truth proclaimed to us by the Gospel: that we are not alone, that the Spirit of God joins us together as one.

An event such as we celebrate today, the 150th anniversary of the founding of this parish, helps us to lay hold of that truth, to grasp the depth of its mystery, and to see its implications for our lives. For our unity in the Spirit extends not just to one another, whom we are to love with patience and eagerness, but also to those who have come before us and to those who will follow after us.

In preparation for this celebration, I have been reading through the Vestry minutes, which we still have from 1875 on, and other historical material. I have found that those who have preceded us in this parish had a number of things in common with us as well as some differences. A frequent item throughout the minutes, for an example of the former, is the election of someone to replace a vestryman, "who had removed from the parish." People moving away has been a constant part of life in Chapel Hill.

Many other things have not changed either. The minutes of June 19, 1934, which happen to have been taken by the rector, Mr. Lawrence, reflect some familiar themes: "Finances in rather bad shape. Receipts about $300 short of what [was] expected. ... Treasurer requested to send out notes in effort to collect money. Matter of leaks in the church was discussed." That was only nine years after this church was built!

Nor have there been any lack of controversial decisions made. The founding of the parish itself and the building of the chapel were controversial. Some in the University thought it divisive and sectarian for all students not to worship together in the University Chapel. In 1912, the controversy was whether to build a parish house and/or a rectory on the parish property; some felt that an additional building would hurt the University. After several parish meetings it was finally decided to build the parish house on the parish lot, but the rectory on the old rectory lot.

A few years later, the question of whether to build a bigger church was controversial not only in the parish, but beyond as well. A ringing editorial in an area newspaper spoke out against it. Having been tipped off by a female parishioner that the picturesque architecture of the chapel might be obscured by being built onto, the outraged writer concluded a long editorial by saying:

"Of course it is none of our business what the Episcopalians of Chapel Hill do to or with their building; but we can't resist the impulse to wish the recalcitrant sister who called the matter to our attention complete success in her opposition to the progress that would disturb a tendril of the ivy which clings to the little chapel, which is in itself a seven-day sermon more potent than any we ever remember having heard inside it."

On Wednesday evening at Evening Prayer, many of us heard Emmet Gribbin tell of the controversy that raged here when he was campus minister, 50 years ago, some 30 years after that editorial, between the "pro-ivy forces" and the "anti-ivy forces." Obviously the "anti-ivy forces," of which Emmet was a part, ultimately won out, but unfortunately for him, not until several years after he had left!

Besides regular parish controversies, another thing that has not changed is the cooperative spirit between what we now refer to as the downtown churches, manifest so generously to us during both last summer's and our present renovations. The minutes of April 30, 1917 reveal that the Vestry offered to the Presbyterian Church the use of both what we now call the chapel and the then-new parish house for use during the construction of the new Presbyterian Church.

But if some things have not changed, other things have. The minutes are full, for example, of rectors' resignations. Every year or two, it seemed, the Vestry would have to call a new rector, and frequently, several calls would be issued before one would be accepted. In 1887, for example, no less than nine calls were issued before the 10th choice, the Rev. R.E. Wright of Philadelphia, accepted. He, however, resigned after one week in the parish, saying that "the ways and customs of this diocese were so different from what he had been accustomed to that he did not think he would be able to do the good he would like in the parish." After an 11th call was declined, the 12th choice accepted and stayed for one year! Alfred Lawrence, who came in 1921, and who broke the mold by staying 23 years, was himself the sixth person called by that Vestry.

The Vestry not only spent a good deal of time calling rectors, they also had a rectory to worry about and maintain. The minutes of Sept. 7, 1884 reveal that "The Junior Warden was authorized to rent the Rectory to Mr. Charles Malone at $6.25 per month payable in advance." It goes on to say, "The Warden was directed to supply the parts of the Rectory Fence requiring renewal of Barbed Wire." This was apparently to protect gardens from the pigs who roamed freely in Chapel Hill!

Other vignettes from the minutes that show how parish life has changed include these: The minutes of June 26, 1898 state that after issuing a call to be rector to a man in Morganton (who subsequently declined it!) the Vestry "ordered that notices about bicycles be posted. On failure [of] bicyclists to give proper heed, it was decided that the church yard would be closed as to prevent its use as a bicycle path." On September 25, 1917, St. Hilda's Guild requested permission of the Vestry to give a fund-raising bridge party in the Parish House. "After considerable discussion" the request was granted. The minutes of six weeks later, however, state that "In view of the Bishop's objection to the use of the Parish House for card parties ... St. Hilda's Guild had withdrawn its request." It went on to say that "It is also the wish of the Bishop and his advisers that the Parish House be not used for dancing." Later, whether motion pictures could be shown in the parish house became the issue. And finally, I share with you this sentence from the minutes of the Vestry meeting of May 14, 1919: "Mr. J.A. Holmes and Mr. H.C. Wills were appointed a committee to investigate the advisability of furnishing the several pews with hat-hooks and were clothed with the power to act upon their investigations."

Despite changing times, and not only because of the similarities which bind us, we are one in the Spirit with our predecessors in this parish. Not only because we share the same name, "the Chapel of the Cross," and the same history; not only because we share the same parish lot and buildings; not only because, despite many changes, we share the same basic worship. Our unity with those whom we celebrate and give thanks for on this 150th anniversary runs much deeper than that. It is based on one "call, one Lord, one faith, one baptism." It is given to us by the "one God and Father of us all, who is above all and through all and in all."

Because of that unifying life and love of God, we share also with them the call or mission proclaimed in today's Gospel: "I do not pray for these only," Jesus says, "but also for those who believe in me through their word, that they may all be one; even as thou, Father art in me, and I in thee, that they may also be in us, so that the world may believe that thou hast sent me."

That mission, accepted by those who went before us, and lived by them both imperfectly and wonderfully, is now ours. We are now, as the founding document says, "the congregation of Christian people" in this place. We are to be the ones who are so one with one another and with God, so forbearing of one another in love, that the world may come to know that the Father has sent his son, Jesus.

We are a diverse congregation, with different worship styles and theological viewpoints, different budget and staffing and building priorities, different perspectives on moral and social and political issues. If we were each choosing who would belong to this parish, we might each of us leave out at least some of the others who are here. No doubt some of you may wish that I had followed the example of the many priests who declined to serve as rector of this parish, rather than that of the few who have accepted!

But our unity is not based on our similarities or on our agreements or on our mutual attractiveness. Rather it overflows from our one "call, one Lord, one faith, one baptism, one God and Father of us all." Acting out of that profound mystery rather than out of our illusion of isolation, we are to "lead a life worthy of the calling to which [we] have been called, with all lowliness and meekness, with patience, forbearing one another in love, eager to maintain the unity of the Spirit in the bond of peace."

We are to be eager to maintain that unity not only with ourselves, and not only with those who have gone before us, but even with those who are to follow after us. One of the great benefits of a celebration like this is the perspective it gives. Those who founded this parish, those who saw it through hard times, those who celebrated its 100th anniversary, whether they knew it or not, were not doing something which affected merely themselves. As all of us here can attest in one way or another, their actions and their faith have had a profound effect on us. And so will ours on future generations.

Some of these children who are singing in the choir this morning, and reading a lesson and participating in the service, will be here for the 200th anniversary of this parish, as will some of their children and grandchildren. They will talk of the common struggles and the peculiarities and the contributions of those who preceded them. And if we have grasped our unity with them and our obligation to them and our call to prepare the way for them, then they, too, will find themselves equipped to be "the congregation of Christian people" in this place. They, too, will hear the words of the Gospel addressed to them, "I do not pray for these only, but also for those who believe in me through their word, that they may all be one; even as thou, Father, art in me, and I in thee, that they also may be one in us, so that the world may believe that thou hast sent me." Amen.

Ephesians 4:1-6; John 17:6a, 15-23

Praying to Forgive
The Fourth Sunday after Pentecost
June 23, 1996

I have to say that during the month of June, coming to church has not been as much fun as it usually is! I do not doubt that is true for all of us.

Just three weeks ago I told you that we had uncovered evidence of disturbing financial misdoings. The next week a printed statement announced the discovery that Brian Mullaney, our former financial secretary, had definitely embezzled $12,000 and quite possibly well over $300,000. This week's "Crossings" is again the bearer of bad news: the final total seems to be between $460,000 and $480,000. Over a three-year period, Brian systematically misappropriated probably hundreds of parishioners' checks into a little-noticed petty cash account which only required one signature, and then forged over 140 checks to himself, each one for thousands of dollars.

Until you have looked at each of the 140-plus forgeries as I and the Vestry have, and held them in your hand, it is hard to realize the enormity of this crime. Until you have inspected meticulously doctored copies of the account's statements, cleverly altered by cutting and pasting to fool the auditors, it is difficult to grasp the duplicity and deceit involved. Until you think about the purposes that money was intended to support — worshipping God, proclaiming the Gospel to a world badly in need of it, teaching others including our children about the Christian faith, helping people of all ages to care for one another, ministering to the needs of those with AIDS or without food or shelter or homes or decent neighborhoods, not to mention being good stewards of the buildings and the staff entrusted to us for these purposes — it is impossible to fathom the heinousness of this sin. Until you understand that all of that money seems to be gone, squandered on lavish parties and gifts and travel and limousines, it is difficult to comprehend the depth of this betrayal.

I know I am speaking bluntly here, but I think it necessary. It is not my intent to judge Brian; both the civil and the heavenly courts will certainly do that. And it is a mark in his favor that he has voluntarily returned and is cooperating in the investigation.

Nor do I mean to inflame us beyond the anger we already have, but rage seems an appropriate response. It is an outrageous situation. We also feel humiliated and betrayed. I certainly do. The question is, as Christians, what do we do with our rage and our humiliation and our feelings of betrayal? I ask this question, not just of us as individuals, but of us as a parish who are suffering in this together.

The temptation, of course, is to use these emotions in ways that are destructive of ourselves or of others. Denial, for example, of what has really happened or how we are internally responding to it, can only make the situation worse, similar to the effect of a non-diagnosis of a physical ailment. I hope the Vestry's immediate response and release of information is helping us avoid that dangerous trap. My remarks today are meant to help us beyond that denial.

Lapsing into the posture of a victim, feeling sorry for ourselves and disengaging from others in the parish is another destructive reaction. We can give in to our urge not to trust anyone and accept defeat by giving up. Again I hope that the Vestry's lead in pursuing the legal process and in exploring avenues for restitution will counteract that temptation to passivity. All of us need to pull together, not apart, to support one another, to reestablish the trust, to rebuild the financial strength of the parish.

Becoming defensive and refusing to learn from our mistakes is another harmful response. While none of us is guilty of this crime, some of our financial policies and procedures were not adequate to its prevention and need to be changed. No system can be completely impervious to all willful evil intentions, but the finance committee of the Vestry is hard at work reviewing and revising our financial controls to avoid any future recurrence.

Finally, our biggest temptation is to vent our rage and humiliation and betrayal by fixing blame and harboring resentment. This can be aimed at Brian or even others we may hold responsible. Nothing assuages our wrath more than to blame it on someone else. Blame (which is not the same as properly holding someone accountable) is like soothing liquid on our scorched throats.

The difficulty is, of course, that soon that refreshing solution becomes like saltwater: It poisons us, but the more we drink the more we want. Blame and resentment and failure to forgive become much more damaging to us than to the person we intend to hurt.

Scripture, of course, is full of enjoinders to forgive. We are to forgive others from our hearts, as our Father has forgiven us. We are to turn the other cheek, to forgive 70 times seven times, to learn from Jesus who forgave his murderers and betrayers from the cross. In a moment we will ask our Father to "forgive us our trespasses as we forgive those who trespass against us," a chilling thought if we are honest.

An article on Pentecost Sunday in the *Baltimore Sun* titled "The Power of Forgiveness" had as its subtitle this sentence, "Psychologists and therapists are beginning to understand that forgiving is not only a theological concept but also an act of will that can heal the heart and mind." It went on to say in part:

> "Humans cannot forget, but we can forgive. Yet most often we choose not to. We dress our revenge up and call it justice. We say it is the right of the victim to be angry, to hate. We refuse to yield that high moral ground of the unjustly injured.

> "We want people to change before we forgive them, to grovel, to make restitution. And when they do not, we declare they do not deserve our forgiveness — forgetting that forgiveness was invented for those unworthy of it [and as Christians we would have to add, "including ourselves"].

> "In our disposable culture, some find it simpler to cut the offending party loose and move on, whether it be spouse, parent, friend, or foe.

"That's because forgiveness is hard work. It comes at the end of a long and painful process, and it must be renewed every time memory pricks. Most of us find a middle ground. We let go of the past, but we don't forgive. It may be that what we do only resembles forgiveness, but is actually accommodation."

The article went on to say, "Forgiveness may, as many believe, require the touch of God on the human heart, a moment of grace, to achieve." We are surely among the many who believe that, but it is not a cheap grace. As some of you heard me say, spiritual writers tell us that if we cannot honestly ask for the grace of forgiveness, we are to ask for the grace to want to forgive. And if we cannot sincerely ask for that, we are to ask for the grace to want to want to forgive, going as far back as we need to! In this case, I still find myself stuck on asking for the grace to want to want to forgive, but I am still praying and I expect to for a while.

That is what I call on all of us to do. While we did not ask for this situation — it was certainly thrust upon us against our will — God can use it to teach us what it really means to be a Christian parish. Coming to church is not always fun because there are hard issues to deal with, hard disciplines to follow, hard struggles to wrestle with. But it is in that wrestling that we will grow, in that embracing of the cross that we will find life, in that struggling together that we will become a true community. For in the words of the Prayer of St. Francis, "It is in giving that we receive; it is in pardoning that we are pardoned; and it is in dying that we are born to eternal life" (BCP, p.833).

How Dear to Me Is Your Dwelling, O Lord of Hosts!
The Twenty-First Sunday after Pentecost
October 25, 1998

*How dear to me is your dwelling, O Lord of hosts! My soul has a
desire and longing for the courts of the Lord; my heart and my flesh
rejoice in the living God.*

Those opening words from today's psalm may sound familiar to you.
Psalm 84 was also the psalm at our service for the celebration of the
150th anniversary of the consecration of the chapel last Sunday evening.
It occurred then as part of the propers (the assigned scripture) for The
Dedication and Consecration of a Church, adapted for our anniversary.
Today it appears as part of the regular three-year lectionary cycle. That
providential coincidence is enough reason for me to think that I am
supposed to preach on this beautiful text! It surely provides a context
for reflecting on last Sunday's glorious occasion.

And what a moving day of celebration it was! In the morning we had the
opportunity literally to join hands with our fellow believers to create a
human chain that stretched not only beyond the limitations of physical
sight but also beyond the limits we too easily put on who the Church is
and what it is called to be. Young and old, black and white, Baptist and
Episcopalian and in between, each of us, as we reached out to grasp the
welcoming hand of our neighbor, could feel an expanded vision of the
mystery of the Body of Christ.

We did not complete the whole chain. Significant gaps remained
on several stretches of West Franklin Street, where churches are less
numerous. But perhaps those holes can remind us not only of the
distance we have yet to go in fully claiming our identity as Christ's
Body, but also of God's grace which fills in and makes good our human
shortcomings.

Charged by the experience of the morning, we were ready to be elevated
by the liturgy that evening! And what an uplifting service it was. From

the stirring opening notes of the brass and the organ to the moving final pealing of the chapel bell, the presence of the God of what has been, who is also the God of the here and now and of what lies ahead, was palpable. At the end, as parishioners stood in the warm night air, embraced by the flickering candlelight, they lifted up their eyes to the bright stars shining over the chapel tower and raised their voices to the heavens as well, declaring in traditional melody, "The Church's one foundation is Jesus Christ her Lord."

If any of us are ever to catch a glimpse of the depth and the ardor of the psalmist's words, perhaps it was then: "How dear to me is your dwelling, O Lord of hosts! My soul has a desire and longing for the courts of the Lord; my heart and my flesh rejoice in the living God."

Even though, as we acknowledged in Sunday evening's liturgy, "the heaven of heavens cannot contain thee [Eternal God], much less the walls of temples made with hands," still the mystery of God's presence does startle us in profound ways through sacred space. The hallowed walls, thick with the prayers of longing and thanksgiving of many generations, speak silently but powerfully to us, whether we are inside or outside them, of the faithful God who is the same yesterday, today, and forever. As we stood Sunday evening in the courts of the Lord formed by our church and chapel, the words of the psalmist echoed deeply within us: "How dear to me is your dwelling, O Lord of Hosts!"

What reverence we should have for this holy ground! It is "by the side of your altars, O Lord" that we are first made children of God through the waters of baptism. It is within these walls that we hear about and worship the living God. It is at the holy table that we are nourished with divine food. It is in the house of God that we kneel before the bishop to affirm our Baptismal covenant, that we are joined in the covenant of marriage. It is from the Lord's lovely dwelling place that we are at the last committed into the Father's hands.

A former parishioner who was here for the service Sunday evening wrote me this week in gratitude for all that it had meant to her. She said that she and her hostess, both widows, had felt a special closeness that night to their husbands of many years. It struck me that the human chain that we had experienced that morning was a powerful expression of bridging not just linear distance down a street, but also of chronological distance through time. Does not the communion of saints link us with those who have gone before just as surely as we were connected with one another on Franklin Street? Many lines in many dimensions emanate from God's altar.

One line, of course, connects us with the future, as unseen as were the people in the next block from us last Sunday. It would be a mistake if our anniversary only celebrated the past and did not move us into what is to come. Our psalm declares; "My heart and my flesh rejoice in the living God." That God, whom we experienced so powerfully last week, calls us forward to this week and to the next and to the next. Just as the apostles, having been strengthened by the vision of Jesus' transfiguration up on the mountain, returned with him to the plain, so we are to move ahead on our path of faith, fortified by our time in the courts of the Lord.

Unlike the apostles, however, who could not return to their mountaintop often, we can frequently satisfy our desire and longing for our holy ground. We are given the gift of regular access to the house of God, to the dwelling of the Lord of hosts. Each worship service affords us another encounter with the Divine, "For one day in your courts [O Lord] is better than a thousand in my own room." Not every time we worship God will be a mountaintop experience for us, but each one can serve as a reminder and a re-tasting of the richness of the psalmist's words, "How dear to me is your dwelling, O Lord of hosts! My soul has a desire and a longing for the courts of the Lord; my heart and my flesh rejoice in the living God."

Back Home
The Sixth Sunday after The Epiphany
February 13, 2000

It is good to be back home among you! Of course I have not been very far away or gone for very long — just down in Pinehurst for several days for Annual Convention. But it feels like the conclusion of a long journey.

As you no doubt know, on the final morning of convention and on our 10th ballot, we finally did elect the 11th Bishop of North Carolina, the Rev. Michael Curry, former rector of St. Stephen's Winston-Salem, and currently rector of St. James in Baltimore — both predominantly black parishes. When Betsy and I met Michael several weeks ago at the nominee "walkabouts," we instantly liked him. He is a man of deep faith and infectious joy, a dynamic preacher, a visionary. He will bring great gifts to the diocese, and I know I will enjoy and grow from working with him. I am excited about that.

I am also disappointed, of course, since I was also one of the seven nominees being considered; and I feel a bit "road weary" from this year-long journey. And what a twisty, turny road it was! Not only was I in the Search Committee's final 10, but not the final eight, and then re-nominated by other clergy delegates three weeks later, but consider these other odd twists. The "walkabouts," where the delegates were given a chance to meet and hear from the nominees, were diminished in attendance by a winter storm. The convention itself was postponed two weeks due to another storm, the iciest part of which hit Pinehurst, which was without electricity for over a week! One of the nominees who had withdrawn from the process one day after he was announced as one of the search committee's final five and then two weeks later reentered the slate, withdrew again the day before the re-scheduled convention.

As the ballots were handed out the first evening of convention, it was discovered that not enough had been printed; so the first ballot was delayed while others were run off. After we finally voted and the results tabulated, the tellers returned to say that more clergy had voted than were registered. The bishop declared that ballot invalid, and we did not get to vote until the next day. The day after that on the 10th ballot, a longer-than-usual election, the bishop-elect finally received, for the first time in both orders since we had begun voting, the majority of both the lay and clergy votes, the latter without one vote to spare. After many fits and starts, postponements and delays and detours, that part of my personal journey was over.

Now comes dealing with that disappointment, because I did develop a lot of energy and excitement about the possibilities of leading the diocese. While my goal was not to become the bishop but to participate in the process as fully as I could, still as today's Epistle begins (could you believe that?), "In a race all the runners compete, but only one receives the prize" (I Cor. 9:24). And of course that one was not me! I realize that some of my disappointment comes from letting my ego get too involved. I wrote in my journal almost a year ago regarding the possibility of being bishop, "Instinctively I too much look on it as an affirmation, as a capping of success." Despite wrestling with that temptation for a year and repeatedly emphasizing to myself that this was not about me but about Divine dynamic grace at work in building up the kingdom of God, I certainly have not mastered it. I am too competitive for that!

Betsy reminded me at one point in the convention about my favorite Garfield cartoon strip. It begins with Garfield trapping a mouse under one front leg. Then he nails another mouse with the other. Then he snares two more with each back leg so that he is completely spread-eagled. A big fat mouse walks by, and Garfield releases all the others to pounce on him. Then with a knowing feline look he instructs the reader, "It's not the having; it's the getting." It was a helpful reminder. Some of my disappointment comes from an over-involved ego, perhaps more intrigued by the getting than the having, and I am repenting of that as quickly as I can.

The rest of the disappointment, however, comes from having to let go of envisioned and real possibilities. We all deal with that on a regular basis. Our aging bodies no longer allow us to do what we once took for granted. A once-nourishing relationship falls apart. We fail an exam or a course or a job interview. Our parent or our child does not fulfill our expectations. We move from one place to another. Someone we love dies. My pain in this regard is no worse and probably not nearly as bad as many others'. I only share it because I know many of you are concerned about me and wonder how I am doing. I want to tell you that I really am doing all right.

That is partly because of all of you. The support and encouragement I have felt from you has been deeply sustaining. I have felt honored and wanted when you have told me you were praying for me to finish a strong second! (Be careful what you pray for!) I am very grateful for your love and concern.

I am also fine partly because I still have such engaging ministry right here at the Chapel of the Cross. The rich liturgical life, the growing opportunities for racial reconciliation and social ministry, the strengthening Christian education and spiritual formation, the deepening fellowship among all ages, the expanding financial stewardship, and the solid development of the staff and the administration to sustain it all both satisfy and challenge me as rector; and I envision they will for some time to come.

Finally I am sustained in all this by the gift of faith. I believe that God is working his purpose out and that I do not have to be in charge. I believe that God does not abandon me but is continually upholding me and schooling me in life-giving, if sometimes in painful ways. I believe that beyond whatever deaths I may encounter lies the fuller life that Jesus came to bring: life that is deep and genuine and satisfying; life that can spill over into healing, even of leprosy or whatever seems incurable in us; life that never ends.

I count on growing in that faith with all of you. I look forward to whatever opportunities God may give us personally and corporately to lay hold of the life which is life indeed. Together we will continue to learn more fully how to love and serve the Lord. It is indeed good to be back home among you.

Faithful Service
University Day
October 12, 2000

The phone call came Monday morning. The Rev. Susan Heath of Trinity Episcopal Cathedral in Columbia, S.C. and anticipated preacher at this service, called to say that her father had died and that she would not be able to participate this morning. I was very sorry to hear that news — for several reasons. The first was for her personal loss, which even when we are somewhat prepared for it is never easy to take. I remember the death of my own father 28 years ago very well.

The second reason, much more selfish, was my personal sense of panic! Suddenly my role in this unprecedented service was much more demanding, with very little time to prepare, especially since I was to spend most of the intervening three days at our diocese's annual clergy conference, getting to know and to be inspired by our new bishop, Michael Curry. Intense worry set in!

I also felt sorry at this turn of events for our new chancellor, Dr. James Moeser, who requested and helped plan this service and for you, the participants. If the truth be known (and I apologize, Dr. Moeser, if it should not be; but a basic raison d'être of a university is the acquisition of knowledge!), the first choice for preaching at this service was Peter Gomes of Harvard University, named by *Time* magazine as one of the seven best preachers in America. When he was unavailable, Dr. Moeser turned to another good friend, the aforementioned Rev. Heath, who is Canon Theologian at the Cathedral in South Carolina. So we have gone from one of the most respected preachers in America to a theological expert from out of state to the guy next door!

Of course life is what happens when you are planning something else, and I trust some good will come out of this disappointment. In fact, perhaps it is healthy for all of us at the onset of our new chancellor's term, a time of new beginnings for the University, to be reminded that we mere mortals are not in control of our individual or corporate lives.

We can be certain that everything will not happen according to our plans. Our role is not to manipulate events, people and circumstances to accomplish even the best intentioned of designs. Our role is to respond as faithfully as we can to the challenges, the relationships, the opportunities, the disappointments of life. As limited human beings, our call is ultimately not to be successful, but to be faithful.

How we all strive to be faithful will be different. For some of us, that word will have a literal meaning: full of faith. Our motivation, our source of energy, our passion for life will spring from a belief in a higher being, a relationship with God, a reverence for and a devotion to the Divine. That is not required in a university setting, nor should it be. Freedom of inquiry and belief is necessary. But neither as an age-old response to the awe and mystery of life should manifestations of faith be ignored, marginalized, or discouraged. To do so is to miss and to lose a vital dimension of the richness of life.

I am delighted and grateful that Dr. Moeser has given us this opportunity for worship this morning. He approaches his new role as chancellor and the many responsibilities and opportunities that go with it from a distinct faith perspective. For him, as it is for many of us, that is the Christian faith. He sees his leadership role not as an opportunity for self-aggrandizement, but as a call to service. His Baptism, through which he was united to Jesus Christ, who came not to be served, but to serve, fills him with the Spirit of God and empowers him to serve God by serving others. He needs no further commissioning.

But in another sense, on this day of his installation as Chancellor of this University, he desires to recommit himself to Christian service by renewing his Baptismal Covenant. The words of his recommitment come primarily from the service of Baptism in the Episcopal Prayer Book. He reaffirms his renunciation of evil and renews his commitment to follow Jesus as Lord. In five specific questions, he pledges to live out that commitment, serving Christ in all persons, for example, and striving for justice and peace among all people and respecting the dignity of every human being. It is out of Dr. Moeser's desire to recommit himself in a new context and with as many of us who are willing, Christian and other believers and seekers, to give thanks to God and to ask Divine help in being faithful, that we come here this morning.

Let those of us who are Christians not see this blessed occasion as a kind of Christian triumph, as some sort of "scoring one for God" in a spasm of spiritual arrogance. The world does not need nor hunger for Christian imperialism. But neither let others be threatened by this overt expression of Christian worship. It is offered out of heartfelt conviction and with no shame, but also with great respect for all the children of God, with passion for the values that unite us, and with deep humility.

The words from the Book of Micah found on the cover of your bulletin encourage us all to tangible commitment to the service of others, manifest in our lives of justice and of loving kindness. They also urge us to walk humbly with God and therefore with one another. The image of walking reminds us that life is a journey. We are in the process of getting to where we should be. Martin Luther King, Jr. said, "We are not yet what we shall be but we are growing toward it; the process is not yet finished but it is going on; this is not the end but it is the road." As individuals and as the University community, we all have a long way to go. We have not arrived, but we have as the poet notes "miles to go before [we] sleep."

Walking humbly with one another means realizing that we need to change. The changes that we so easily recognize need to happen in others and in our world need to happen first in us. Those changes, toward more authentic justice and deeper loving kindness, for example, do not come easily. A cartoon several years ago in *The New Yorker* showed a man in his pajamas beside his bed praying to God in these words: "I asked You, in the nicest possible way, to make me a better person, but apparently You couldn't be bothered." (That is a good one to think about for a while!) Change, like knowledge, makes a bloody entrance. It rarely happens with no cost to us. Whether as individuals or as a University, genuine and fruitful change will come through facing honestly the obstacles that confront us, through acknowledging responsibilities we would rather shirk, through doing battle, if you will, with our human tendency to complacency and self-satisfaction.

Take on the communal level, for example, the necessary continuing discussion about the mission of higher education. Most would agree that the first purpose of a university is the acquisition of knowledge. But can that be divorced from the other original mission of universities, which of course devolved from the Church, of formation of character? Where has the attempt at "value free" education left us? What is the morality of informing minds without shaping consciences and hearts to use that knowledge well? What is the moral responsibility of the university? Where is, if you will, its soul?

Or on an individual level, take our tendency to avoid others who are different from us, racially, religiously, politically, socially, economically. Do we not miss much of what life has to offer by too easily protecting ourselves from other experiences and other viewpoints? Do we not deprive others of what they might learn from us? Why must our worlds stay so small and insular?

Change, growth, transformation, corporately or individually, does not happen without struggle. We will more fruitfully live into our individual and common missions by facing precisely those realities, responsibilities, and people in our lives that we would rather avoid.

Thomas Merton, in his book *Seeds of Contemplation*, writes about this phenomenon. He uses an image from Christian theology, one I think we can all understand and profit from. I would like to close by offering his thoughts as a final reflection. In the absence of Peter Gomes or Susan Heath, we can at least have Thomas Merton! Dr. Moeser, as you encounter difficulties in your new charge, as you surely will, and as you wrestle with those struggles that will now shape your soul and that of this University, I hope you will find this reflection as strengthening as I have.

> Souls are like wax waiting for a seal. By themselves they have no special identity. Their destiny is to be softened and prepared in this life, by God's will, to receive, at their death, the seal of their own degree of likeness to God in Christ. And that is what it means, among other things, to be judged by Christ.

The wax that has melted in God's will can easily receive the stamp of its identity, the truth of what it was meant to be. But the wax that is hard and dry and brittle and without love will not take the seal: for the hard seal, descending upon it, grinds it to powder.

Therefore if you spend your life trying to escape from the heat of the fire that is meant to soften and prepare you to become your true self, and if you try to keep your substance from melting in the fire — as if your true identity were to be hard wax — the seal will fall upon you at last and crush you. You will not be able to take your own true name and countenance, and you will be destroyed by the event that was meant to be your fulfillment.

Let us pray. Almighty God, we thank you for all that you have done for us. We thank you for the splendor of the whole creation, for the beauty of this world, for the wonder of life, and for the mystery of love. We thank you for setting us at tasks which demand our best efforts, and for leading us to accomplishments which satisfy and delight us. We thank you also for those disappointments and failures that lead us to acknowledge our dependence on you alone. Help us in the words of your prophet, Micah, to respond faithfully to what you require of us: to do justice, to love kindness, and to walk humbly with you and with one another. This we ask you for your love's sake. Amen.

The new parish house, dedicated in 2014

Wrestling with the Divine
The Twenty-first Sunday after Pentecost
October 24, 2004

What a wonderful story in Genesis about wrestling with God! Jacob, on his way to reconcile with his brother Esau, finds himself in an all-night wrestling match with what turns out to be the Divine. This is a genuine struggle, not the staged, histrionic televised matches of today's professional wrestling, with the crowds agonizing with the prolonged close calls of their noble favorites and howling for the blood of the despised villains! Here there are no crowds, no pretense, no agreed-on scripts. Jacob, alone and worried about his future, grapples for hours in exhausting, yet exhilarating, struggle with God. Although his thigh is put out of joint in the process, he receives a new identity through a new name, Israel, and a Divine blessing. He finds that life is at its fullest, not in running away and avoidance, but in total, whole-hearted engagement. Jacob, in becoming Israel, holds up for us the importance of wrestling with the Divine.

That strikes me as a wonderful metaphor for our faith's journey. Life is about struggle and effort, not just comfort as a couch potato spectator! Rather we are to engage with God, with our faith, with the deeper meanings and callings of our lives. Although we risk injury and pain, we are to persist in that struggle. We are willingly and passionately to enter into that enlivening engagement of wrestling with the Divine.

That persuasive metaphor casts light on a number of elements in our individual and common lives. As I have been reflecting this week, I find that wrestling and engaging with God is what is happening around us and what we are all called to be doing.

We received a postcard from David Frazelle a few days ago. In less than six weeks, David will begin as our associate for parish ministry; but you will recall that after his ordination as a transitional deacon in late June, he began hiking the Appalachian Trail from Maine to Georgia, a distance of 2,138 miles! Along the way he has battled an infected toe, a sprained ankle, storms which saturated his sleeping bag, and stretches of loneliness, especially in the beginning weeks of wilderness with no companions. On his postcard, which shows a map of the entire trail through multiple states and which you can see on the parish office door, he writes, "Greetings from Southwest Virginia. I am thinking of you and the Chapel of the Cross more and more these days and am praying for you daily. Only 600 miles to go now. I'm really looking forward to working with you."

In an earlier message, David said that he decided to hike the trail because he "wanted to follow a dream, to have an adventure, and to encounter God in nature and in people." It seems now that he will be among the 10 or 15 percent of those who begin the trail to actually finish. Each hiker is given a nickname on the trail by fellow backpackers, and his, perhaps for obvious reasons, has been determined to be "King David"! I think it could as easily have been "Jacob."

I received another letter this week from a former student here who was confirmed with our Adult Inquirers' Class last May. He is now living in Vancouver, British Columbia, and his struggle is in trying to find inspiring, engaging worship in his new situation. He writes, "One of the main things that led me into the Anglican Communion through the Chapel of the Cross was what I found to be the timelessness of the liturgy. I loved immediately the ancient feeling of the Book of Common Prayer and of the music. ... It made it so clear to me that what we were there to worship was timeless and forever and bigger than what goes on here and now. ... I felt God in the changelessness and commonality of His Church. It grabbed all my guts and I felt like I had finally found home." He goes on to bemoan the Anglican liturgy he has found in his new location so far, characterized in his perception by too much distraction and novelty and not by enough solid grounding. I wrote him back and encouraged him to stay with the struggle, to keep looking for God, even amidst the changes that might at first seem devoid of the Divine.

One form of wrestling that we have been witnessing these past few weeks has been the political debates between local and national candidates. While I wonder if there is any true engagement going on, there certainly has been no lack of lunging and attacking and trying to throw and pin! Whatever your level of skepticism or bewilderment at this grappling, it does remind all of us that *we* are to engage these important and difficult issues with as much energy and integrity as we can, not only within ourselves but also with one another. As Christians and as engagers in life's journey, we are to participate fully, including voting, and then be ready to pull together and to heal divisions, no matter what the outcome of the elections.

This past Monday was the date set a year ago by the Archbishop of Canterbury for the release of the report by the special commission he appointed in light of growing division in the Anglican Communion over the issues of ordaining gay clergy and blessing same-sex unions. Contrary to popular impression, the commission was not charged to settle those particular issues, but rather to address the issues of authority and union within the Church in the face of deep moral disagreements. I am grateful that the commission did not, and I hope with its leadership the whole Church will not take the easy way out and simply declare the wrestling over, naming winners and losers. With God's continued grace may we not shrink from the task of seriously engaging all these issues and one another and the persistent presence and guidance of the Holy Spirit.

Finally, a major wrestling engagement for all of us, individually and communally, is our Annual Giving Campaign, now under way. Each year it is of crucial importance, both to us as individual Christians who struggle with the role and importance of money in our lives and how we use and share it, and to us as a parish, supporting the ministry God calls us to with a forward-looking budget. As the mailing you should have received articulates, the communal consequences of our effort this year are particularly critical. At my request, the Vestry took the bold steps of approving my calling of Tammy Lee to be our associate for campus ministry, of moving Vicky Jamieson-Drake from three-quarter time to full time as associate for pastoral ministry, and of approving the call of David Frazelle to be full time associate for parish ministry, starting in December.

That fulfills a long-needed and dreamed-of goal of having four full time priests on our staff, who through their dedication and gifts and experience can help lead our entire parish to exercise our significant and much-needed ministries. But underwriting these moves as well as the escalation of fixed costs, outreach needs, and facilities maintenance requires an unprecedented 15 percent increase in our Annual Giving Campaign. Not all of us will be able to increase that much; some of us can do even more. The wardens and I and other Vestry leaders, in our wrestling with what God calls us to, have committed to increase our pledges for 2005 by at least 25 percent. I hope that you, too, will wrestle with your individual decisions, that communally we may continue to respond faithfully to the God who engages us.

Unlike our various governments or all businesses or, I am told, some congregations — including some synagogues — we do not assign people how much they must pay. I did, however, have a fantasy last month when the Gospel reading was about the dishonest steward. He was the clever one who summoned his master's debtors and said to one, "Take your bill [of a hundred measures of oil] and sit down quickly and write fifty," and to another, "Take your bill [of a hundred measures of wheat] and write eighty." Would it not be good, I thought, if our treasurer could say to one parishioner, "Take your pledge of $3,000 and write $4,000" and to another, "Take your pledge of $1,200 and make it $2,000" and to another, "It is time for you to begin the discipline of pledging. Sit down quickly and write $500"! But then, where would the struggle be and the wrestling and the getting our bones out of joint and finding in all that the Divine blessing?!

Let me conclude by urging you to see your financial giving as an integral part of your faith journey, to enter into that decision with energy and determination, and, as in all dimensions of your life, to be bold and persistent as, like Jacob and all his spiritual descendants, you wrestle with the Divine.

Genesis 32:3-8, 22-30

The Marriage of Tambria Elizabeth Lee and David Exum Brown
April 22, 2006

> From our first reading: *Ho, every one who thirsts, come to the waters; and he who has no money, come, buy and eat! Come, buy wine and milk without money and without price. ... Hearken diligently to me, and eat what is good, and delight yourselves in fatness.*

What a great passage for a wedding feast! And what a reminder of God's grace and abundance, which underlie our joyful occasion this afternoon. For we have come here from many places, from east and west and north and south, by plane and bus and car and on foot, with hearts full of joy and affection and thanksgiving. We have come because we could not stay away, because our affection for David and Tammy drew us all here like a magnet, because we are exuberantly grateful for what God has been doing and will continue to do for them.

Thirteen years ago, when Tammy was first interviewing for a position here at The Chapel of the Cross, I clearly remember her response to a question about her future intentions and possibilities. "I would like to get married," she said. "But I keep waiting in vain for God to drop down my husband out of heaven in a Glad trash bag!" David, it would have been dramatic and symbolic for you to walk down the aisle today with neck and arm holes cut in black plastic, but you look so much better in a suit! Nonetheless, we would miss the point entirely if we did not grasp the deep reality, Tammy and David, that God has given each of you the gift of the other. You could not make it happen; you could not make it happen earlier (or I am sure you would have!); you did not "earn" each other. You who have no money are given wine and milk with no price. The God of abundance and overflowing generosity has invited you to the wedding feast.

And that brings us to our Gospel reading for today: the wedding feast at Cana, an amazing story about God's liberality and power. Jesus provides another 150 gallons of wine for a sagging celebration, enough for a modest crowd of, say, 300 people, to have another 10 glasses apiece! Given this crowd, we might need that same miraculous help today! (More basically we need a multiplication of the square footage of the dining room!) Part of the point is that God does not skimp, but overwhelms us with generous portions of all that we need. Sometimes we may have to wait patiently! But God is faithful and demonstrates the burning divine love for us with more abundant gifts than we can keep track of or acknowledge.

That this liberality was shown at a wedding feast makes this a particularly appropriate story for us today. We see not only God's generosity but also God's efficacious power. Ordinary water, set aside for simple purification purposes, was transformed by the divine intention into fine wine. Something commonplace and good became something extraordinary and excellent. That same grace is at work in your lives, David and Tammy. Through your vows to one another, God takes, if you will, your ordinary human relationship, and transforms it into something extraordinary: a lifelong commitment which reflects God's unbreakable covenant with us. Through God's grace, the water of your ordinary daily lives becomes the fine wine of witness to God's generous and transforming love.

This past Sunday we celebrated the great feast of Easter, and we continue that celebration throughout the great 50 days. Easter proclaims to us the amazing mystery that Jesus has overcome sin and death and includes us in his victory. Today's service makes real and strengthens that Easter hope. As the generous and triumphant God summons us all to this wedding Eucharistic feast, a foretaste of the heavenly banquet, we give thanks for God's abundant and powerful grace. We are especially grateful for your cooperation with that grace, David and Tammy, which encourages us to respond more attentively and faithfully to God's persistent invitation. Since "Christ our Passover is sacrificed for us, therefore let us keep the feast. Alleluia!"

What Is It?
Inter-Faith Council for Social Services Sabbath Weekend, Kehillah
Synagogue
February 4, 2007

Good morning. I am very happy to be with you this morning and to
see all of you. In my 25 years in Chapel Hill, I have worshiped in this
building several times before, upstairs in the main sanctuary. The first
was at an ecumenical Thanksgiving Day service in the late 1980s. This
was the Chapel Hill Bible Church then, of course, and I as the President
of the Chapel Hill/Carrboro Ministers' Association asked the pastor if
he and his congregation would be the host that year. Then, perhaps
as a sign of things to come, I invited Rabbi John Friedman, my good
friend from Judea Reform in Durham, to be the preacher! John came
about the same time I did, 1982, and his two children are exactly the
same ages as my two boys, and they were in class together all the way
through Durham Academy. At any rate, John gave a fine sermon on
forgiveness that day. I still remember it because he even quoted Jesus
from Luke's Gospel. So Rabbi Jen is not the first Rabbi to preach here!

My other time in this building was more recent. It was on a Sunday
evening a year or so ago to help the Episcopal Church of the Advocate
celebrate an early anniversary. That is a fledgling congregation the
Chapel of the Cross has helped to get started, and I am very grateful
to all of you here for letting them use your space. Lisa Fischbeck was
sponsored for ordination by the Chapel of the Cross 15 years ago, and
we are thrilled that she is the founding priest of this fourth Episcopal
congregation in Orange County. Eventually she and her folks need to
find a permanent location, but thus far they have really enjoyed using
your fine space, which they find flexible enough both for their worship
and for their dinner and fellowship afterwards. I think some of them
have had trouble adjusting to kosher food, but that won't hurt them any!

I am happy to represent in some sense the Inter-Faith Council for
Social Services this morning, although some of you are already well-
connected there. This is the first time I know of that we have observed

IFC Sabbath Weekend by exchanging clergy, and I think it is a great idea. I particularly liked being assigned here today, not only because I get to know you better, but also because being here on a Saturday allows me to be present at my own congregation tomorrow to welcome the preacher assigned to us! That will be Pastor Ruth Harper Stevens of University United Methodist. I think that same dynamic works for Rabbi Jen as well; and in fact it will work very well for her every year, but next year I won't be so lucky!

The IFC holds a special place in our hearts at the Chapel of the Cross, not only because of the wonderful work it does and because it brings people of different religious traditions together in a common ministry, but because we were privileged to be in on some of its most important history. In the 1960s, a handful of churchwomen in Chapel Hill got together to talk about the need for a unified approach to responding to the poor. They met with some of their local pastors at the Chapel of the Cross, and out of that first meeting was born the Church Council for Social Services.

Early on it transitioned into the Inter-Faith Council, and as it grew it branched out from offering groceries and financial assistance, eventually, in the early 1980s, to providing lunch out of a rented building and wanting to offer shelter and all three meals. No progress was being made on this front until later in the 1980s when the ecumenical Thanksgiving Service happened to be at the Chapel of the Cross. The Rev. Bob Seymour, founding pastor of Binkley Baptist Church, was the preacher. His text was "Singing the Lord's song in a strange land" from the psalms. In the front row, customarily in those days, was the mayor of Chapel Hill, who always read the Presidential Proclamation each year about Thanksgiving Day. At that time the mayor was Jimmy Wallace. I remember Rev. Seymour waxing eloquent about the plight of the poor among us, and at one point he leaned over the pulpit and pointed to the Honorable Mr. Wallace and declared, "And yes, Mr. Mayor, it is a scandal in this prosperous community of Chapel Hill that we do not have a permanent shelter with which to house the homeless and feed the hungry!"

The next week Mayor Wallace appointed Rev. Seymour the chair of a task force to find a permanent shelter, which eventually worked out the

25-year lease for the renovation and use of the old Town Hall, still in use — at least for a while longer. It has continued to grow so that this past year, as you may have seen in printed material distributed for this weekend, we housed over 800 homeless people and served over 85,000 meals. Thank you so much to any of you who have helped with IFC this year, and if you have not, I hope you will consider giving of your time or of your money or both! Because feeding the hungry and providing for those with no homes is both a responsibility and a privilege we all share. It is divine work; it is what God does for us. God gives us food and shelter, and through us God wants to provide food and shelter for all God's children. Even if we have never worried about the next meal or protection from the weather, certainly our ancestors did.

Take the congregation of the people of Israel in today's assigned scripture from Exodus. They had no food, no shelter. It was hard work wandering in the desert, and finding food out there for hundreds of thousands of people was not easy! Being better-fed slaves was beginning to look pretty good again, and the people were grumbling against God and against Moses. They longed for "the fleshpots of Egypt," a memorable phrase to come out of this story, as well as "manna from heaven." So in the evening God fed the people with a plethora of quail. (I know "covey" is the right word for a group of quail, but this amount was way beyond "covey"!) And in the morning after the dew burned off, the people discovered a "fine, flake-like" substance, and they asked, "What is it?" The Hebrew phrase for that question, of course, is "manna," which became the name for this divine gift.

The account of this story in the book of Numbers states that "manna was like coriander seed and its appearance like bdellium (a gum resin). The people went about and gathered it, and ground it in mills or beat it in mortars, and boiled it in pots, and made cakes of it; and the taste of it was like the taste of cakes with oil. When the dew fell upon the camp in the night, the manna fell with it" (11:7-9). One commentator, from a Southern church no doubt, referred to all this sustenance just lying there available as the first instance of "dinner on the ground"!

The point is that despite the people's grumbling and lack of gratitude for their deliverance from Egypt, God went to great lengths to feed them day after day and to protect them with the pillar of cloud. It wasn't that they were so good and cheerful and pleasant to be with that they "earned" their food. God just fed them, grumbling or not. Some of the hungry today follow suit. Many are pleasant and well-mannered. But some, we think, should be more grateful and don't deserve our efforts to feed and house them. But why should we expect any more than God received in the account of Exodus and often receives now? When we feed others because they are hungry, deserving or not, we are doing what our Father teaches us to do. We are being God's children.

One last point: I find it very interesting that "manna" means, "What is it?" At first, they were not sure this was something they wanted. Like the wandering people of Israel, I think we are often uncertain about the gifts God gives us. Somebody asks us to take on some responsibility, and we think, "The last thing I need is something more to do. What is that?" Frequently we find, however, that that invitation becomes a significant encounter with grace for us and a real means of divine nourishment. Or we meet somebody to whom we do not take an immediate liking, yet that person eventually becomes someone from whom we learn much about the grace of God. More manna from heaven. Or more seriously we find ourselves in a crisis situation, feeling out of control. The events happening to us do not seem like gifts, and we ask the question of the hungry people of Israel, "What is this?" Just because, from our anxiety and our narrow perspective, we question something's value, does not mean that it cannot be manna for us and actually sustain us for another day in our wandering journey towards the Promised Land.

We may feel that way about volunteering to work at IFC, in the kitchen or in the office. "What is that?" we might ask. "Who needs it? I am not sure I would like that." But others of us who have felt the same way have discovered that even if it is not always easy, we receive much more than we put into it. We find our perspective changed, our understanding of others widened, our gratitude for the blessings in our lives widened. "What is it?" An opportunity to serve others might just be for you manna from heaven.

A Mountaintop Experience
The Last Sunday after The Epiphany
February 18, 2007

The Last Sunday after the Epiphany, just before Lent begins, always proclaims the Gospel story of the transfiguration. Jesus, the human companion of Peter and John and James, took them up on a mountain and was suddenly transfigured before them. "His face shone like the sun," Matthew tells us, "and his garments became white as light." His divinity was overpoweringly apparent. God's transcendent presence was clearly perceived in this awesome, mountaintop experience.

Just about a year ago, many of us had a similar epiphany in this very chapel. No, we did not see Jesus or Moses or Elijah or hear the divine voice coming out of a cloud! But for the 270 of us who packed the pews and the loft and the aisles and the window wells of this chapel that afternoon, there was a palpable sense of God's presence, of God's Spirit at work, of the radiance of God's glory shining through the ordinary of our everyday existence.

The occasion, of course was the 30th anniversary of the first Eucharist celebrated by the Rev. Dr. Pauli Murray in this very chapel where her grandmother, Cornelia, had been baptized as a slave. In January of 1977, Pauli, at the age of 66, became the first African-American woman ordained an Episcopal priest, and when she presided at our altar a month later, she was the first woman of any race to do so in the state of North Carolina.

Now a scant 30 years later, another woman, the Most Reverend Katharine Jefferts Schori, the first female presiding bishop and the only female primate in the entire Anglican Communion, stood in Pauli Murray's proud shoes (the title of her book about her family history) and led us in giving thanks for God's saving presence and persistent grace. "You and I stand here today in proud shoes," Bishop Katharine said, "because of her dream. I know that I stand here today only because she stood here before me. Her proud shoes have carried many others down the road to freedom."

Our own bishop, Michael Curry, the first and still only black diocesan bishop in the South, proclaimed Jesus' Gospel commandment to us to love one another as Jesus loved us, from this same eagle lectern from which Pauli read out of her grandmother's bible. The lectern, of course, is inscribed in memory of Mary Ruffin Smith, who presented Cornelia at age 10 for baptism. Standing in silent witness for well over a century in this sacred space, upholding the word of God, even that unmoving lectern seemed transformed, shining forth with the brightness of that inspired word more fully manifested than ever before. We had heard Jesus' words many times, "This is my commandment, that you love one another as I have loved you." Now they took on an even fuller meaning.

Manifest in the historic presence of Pauli Murray and of Cornelia and of Mary Ruffin Smith, manifest in the strong but humble witness of Katharine Jefferts Schori and of Michael Curry, manifest in the rapt, crowded gathering in the chapel of young and old, black and white, male and female, "one another" became real and visible and incarnate. "One another" excludes or discounts or dismisses no one. "Love one another as I have loved you" enfolds everyone within the reach of its saving embrace. Each of us is God's beloved. Each of us is to make that love real to *all* the others.

Pauli Murray's sense of being beloved, of standing in proud shoes, began with the baptism of her grandmother in our chapel in 1854. This cherished memory, Bishop Katharine declared, "said that yes, even that girl owned by another was God's beloved and worthy of God's own gift and adoption. That ancient dream planted in her family and history shaped Dr. Murray's life, and her ministry both lay and ordained." What a seed was planted in that service of baptism in this chapel over 150 years ago! How God has touched and transformed lives in many generations because of it.

Every time we baptize another person in this chapel, we are claiming one more child of God. Every time we pour water on one made in God's image, we are declaring that person beloved of God. Every time we mark another child as marked as Christ's own forever, we are sending forth into the world another witness to the powerful and transforming love of God.

Baptism is a mountaintop experience. Baptism is never ordinary. Baptism transforms the everyday reality of our lives and reveals the Divine presence, the Divine dynamism alive in creation, the Divine love surging through all God's children.

As those who have been baptized in the Name of the Father and of the Son and of the Holy Spirit, let us each claim our own identity as God's beloved. Let us each open the eyes of our faith to behold God in all of God's redeeming work. Let us each ask God to transform our lives that we may all stand in proud shoes and love one another as Jesus has loved us.

Matthew 17:1-9

God's Recalculating
The Third Sunday after the Epiphany
January 27, 2008

Immediately they left their nets and followed him.

Did you ever wonder what would have happened if Peter and Andrew and James and John had responded to Jesus differently? How would history have been altered if Matthew had written, "They looked at Jesus as if he were crazy and went right on working with their nets"? Would Jesus only have had eight apostles, or would he just have added different ones? Would the Church have flourished as well and as far and wide and altered the course of history as much under different leadership? Would the eventual authorized English translation of the bible, if there was one, (with James out of the picture) have been known, say, as the King Benjamin Version? Would my predecessor as rector, Peter James Lee, if he were even a Christian, been called perhaps Gamaliel Jacob Lee?

How would God have handled such a setback to the Divine plan as these potential disciples' refusal? In fact, the deeper question I want to get to is, how does God work out salvation in the face of human free will? What happens when we, knowingly or not — the difference between sin and error — defy God's will? Are we doomed? Does it all come crashing down around us?

During my theological studies in seminary, I had a professor who challenged us on our theology of God's will. We all accepted the notion that God does have a will and that living our earthly lives involves trying to discern that will. But what happens, he asked us, if we get that wrong? Is your notion, he pressed, that God has carefully lined out a path for you to follow, and that as long as you dutifully walk that path, you are safe; but that the moment you step off it, you are liable to set off a mine which explodes in your face? Land mine spirituality, he called it: Cross God and you will pay for it. Instead he called us to consider that the God who creates us and loves us into being, although he is not a deist god who simply sends us off to do our own thing, honors and respects our wills

52

and in some sense partners with us and invites our co-creative efforts. While God knows what is best for us and wants what most brings us life, God also works with the circumstances of our lives and our good and bad decisions to bring good out of it all, even when we fail. "We know," Paul wrote the Romans, "that in everything God works for good with those who love him, who are called according to his purpose" (Romans 8:28).

You may be familiar with the rather recent phenomenon known as the Global Positioning System or GPS. When you are driving to an unknown destination, it maps out directions and talks you through them at each needed turn. On a recent trip, my sons had ours set for a male voice with an English accent, whom they dubbed "Daniel." Driving up to and into New York City was almost a joy with Daniel, and it occurred to me that if we all were this tuned in to God and as careful about seeking and finding God's directions, this would be a much better world! But then something very interesting happened. A detour forced us to take a different bridge into the city than the one planned, and we had to disregard what Daniel was telling us. I half expected him to say in an angry voice, "Wait. You're not doing what I told you!" Instead, each time we did not take the U-turn he suggested to take us back to the original plan, he would say quite calmly, "Recalculating." Which took me back to my theology professor 35 years ago: In some real sense we cannot ultimately thwart the will of God. Like Daniel, God is just patiently recalculating.

To some degree, Jesus does that in today's Gospel. When he heard that John, his cousin, had been arrested, Mathew tells us, "He withdrew into Galilee; and leaving Nazareth he went and dwelt in Capernaum by the sea." A change in venue seemed called for. When Jesus was first born and Herod tried to take his life, Joseph was warned in a dream to flee to Egypt for a while until it was safer. Recalculating. Had Peter and the other brothers not followed Jesus' invitation the first time, perhaps he would have tried again until they agreed; we do not know. But it is safe to say that God has the resources and the love and the perseverance to work all things for good. Even if we take a wrong turn, God is recalculating.

This is true for us communally as well as individually. Last year we went through a whole process trying to discern whether or not God is calling us as a parish to express our pastoral care for our gay and lesbian parishioners by making available the blessing of their lifelong unions. The final decision, which was mine to make as your rector with your and the Vestry's advice, is that we will. The grace and fruitfulness that have come from that process and from the one service of blessing that we have had thus far lead me to believe that God's Spirit was in that decision and that we got it right. But if we have any humility at all, we need to be open to the possibility of our misreading God's directions and taking a wrong turn. If so we trust that God is patiently and compassionately recalculating.

Over five years ago, the Vestry and I began another process of asking what God would have us be and do as the Chapel of the Cross. Out of that seeking came the work of a number of committees and numerous discussions among the wider parish about our programs and about our facilities. Our best discernment is that God is calling us not to be complacent with what we have achieved in over 165 years, but to stretch ourselves to build literally new foundations for our expanding ministry. We believe God is calling us to a new boldness and generosity in being "A Light on the Hill," a witness to the campus and to the whole community of God's reconciling love, and by "Building to Serve." What will be the final outcome, of course, is still in the future; but we proceed with confidence and with joy, knowing that God is with us, no matter what, and that if any recalculations are needed, they will be made clear over time.

A week from tomorrow, as many of you may know, I will be starting a three-month sabbatical of renewal and refreshment. I look forward not only to that time, but also to being back with you starting on the Feast of the Ascension on May 1. I have no doubt that with the leadership of the rest of the staff and of the Vestry and the continued strong participation of all of you, these Lenten and Easter-filled months will be times of fruitfulness for this parish and for those we serve. God does not take sabbaticals, of course, and you can be assured that God's Spirit will continue to work among you, recalculating as necessary, as you faithfully carry out the ministry God calls us to do. To God be the honor and the glory and the power and the majesty for ever and ever. Amen.

Matthew 4:12-23

The Chapel — 160 Years
October 19, 2008

One hundred and sixty years ago today, on October 19, 1848, this chapel was officially consecrated by the second bishop of the young Diocese of North Carolina. Abraham Lincoln was not yet 40 years old and was still five presidents away from taking office. Electricity and indoor plumbing and automobiles were far in the future. Slavery — by most — was accepted as a way of life.

Ten years before that service, in 1838, the Rev. William Mercer Green, a UNC graduate, had resigned as rector of St. Matthew's, Hillsborough, and accepted an appointment as Professor of Belles Lettres at the University. After four years of gathering other faculty and spouses and students around him for worship in homes, he led them to the formal step of incorporating themselves as an Episcopal congregation. They soon set about purchasing land and, with the help of a nationally known architect, Thomas Walter, designing and building the chapel. What a bold and imaginative vision they developed! Keep in mind that the handful of University buildings, which then constituted the campus, were fairly conventional rectangular affairs. How striking the gothic chapel with its crenellated tower and buttresses and arched, beautifully traceried windows must have been! At least when it was finally finished!

The money ran out and for several years, without any roof or floor, the walls enclosed only dirt and leaves and snow instead of the dedicated worshippers who continued to meet in homes. Finally, five years after it was started, the chapel was dedicated to the worship of God and to the service of God's people. Both for those who entered its gates with praise, as we sang in our opening hymn, and those, especially students, who merely passed by it on their daily routines, the very presence of the chapel spoke of the majesty and the mystery and the mercy of God. That is called the proclamation of architecture.

But the imaginative and bold vision of these early parishioners was not limited to the physical structure of the church. It manifested itself also in their sense of who made up the Church, who constituted the Body of Christ, who was "in" and who was "out." When they signed the articles of incorporation in 1842, which required by national canons the signatures of 12 men, they obediently complied; but expressing their vision of the comprehensiveness of the Church, they also included on the document the signatures of 12 women.

The incorporation of the slave loft into the construction of the chapel — although such segregation and the practice of slavery itself rightly horrified later generations — made it possible at that time for slaves to be included in the worship and education of the parish. Most of you know that Cornelia Fitzgerald, who was baptized in this chapel and sat in the loft, later helped raise her granddaughter, Pauli Murray, who became the first African-American woman ordained an Episcopal priest. When she presided at our chapel altar in 1977 at her first service of Holy Communion, she was the first woman to celebrate the Eucharist in the state of North Carolina, and so helped heal and widen the circle of the Body of Christ even further.

A story many of you do not know is that our chapel even opened its doors to the dreaded Yankee occupiers immediately following the Civil War! When Brigadier General Smith Atkins of Freeport, Illinois, called on the president of the University, former Governor David Swain, to pay his respects, the General and Eleanor Swain, one of the daughters, were dramatically smitten with each other. After a whirlwind courtship, which included the Union military band setting up on the Swains' front lawn to serenade Eleanor, a communicant of our parish, they were married in our chapel on August 23, 1865 (according to William Meade Prince in *Southern Part of Heaven*). The chapel has been a House of Prayer for all people!

After the following low period of Reconstruction, the chapel, along with the University, began again to thrive and grow. Kemp Plummer Battle reopened the University as its President and served as senior warden of our parish for many years. He arranged for his boyhood friend, Joseph Blount Cheshire Jr., to have his first clergy assignment here in the late 1870s. Mr. Cheshire wrote in his autobiography that during those three years he frequently caught rides on the mail hack over to Durham, "a very busy town of perhaps two or three thousand inhabitants … beginning to be of importance for the manufacture of smoking tobacco," where he founded St. Philip's. He later served as bishop of the Diocese for 39 years.

In time, the chapel became inadequate to handle the number of parishioners, and shortly after firing the rector in 1920 for "not visiting students enough," the Vestry again hired a nationally known architect, Hobart Upjohn. They continued the bold, imaginative vision of our founders but adopted a very different paradigm in designing and constructing the church, underwritten by philanthropist William Erwin and dedicated by Bishop Cheshire in 1925. A wonderful new expression were the stained glass windows to the left and right of the altar, which capture in lesser-known scriptural stories the continuing ministry "DNA" of the Chapel of the Cross.

The one on the left shows Peter risking ritual defilement by going into the house of Cornelius, a Roman centurion, to baptize his family. A divine vision has helped him understand that forgiveness and salvation are for all people and that in his words at the bottom of the window, "God is no respecter of persons" or in another translation, "God shows no partiality." Our legacy from the founding of our parish on has been to welcome all people and, in the words of the Baptismal Covenant, to "strive for justice and peace among all people, and respect the dignity of every human being."

The window on the right features Paul in Athens, the intellectual center of ancient civilization. Many gods are worshiped there and their statutes literally put up on pedestals, but in case the Athenians missed one who might be offended, they also erected an empty pedestal "to the unknown God." Paul ingeniously informs them that the God they do not know is Jesus, and tells them his story. Founded on the campus of the first public university in the United States to open its doors, we too at the Chapel of the Cross are to proclaim the Gospel in ways that people hungry for education can understand and accept. We cannot simply be satisfied to be part of a parish that has done this for generations. Our anniversary celebration today is not merely a recounting and relishing of the past. It must also energize and engage us for the future.

A letter from Mr. Erwin in 1922, articulating his reasons for donating the land and the money for constructing the church, reveals that plans at that time called for the chapel to be converted into "an auditorium of the Parish House plant."

Thank God they could not bring themselves to do that! For the chapel remains the soul of this parish, both our link to our past and a living embodiment of the worship and the ministry that we are privileged to inherit and to be called to. Let us, with Jacob in our first reading, awake from any sleep that may obscure our eyes and acknowledge for ourselves, "Surely the Lord is in this place, and I did not know it. ... How awesome is this place! This is none other than the house of God, and this is the gate of heaven."

Genesis 28:10-17

Always Be Steady … Fulfill Your Ministry
The Celebration of 40 Years of Service by Dr. Wylie S. Quinn III
The Twenty-First Sunday after Pentecost
October 17, 2010

Preach the word, be urgent in season and out of season, convince, rebuke, and exhort, be unfailing in patience and teaching. … Always be steady, endure suffering, do the work of an evangelist, fulfill your ministry.

Today we have the unique privilege of celebrating 40 years of dedication in the service of God and in the employment of this parish. Dr. Van Quinn has served as our organist and choirmaster for four decades. If you read the article in the October *Cross Roads* announcing today's celebration, you saw speculation that there might be elements of a roast in the address from the pulpit! But not only would that stray outside the purpose of the sermon, which is to proclaim the Gospel and to make the mystery of God present among us, but even more significantly, Van's shy and withdrawn personality just does not lend itself to any eccentricities or outrageous behavior. Despite our 28 years together, I simply have not found any good material with which to roast him! I will start taking better notes now in anticipation of his 50th anniversary!

If this sermon is not a roast of Van, neither is it a toast — for the reasons already mentioned about the purposes of the sermon. As much as this occasion is about Van and his life among us, in a larger sense it is about God, especially about God's incredible gift to us of music, and about the challenges of faithful service to which God calls all of us.

Let me begin then with God's gracious gift to us of worship and music. I count it a great blessing that music integrated into worship has long had a major role in the ministry of this parish. And of course, music has played universally a significant part in Christian worship since its early days. Music resonates inside us and connects us to our inner souls in a mysterious but undeniable way. It allows us to praise God from the depths of our being. St. Augustine even declared that the one who sings prays twice.

St. Basil, writing delightfully in the fourth century, emphasized music as a teaching vehicle, as a way to learn scripture and important Christian truths, even when we might not want to!

> Whereas the Holy Spirit saw that mankind is unto virtue hardly drawn, and that righteousness is the less accounted of by reason of the proneness of our affections to that which delighteth; it pleased the wisdom of the same Spirit to borrow from melody that pleasure, which mingled with heavenly mysteries, causeth the smoothness and softness of that which toucheth the ear, to convey as it were by stealth the treasure of good things into man's mind. To this purpose were those harmonious tunes of psalms devised for us, that they which are either in years but young (the children), or touching perfection of virtue as not yet grown to ripeness (the rest of us!), might when they think they sing, learn. O the wise conceit of that heavenly Teacher (Basil concluded), which hath by his skill found out a way, that doing those things wherein we delight, we may also learn that whereby we profit!

Just think of the 40 years worth of junior choirs who have learned so much about their faith through the hymns and the anthems that Dr. Quinn has chosen for them and drummed into their hearts and minds!

But music has not simply been viewed in Christianity as a teaching tool. Many centuries later, Richard Hooker, the Anglican Divine, wrote convincingly and beautifully of the power of music itself, even without words, to stir us and to connect us with the Divine Mystery.

> Touching musical harmony whether by instrument or by voice, it being but of high and low in sounds a due proportionable disposition, such notwithstanding is the force thereof, and so pleasing effects it hath in that very part of man which is most divine, that some have been thereby induced to think that the soul itself by nature is or hath in it harmony...

> Although we lay altogether aside the consideration of ditty or matter, the very harmony of sounds being framed in due sort and carried from the ear to the spiritual faculties of our souls,

is by a native puissance and efficacy greatly available to bring to a perfect temper whatsoever is there troubled, apt as well to quicken the spirit as to allay that which is too eager, sovereign against melancholy and despair, forcible to draw forth tears of devotion if the mind be such as can yield them, able to move and moderate all affections (Laws, Book 5, Chapter 38).

I know that not just those in our choirs, but all of us who have sung God's praise along with them or listened in quiet reverence to their inspiring offerings, can affirm this power of music attested to by Hooker, which has moved us here many times so deeply in our spirits.

That is a gift from God not to be taken for granted. To quote a more contemporary theologian, when Peter Gomes, Plummer Professor of Christian Morals at Harvard University, preached here at Evensong on Pentecost five years ago, he began his remarks by praising the quality of the music. "I travel all around our country," he said "and even in Europe. You do not know how mediocre the music programs are in so many places! But here at the Chapel of the Cross, the music is of a remarkable quality. It contributes to the whole experience of worship and leads us more easily to surrender ourselves to God. Do not take that for granted," he admonished us, leaning across the pulpit. "Appreciate it. Give thanks for it. And pay for it!" As we move forward with our joint annual-capital campaign, that is a message from an outside observer that we all need to hear!

Moving on to the challenges of steady and faithful service, the words of Paul with which I began this sermon, first of all describe the remarkable achievement of Dr. Quinn in completing 40 years of service: "Always be steady … fulfill your ministry." Steady is certainly what his ministry has been, not only recruiting and planning and rehearsals and voluntaries and hymns and service music and anthems and motets week after week, year after year, decade after decade, but also his continual teaching, his pastoral care for those under his charge, his witnessing to the faith, plus numerous weddings and funerals and other special services of various kinds — the numbers are too scary to add up! He has in many and various ways preached the word, been urgent in season and out of season, convinced, rebuked, and exhorted, as his choirs will attest! Perhaps I should stop there with our quote because, as Van would be the first to tell you, he has not always been "unfailing in patience." But that has kept him humble, knowing deeply, as all of us must, his dependence on God's merciful and bountiful grace, and it has kept him even more motivated always to be steady and to fulfill his ministry.

Those words of Paul also urge all of us to respond to God's call with equal determination and faithfulness. Few of us are musicians; few of us are asked to be in the same place over such a long period of time. But all of us are called to respond faithfully; all of us are called to live lives of service; all of us are called to dedicate ourselves to God and if to God, then to all of God's people. All of us are called to worship God in the beauty of holiness, to sing out our praise and thanksgiving and so to pray twice, and going forth into the world, to show forth our praise "not only with our lips, but in our lives."

At the end of this service, we will sing a hymn with a familiar tune (*Engelberg*) but whose words we have never sung before. They are most appropriate, however, to this celebration and worth emphasizing. Let me ask you to turn to hymn number 420 and read the stanzas aloud with me.

> *When in our music God is glorified, and adoration leaves no room for pride, it is as though the whole creation cried Alleluia!*
>
> *How often, making music we have found a new dimension in the world of sound, as worship moved us to a more profound Alleluia!*
>
> *So has the Church, in liturgy and song, in faith and love, through centuries of wrong, borne witness to the truth in every tongue, Alleluia!*
>
> *And did not Jesus sing a psalm that night when utmost evil strove against the Light? Then let us sing, for whom he won the fight, Alleluia!*
>
> *Let every instrument be tuned for praise! Let all rejoice who have a voice to raise! And may God give us faith to sing always Alleluia! Amen.*

2 Timothy 3:14-4:5

Grateful Children of God
The Seventeenth Sunday after Pentecost
September 23, 2012

Jesus was quite drawn to children and they to him. In today's Gospel, he took a child in his arms and identified himself with that child. He declared to his disciples, "Whoever receives one such child in my name receives me; and whoever receives me, receives not me but him who sent me." In so doing, Jesus revealed that he so identified with children that what people did to them they did to him; and he also made clear that his primary sense of identity was as the child, the son, of his Father. As a devoted and loving child, his primary focus was to do the will of his Father, to imitate his Father, to be in union with his Father.

There is something in that single-minded devotion of a child which Jesus would have us pay close attention to. True life, he is saying, comes not from serving ourselves, from trying to be the greatest and lording it over others, but from serving our divine Father and therefore serving others. It is through that simple devotion and focus on living as God's child that we can find true fulfillment.

This morning I want to focus briefly on one very important aspect of that childlike simplicity, and that is the gift of gratitude. Being genuinely grateful for what is given is an acknowledgement of our childlike status before God. Like all children, we receive all that we have been given. We did not give ourselves the gift of life, nor the gift of our bodies and souls and all the capacities that they give us, nor the gift of the earth and all its beauty and sustaining resources, nor the gift of other people, nor the gift of all the circumstances of our lives. All of that comes from God, from whom all blessings flow. Our response is to give God thanks and to use as well as we can all that we have received. Like unspoiled children, we are not to complain about what we have or that it is not enough, but to relish and make use of all the gifts the Father lavishes on us for as long as they are given to us.

For no earthly gift lasts forever. A sunrise lasts a few minutes; a meal, at most an hour. A pet may live a decade or so; even a spouse is parted from us by death, as will be all our friends and family. As children of God, however, we trust and believe that the Giver of all gifts is always with us, always ready to give us more of the Divine self, always leading us to new life. Gifts may come and go, but the Giver lasts forever.

We are constantly coming to endings and new beginnings. They are inseparable. Something cannot begin without something else ending. Each night we let go of one day and prepare for the gift of another.

Tonight we come to one such ending and beginning in the life of our parish. In the liturgy of the Blessing of the Ground, we will give thanks for parts of our building and for trees that we will soon say goodbye to. We will also give thanks and ask God's blessing on the new section of the building and the playground and trees that are to come. As I shared in this month's *Cross Roads,* while I am very excited about these long-needed facilities and their positive impact on our many ministries, still "it is not easy to say good-by to the familiar and the cherished." But we do so as grateful children of God, thankful for both the past and the future, and we do so focused not simply on the gifts, but on the Giver, who makes all things new.

Ending and beginning, losing one's life and finding it, dying and rising: the essence of life for us who are called, and who aspire to live, as simple, grateful children of God. Each time we come here to worship God we celebrate endings and beginnings; we offer up what has been and we look for what will be. Tonight it will just be more obvious.

As we prepare now for that transition, we do so in the context of Holy Eucharist, which is, of course, about dying and rising. In this sacramental mystery, Jesus' death and resurrection is made present again, and through his victory we are caught up with him into new life, into a new beginning. Just as the consecrated food of bread and wine dies to itself and loses its identity to new life in us, so we are subsumed into Christ's Body and become one with God and with one another. Week after week we live out this paschal mystery in this foretaste of the heavenly banquet. "As often as [we] eat this bread and drink the cup, [we] proclaim the Lord's death until he comes."

Ending and beginning, losing one's life and finding it, dying and rising: the essence of life for us who are called, and who aspire to live, as simple, grateful children of God.

Mark 9:30-37

II

Feasts and Fasts: The Liturgical Year

Nonstop Repentance
The Second Sunday of Advent
December 6, 1987

During the recent fund campaign for WUNC radio, listeners were challenged at one point to call in, along with their pledge, one word which they thought best described the 1980s. A number of interesting responses were received, including "fibrous," "biodegradable," and "deficit." The winner, which was declared to best characterize the 80s, was "kakistocracy," a word which was defined as "government by people least equipped to do so!" Who am I to argue with such an apt word?

But the entry which interested me most was submitted by our own associate for parish ministry, Nancy Reynolds Pagano. Her choice was "nonstop." I don't know about you, but that word strikes a deep chord in me.

Life in the 1980s is certainly nonstop. There are places to go; people to see; things to get done; errands to run; projects to start; service to be rendered; books to be read; speakers to be heard; shows to be seen; labor-saving devices to be hauled to the repair shop and picked up again; bills to be paid; social obligations to be fulfilled; new ideas to be studied; letters to be answered; and lists to be made of the things that we did not get done today, and are not, incidentally, likely to finish off tomorrow.

We may lament this state of affairs, and wish that our lives could be simpler, that we had more time to take things at a leisurely pace. But the fact is that things are not likely to change. We keep assuming they will. "If I can just make it to the holidays," or "to next semester," or "to the summer," or "to retirement." But retired people tell me that they can't figure out now how they ever used to have time to make a living!

The truth is that our lives are going to be busy, and perhaps busier, continuing at a nonstop pace, far on into the future. That is a fact to face, reality to reckon with. The question becomes, "How do we deal with that reality?" I am afraid that the answer is for too many of us (and I certainly include myself): "Not very well." Rather than taking available means to gain some perspective on our lives, we occupy ourselves with more tasks. Rather than utilizing any rare, silent times we may have to face ourselves and God, we fill them up with diversions. Rather than simplify our lives, we clutter them. Listen to these words from an article in the *Chapel Hill Newspaper* a few years ago by, of all things, a Hollywood reporter:

"Americans, more than any people on earth, are entertained to death.

"Television and cable run 24 hours a day. Many theaters are open around the clock. Restaurants, elevators and automobile radios blare canned music ceaselessly. Factories and business offices pipe in music.

"Walkman and other tape recorders, not to mention portable radios, are part of the American street scene. It's as if the populace had grown earphones and antennas. Even joggers wear them.

"Airports have small quarter-operated TV sets for travelers who cannot sit still for half an hour awaiting their flights. In flights there are, of course, earphones and movies. Professional football's sidelines are marked by half-naked women kicking their heels in the event fans get bored watching Dallas kick the kapok out of Houston.

"Silence has become a sin in the United States. Diversion is all."

"Diversion is all." Ironically, we heap on our already hectic lives noise, clutter and distraction. We go to great lengths to avoid silences: times when we may be confronted with the noise inside of us, times to listen for what God may be saying to us, times to achieve some intimacy with ourselves and with God.

The readings for this Second Sunday of Advent urge us to repentance. "In the wilderness prepare the way of the Lord," says Isaiah, "make straight in the desert a highway for our God." In his letter, Peter assures us that "the Lord ... is forbearing toward you, not wishing that any should perish, but that all should reach repentance." Mark tells us that "John the baptizer appeared in the wilderness, preaching a baptism of repentance for the forgiveness of sins."

Perhaps the repentance that is asked of us is not so much from killing and stealing and lying and more easily identifiable sins, but from occupying ourselves with so much that we leave no room for God. Perhaps we need to repent of, that is "turn away from" our being content with never questioning, never struggling to see who we are, and why we are here, and what is asked of us. Perhaps we are to repent of our constant reliance on our own strength and resources to bring us through life's difficulties, never allowing God to find us in our brokenness, and lift us up, and breathe new life back into us.

When we become too busy and preoccupied, then we pass by the reality of the loving God, who longs to break through our negligence and shortsightedness, who says to us the same words he uttered to his chosen people through his prophet Isaiah, "Comfort, comfort my people, says your God. Speak tenderly to Jerusalem, and cry to her that her warfare is ended, that her iniquity is pardoned."

When we are accustomed to relying only on ourselves, then we miss the hope that Isaiah offers: "Behold, the Lord God comes with might, and his arm rules for him; behold, his reward is with him, and his recompense before him." And lest we think that God is only powerful and not gentle, Isaiah adds, "He will feed his flock like a shepherd, he will gather the lambs in his arms, he will carry them in his bosom, and gently lead those that are with young."

When we become so focused on our own lives and our own importance, we deprive ourselves of the liberating perspective which God offers us through Isaiah, "All flesh is grass, and all its beauty is like the flower of the field. The grass withers, the flower fades, when the breath of the Lord blows upon it; surely the people is grass. The grass withers, the flower fades; but the word of our God will stand forever." When we can see our smallness and relative unimportance in the face of the Lord with whom "one day is as a thousand years, and a thousand years as one day," then we are freed from the tyranny of self-centeredness and self-service and self-reliance to worship and serve and depend on the God of heaven and earth.

God is the center of the universe, and not we and our brief lives, which we take all too seriously. It is God's power and love and forgiveness in which we put our trust, not our own meager efforts. "It is he that hath made us and not we ourselves."

Let the season of Advent, then, be a reminder for us of our need to repent. Let it be a special time of silence and attentiveness. Let the scripture readings of these Sundays speak to us of the God before whose power and holiness we are as nothing, yet who seeks us out, and forgives us, and comforts us, and leads us. Let our getting ready for Christmas be truly a preparing of the way of the Lord. Amen.

Isaiah 40:1-11
II Peter 3:8-15a, 18
Mark 1:1-8

A Desire for the Divine
The Second Sunday of Advent
December 10, 2006

When you see the silent candle burning, you are no longer caught in the obsession with darkness, and a desire for the Divine sweeps you upward.

Johann Wolfgang von Goethe, in his striking poem, *The Holy Longing,* captured a deep Advent theme in these few words: "When you see the silent candle burning, you are no longer caught in the obsession with darkness, and a desire for the Divine sweeps you upward." All this past week, we have been lighting in the darkness the solitary first candle in our Advent wreaths, pointing us to the One who is to come. The quickening of that flame in the fading December light, perhaps accompanied by the plaintive musical cry of "O come, O come, Emmanuel," has indeed awakened hope within us. Despite the surrounding darkness, it has reconnected us with the deep desire for God inside us and swept us upward to our source of hope and salvation, the God in whom we can trust.

Now we begin the second week of that expectation and longing, and another candle, another witness to God's continual coming among us, invites us away from our obsession with darkness. Do not be overcome by what closes in upon you and weighs you down, it seems to say. Focus on the light, the promise of life and nurturing warmth. Let the spark of the Divine in your soul lift you up out of the darkness. Let it connect you with your desire for the Divine and reaffirm your identity as a child of God. Let it reignite within you your yearning for a higher engagement with God.

This advent has been a particularly poignant time for me. In part this comes from the weeklong clergy refreshment conference known as CREDO, which I attended just before Thanksgiving. It was a wonderful opportunity to reexamine and renew my spiritual life and my vocational health and to worship and converse with other Episcopal clergy from throughout our Church. As a result I find a new freshness and a new vitality in prayer and in the liturgy and in the preparations associated with this advent season.

But an even more significant factor has been my relationship with a close friend of mine, Stan Tabor, and with his family, all members of our parish. Our friendship goes back over 25 years and started in our Seattle days. Each couple serves as godparents for one of the other's children. Eighteen months ago, Stan was diagnosed with brain cancer, metastasized from a melanoma. For a year and a half, a battle has been waged in his body, utilizing surgery, full brain radiation, targeted radiation numerous times, chemo therapy of various kinds, even an experimental treatment in which vaccine made from a harvested tumor from his chest was injected back into him at two-week intervals for several months. Not yet 60, Stan has fought the good fight and succeeded in participating in his second daughter's college graduation and his son's graduation from high school. They have had wonderful family times and have taken several trips together.

As Advent began last week, Stan came under hospice care. The shortening of these December days has taken on a new dimension for him and for all of us. But he has not given up living. He has not given up believing or praying or loving. As I sat and listened to him talk with the hospice chaplain, I was struck with the deep sense of gratitude Stan feels for this unusual time, for the gift of his family and their special times together, for the support of so many friends who have shared this unique time with him. Life has become very real for Stan, and death as a real part of life, and the life that lies beyond death. These are not just concepts anymore. Although not without his moments of fear and anger and doubt, Stan has quietly and inspiringly grown in his faith and trust in God, who has not abandoned him, who created him and claimed him as a child at baptism, who overcomes death and offers unending life. As his friend and priest, who has been privileged to share his journey with him, I find myself deeply touched by Stan's faith and gratitude. *I* am more ready to find the good in each day, where God has come nearest us, to prepare the way of the Lord, as we hear in today's Gospel, to let the desire for the Divine sweep me upward into fuller life in union with God and with others.

As we light this week the second candle in our Advent wreaths, in anticipation of the third and then the fourth to make a full circle, let it beckon each of us into a deeper advent, a more real sense of God's presence within and among us. When we see the silent candle, in Goethe's words, may we no longer be caught in our obsession with darkness, but may our desire for the Divine sweep us upward.

I close with what has come to be the CREDO prayer, helpful at any time of the year, but perhaps particularly appropriate for us during Advent. Let us pray.

Holy God, be in my mind that I might let go of all that diminishes the movement of Your Spirit within me. Discerning God, be in my eyes, that I might see You in the midst of all the busyness that fills my life. Loving God, be in my heart, that I can be open to those I love, to those with whom I share ministry and to the whole human family. Gracious God, be in that grace-filled silence that lies deep within me, that I might live in Christ as Christ lives in me. Amen.

Advent Hope
The Second Sunday of Advent
December 9, 2007

A new student at Carolina was having a very difficult time adjusting to the social and academic demands of college life. He felt scared and awkward and alienated. He did not want to be here, and he kept to himself as much as he could. Discovering our chapel, he spent long hours just sitting before God. For weeks and months, any time he could come and find the chapel empty, he would gratefully sink into its sacred solitude, leaving only if someone else should enter. His isolation and alienation were made bearable only by the comfort he found in the chapel. Out of the strength that refuge brought him, he gradually began to adjust to college life and to find his way. That was over 40 years ago.

Upon graduating from the University in the late sixties, Clifton Daniel entered Virginia Seminary and was ordained a priest. Ten years ago he became bishop of the Diocese of East Carolina. Ten days ago as preacher in our chapel for the concluding Eucharist of the Province Four Bishops annual meeting, Bishop Daniel looked back on that difficult time in his early student days. He reflected to those of us present that the hours spent in our chapel probably saved his life. Somehow the grace and the strength he eventually absorbed there formed the seeds of his calling to ordained ministry and enabled him to respond to his life's vocation.

I tell you that story not only because I think it is critical for all of us to know how important is the ministry of the Chapel of the Cross and how significantly through the decades and continuing on, people's lives have been changed by their encounters with our sacred spaces, our liturgy, our many and varied ministries. So often, as is the case with Bishop Daniel, these changed lives also have far-reaching effects on still other lives; all of which grew out of the faithfulness and the vision and the stewardship of parishioners of the Chapel of the Cross, whose mantle you now carry.

But more importantly on this Second Sunday of Advent, I tell you this story because it is very much an Advent story. It is a story of waiting and hoping and needing a Savior. It is a story of trying to be attentive to God in the midst of brokenness and with the deep realization that we cannot save ourselves. For all of us could be the young student, Clifton Daniel.

We may not think we are. We may think we are more self-sufficient than that, more able to cope with what life throws us, more able to adjust to difficult circumstances. And of course there is truth to that perception. God has given us many strengths, many resources to bring to life's challenges and struggles.

But Advent is a time to reflect on our need for God, on our relative powerlessness, on our dependence on God's power and grace. In the face of difficult relationships, of addictions, of past failures, of significant losses, of the power of war and of poverty and of drought, of our limitations, of the inevitability of death, of being — in the words of next Sunday's well-known Advent collect — "sorely hindered by our sins," we are unable to save ourselves. We can, like an ill-adjusted student, only look to God with expectancy and hope.

Dietrich Bonhoeffer, imprisoned by the Nazis during World War II, felt this same helplessness. He wrote in a later-published letter: "Life in a prison cell reminds me a great deal of Advent. One waits and hopes and putters around. But in the end, what we do is of little consequence. The door is shut, and it can only be opened from the outside." Whether we envision ourselves locked in a prison cell or voluntarily sequestered in the chapel, the metaphor is the same: We await God's saving and liberating power. "O come, O come, Emmanuel, and ransom captive Israel, that mourns in lonely exile here until the Son of God appear." "How long, O Lord, how long?" we ask in our alienation and powerlessness, but with Advent hope.

For Advent, while facing reality truthfully and humbly, is not a time of despair. It is not a season for self-indulgently wallowing in our difficulties and looking forward to a bleak future. It is instead an opportunity to face the reality of our lives honestly and to believe in God's power and love and forgiveness. It is a time to realign our hope.

For neither is Advent a period of passivity or abandoning all initiative. We do not simply throw our hands in the air and give up on life's daily battles and abandon all such good works as God has prepared for us to walk in. No, Advent hope is active. While it is focused on God and not on ourselves, it also makes room for God to act. It requires us to be attentive and to be patient and to watch. Advent hope mobilizes us and refocuses us. It calls us away from mere reliance on ourselves and to look to God for our salvation and our strength. It would have us seek out sacred space, like the lost student, and to let God find us and nourish us and call us to believe and to respond and to serve others. Advent hope wells up within us in, sometimes a distant, but clearly irrepressible joy, "Rejoice! Rejoice! Emmanuel [God with us] shall come to thee, O Israel."

Do Not Look for Another
The Third Sunday of Advent
December 12, 2004

Are you he who is to come, or shall we look for another?

This question of John the Baptist, impatiently waiting in prison, is also a question for us, but not so much in terms of our finding the Messiah. As baptized Christians, we have already accepted Jesus as the Lord and Savior. We know he is the Son of God, the one who has come. Rather the question for us concerns how this Christ continues to be revealed to us. In whose face do we find the face of Jesus? Whom are we given to love that we might love him? We look at many human faces and ask each one, "Are you the one who is to come, or shall we look for another?"

Last Sunday morning, vested and waiting at the back of the church for the procession to start, I noticed two men making their way down the side aisle from the transept door, looking for a seat in the back. Even though their clothes were clean, their appearance said, "street people." I made a mental note that they would probably seek assistance during the course of the morning and unconsciously braced myself. Sooner than I expected, even as I stood at the baptismal font during communion for the anointing and laying on of hands, one approached me and said, "Father, can I see you after the service?" "No," I told him truthfully, "I have a class to teach." Later, I found out that Ted, as he identified himself, had located David Frazelle (the "new kid on the block," who did not yet have further obligations during the coffee hour!) and told him that he and his friend would be coming to see me the next day. His friend did indeed come to my office Monday morning, but only to tell me that Ted had died suddenly during the night at the shelter. They had been strengthening one another as they searched for employment and tried to get back on their feet, and he would miss him dearly.

"Are you the one who is to come, or shall we look for another?"

A few days later I received a phone call from a woman in our parish, who over the last few years has seemed to develop a penchant for disagreeing with just about every rectoral decision I make. She wanted to tell me why she was opposing the latest proposal I had made to one of our major committees. I struggled to listen to her reasoning, trying not to argue but to understand her concerns — but not very successfully. It was very hard not to connect it with earlier conversations.

"Are you the one who is to come, or shall we look for another?"

That evening my wife and I went out to dinner. Shortly after we were seated a young couple from our parish, with their one-year-old, was shown a table not far away. We waved at each other, but soon the toddler began expressing his hunger, and I kept looking over there. Betsy suggested that that might make the parents uncomfortable. "No," I said, being a sucker for little children, "I am hoping they will bring him over here for a change of scenery." "I am your wife and dinner companion," she replied. "You should be paying attention to me." She was right.

"Are you the one who is to come, or shall we look for another?"

Every day Jesus comes to us in the faces of other people, some familiar, some not, some easier to love than others, some very difficult. It is not that God will love us less if we do not respond well. God's great love surpasses any of our human limitations. But we will miss that opportunity to return God's love by being attentive to the Christ in another. Do not ask the one in front of you, "Are you the one who is to come, or shall we look for another?" Do not look for another.

Matthew 11:2-11

Underappreciated Gifts
The Fourth Sunday of Advent
December 22, 2013

As we have been preparing for the annual celebration of the coming of Jesus, it has been a great pleasure to have back in its place in our church the Nativity window over the Franklin Street door. While we may have taken it for granted in earlier celebrations of Christmas, to be without it for several years during its prolonged restoration was particularly regrettable and disheartening, especially since the insulation that long filled its space had no artistic merit whatsoever, in fact quite the opposite!

But now that the necessary work was finally completed and we are again inspired and uplifted by our priceless Nativity window, it is good to give thanks to God for this cherished gift and to appreciate its presence in our lives. I give you all permission to turn around and appreciate it yet again! At the children's pageant yesterday, my grandson, Walker, noticed the king kneeling to the left of Jesus and declared him to be "Santa!" Given our Gospel this morning, do take note of Joseph's place in the scene. Although we may not notice this beautiful art often, particularly on a cloudy morning, it not only points us to the deep mystery of the Incarnation, the awesome reality of the Divine Word becoming flesh and dwelling among us, it also now symbolizes for us so many other gifts with which God fills our lives and which we can so easily take for granted and underappreciate.

Within the window itself, perhaps the least notable and least striking figure in the nativity scene is Joseph. He is shown in the central panel, but is greatly overshadowed, standing in the background behind Mary and Jesus. That is certainly consistent with how his role has been viewed by Christian theology and art. While Jesus is the Savior of the world and Mary his mother is (in Greek) the *theotokos* or God bearer, Joseph is regarded as Jesus' legal father, a less prominent role, although one that does establish Jesus as of the royal lineage of David.

Most of scripture ignores Joseph, including Paul's Epistles, the earliest Christian writings, and Mark's Gospel, the oldest of the four versions. John makes only a passing reference to Joseph's existence. Only Matthew and Luke in their first two chapters include information about Joseph. Even there he is never quoted, not an insignificant omission from an inspired narrative relying on words to express God's self-revelation. After the infancy narratives and the one story about the pre-teenage Jesus being "lost" and then found in the temple, Joseph disappears from the Gospel narratives altogether, no doubt having died well before Jesus began his public life. So Christian theology and art have followed scripture's lead and not paid much attention to Joseph's role in salvation history.

But when one of the few scriptural stories about him surfaces in the lectionary, as it does in the Gospel on this Sunday before Christmas, it reminds us that Joseph's role was not at all insignificant and that he is another of those rich, underappreciated gifts of God for us to be more attentive to.

After all, although Joseph is not presented to us as Jesus' biological father — revealing the divine truth that only God can make God present among us; we cannot, so to speak, give God to ourselves — although Joseph is not his biological father, he is, along with Mary, the one who raised Jesus, who cared for him and protected him and taught him. Our story today shows us several inspiring traits Jesus would have absorbed and learned from Joseph.

When Joseph found out that Mary was with child while they were as yet only betrothed, he knew the law that called for divorce and possibly even death. But Matthew calls him "a just man and unwilling to put her to shame." Joseph wanted to uphold the law, but to do so compassionately and quietly, with no vindictive judgment.

Think of Jesus' response decades later when they brought him a woman accused of adultery, demanding that she be killed. "Let him who is without sin cast the first stone," he said. And as they walked away one by one, putting down their stones, he said to her, "Neither do I accuse you. Go and sin no more." The compassionate righteousness of Joseph had been "caught" by Jesus as he learned from him each day and "grew in wisdom and age and grace before God and man."

Or consider Joseph's openness to God's direction. When the angel assured him in a dream that Mary had not been unfaithful but that the child was the work of the Holy Spirit, a son who would "save his people from their sins," Joseph put aside *his* compassionate plan for Mary and "did as the Angel of the Lord commanded him," taking her as his wife. Following several other subsequent divinely inspired dreams, Joseph also listened to and obeyed God, taking the child to Egypt for protection against Herod and later returning with him to Nazareth when it was safe. Joseph faithfully listened for and obeyed God.

Think of Jesus' devotion to his heavenly Father's will. "I seek not my own will, but the will of him who sent me" (John 5:30). "My food is to do the will of him who sent me" (John 4:34). "Whoever does the will of God is my brother and sister and mother" (Mark 3:35). In the Garden of Gethsemane, the night before he died, Jesus prayed that this cup might be taken from him; but his final prayer was, "Not my will, but thine be done" (Luke 22:44). In the prayer Jesus taught his followers (which we pray every service for which we gather in the Episcopal Church), we say, "Thy will be done on earth, as it is in heaven." That passionate devotion to God's will, so characteristic of Jesus, was first learned from Joseph, whose role was confined to the early but very important formative years of Jesus' life on earth. And Jesus passed on to us what he first learned at the knee of Joseph.

On this Fourth Sunday of Advent then, when we make our hearts ready, as the carol says, to "prepare him room," let us be thankful for all God's underappreciated gifts to us, for our Nativity window, restored to its place of witness, for faithful Joseph, who helped form the compassionate and obedient Jesus, and for the Incarnation itself, the turning point of human history, when Jesus became Emmanuel, God with us. "Glory to God whose power, working in us, can do infinitely more than we can ask or imagine: Glory to him from generation to generation in the Church, and in Christ Jesus for ever and ever."

Matthew 1:18-25

God's Power Revealed in Powerlessness
Christmas Day, 1988

Paul Tillich, in his collection of sermons called *The Shaking of the Foundations*, uses an image which I find immensely helpful, especially in this Christmas season. He observes that the Greek word for "truth" means "making manifest the hidden," and he asserts that that truth is not apparent, but must be unveiled and discovered. This is not an easy or a natural process for us, Tillich says, for truth dwells in the depth, while we tend to stay on the surface. The surface, of course, moves continuously about like waves on the ocean, filling our lives with delusion; but the depth, which is the abiding place of truth, is eternal and certain, not disturbed by shifts and changes.

The challenge for us, then, is to penetrate that depth, to go below the surface to discover the truth that God would reveal to us. Especially at Christmas, when it is so easy to become lost in the waves of glitter and presents and activities, it is necessary for us to re-enter the depth and to be confronted again with the truth of Christmas.

The story, as it is told by Luke, is a deceptively simple one; yet there is much for us to probe on a deeper level. Jesus, having been conceived in the womb of his mother by the Holy Spirit, was born in a stable in Bethlehem, the Son of God. This event was heralded by angels to nearby shepherds, who came and saw and "returned, glorifying and praising God."

But not everyone responded so openly or so positively to God's uniquely manifested presence. All who heard the shepherds "wondered" or "were astonished" at these things. Astonishment is a standard reaction in the Gospel (cf. Luke 1:21, 1:63), and it does not necessarily lead to faith.

Matthew is much more specific about those who rejected Jesus by adding the story of Herod's killing all the newborn male children, resulting in Jesus' "exile" in Egypt. John wrote in the Prologue to his Gospel that "he came to his own home, and his own people received him not." This pattern of the proclamation of God's Good News in Jesus being met with some who resisted and some who accepted is repeated over and over in the Gospel. Not only at his birth, but also at his Baptism, during his public ministry, and at his death and resurrection, scripture tells us that Jesus was met with both rejection and acceptance. "Some (seed) fell on the rock ... and some fell into good soil and grew." (Luke 8:6-8)

The same choice as that which faced those first participants in the Christ event confronts us when we encounter God's Word: Will we only marvel at all these things, refusing to know and accept Jesus, or will we receive him that he may, in the words of John, give us "power to become children of God"?

"Power to become children. ..." Those are strange words to be joined together. Children are not very powerful, or so it seems. What is this power of God, and what are we asked to become?

God's power is not like the power of the world, which may explain why Jesus found, and finds, so much rejection. Whereas the world defines power in terms of domination, of control, of imposing one's will upon others, God exercises the power of love, of goodness, of servanthood.

The power of God was manifest in Jesus, not as one who manipulated others or used them for his own ends, but as one who came to serve and to bring new life. Jesus was sent to us, not as a conquering ruler commanding the attention and the adulation of all. Rather he came as a helpless infant in an obscure village, whose identity was revealed only to a few shepherds. The Kingdom which he later preached to those who would listen was spread not by the rich and the powerful, but by those whose only power came from God's Spirit which filled them. God's power was made perfect in their weakness.

That is most difficult for us to accept. That the all-powerful God can and does and wants to work through our weakness does not sit well with us. We want to cover up or compensate for our weaknesses, not offer them to God to be transformed. We are not prepared to admit that apart from God, we can do nothing. We do not want to own our powerlessness. Surely the power of God could be manifested in another way? Would it not be far better to maximize our own strengths and operate out of those? Is it not a contradiction to say that the powerless have any power?

I recently came across a true story recounted by Christopher de Vinck that may lead us to the truth that lies far below the surface.

"I grew up in the house," de Vinck begins his story, "where my brother was on his back in his bed for almost 33 years, in the same corner of his room, under the same window, beside the same yellow walls. Oliver was blind, mute. His legs were twisted. He didn't have the strength to lift his head nor the intelligence to learn anything."

De Vinck goes on to explain that fumes from a leaking coal-burning stove had overcome his pregnant mother in 1946, and that although his father had quickly carried her outside and revived her, they gradually found out during the first few months of Oliver's life that there was nothing that could be done for him. His parents refused the solution of an institution, and they cared for him at home.

"We bathed Oliver. Tickled his chest to make him laugh. Sometimes we left the radio on in his room. We pulled the shade down over his bed in the morning to keep the sun from burning his tender skin. We listened to him laugh as we watched television downstairs. We listened to him rock his arms up and down to make the bed squeak. We listened to him cough in the middle of the night.

"Oliver grew to the size of a ten-year-old. He had a big chest, a large head. His hands and feet were those of a five-year-old, small and soft. We'd wrap a box of baby cereal for him at Christmas and place it under the tree; pat his head with a damp cloth in the middle of a July heat wave. His baptismal certificate hung on the wall above his head. A bishop came to the house and confirmed him.

"Even now, five years after his death ... Oliver still remains the weakest, most helpless human being I ever met, and yet he was one of the most powerful human beings I ever met. He could do absolutely nothing except breathe, sleep, eat, and yet he was responsible for action, love, courage, insight. When I was small, my mother would say, "Isn't it wonderful that you can see?" And once she said, "When you go to heaven, Oliver will run to you, embrace you, and the first thing he will say is 'Thank you.'" I remember, too, my mother's explaining to me that we were blessed with Oliver in ways that were not clear to her at first. … We were blessed with his presence, a true presence of peace.

"When I was in my early 20s, I met a girl and fell in love. After a few months, I brought her home to meet my family. When my mother went to the kitchen to prepare dinner, I asked the girl, "Would you like to see Oliver?" for I had told her about my brother. "No," she answered.

"Soon after, I met Roe, a lovely girl. She asked me the names of my brothers and sisters. She loved children. I thought she was wonderful. I brought her home after a few months to meet my family. Soon it was time for me to feed Oliver. I remember sheepishly asking Roe if she'd like to see him. "Sure," she said.

"I sat at Oliver's bedside as Roe watched over my shoulder. I gave him his first spoonful, his second. "Can I do that?" Roe asked with ease, with freedom, with compassion; so I gave her the bowl and she fed Oliver one spoonful at a time.

"The power of the powerless," de Vinck concludes. "Which girl would you marry? Today Roe and I have three children."

We are not unlike Oliver. In truth we cannot do much more than breathe, sleep, and eat. We are not in charge of what happens to us. We cannot heal ourselves. We cannot control the response of others to us. Yet the power of God, the love of God, the goodness of God, working in us and in the hearts of others, can do infinitely more than we can ask or imagine.

As children of God, what are we asked to become? The almighty and transcendent God, who came to us as a helpless baby, invites us to accept our own powerlessness. God beckons us to probe below the surface of our self-sufficiency to discover our need for, and our rootedness in, and our union with God. The One who created all of us and redeemed us and fills us with life which will never end impels us to accept all men and women as our brothers and sisters, as co-equal children of our one Father.

On this feast of Christmas, when we behold the mystery of the Word made flesh and penetrate its depth, we are faced with an unavoidable choice: Will we continue along our own way, depending on our own strength, ignoring God's invitation; or will we choose to accept the Savior whom God sends to us, to receive him, to be filled with the power to become children of God?

Glory to God whose power, working in us, can do infinitely more than we can ask or imagine: Glory to him from generation to generation in the Church, and in Christ Jesus for ever and ever. Amen.

Ephesians 3:20, 21

He's Here Already!
Christmas Eve 1990

He was in the world, and the world was made through him, yet the world knew him not. He came to his own home, and his own people received him not.

We might transpose these words of John from tonight's Gospel and put them into the present: "God is in the world, yet the world, created and sustained by God, knows him not. He came to his own home, and his own people still receive him not."

Perhaps we simply do not see evidence of God at work in the world. Our vision is filled with terrifying pictures of impending war in the Middle East, of a gloomy economic scene, of increased drug use and violence and racism. The news seems to worsen every day, and along with it, any sense of hope that we might have. If we think of the Divine at all in connection with any of this, it is perhaps only to wonder, "Where is God?"

Our situation and response is not unlike that of the world into which Jesus was born. While there was a relative peace, it was at the cost of an oppressive military occupation. The Jews longed for deliverance, for a restoration of the Kingdom of David, for the one who would come to establish God's righteousness. "Where is God?" they wondered. "Why doesn't he come?"

The answer to that question was announced in a flash of angels in the night singing the glory of God and proclaiming the birth of the Savior. But not many witnessed that surprising and luminous epiphany. Moving from the sublime messengers to the ridiculous, the news was announced to most Bethlehemites by a motley bunch of shepherds. Shepherds were so despised in Jewish society that they were not allowed to testify in Jewish courts, so what did they know? The world paid them no heed. People went back to bed, their hope unaroused. The good tidings of great joy, except for a very few, went unheard.

Where do we, and did the world before us, go wrong? Why have those created by God not been able to recognize him? Why have God's own people not been able to receive him, and have continued to wonder, "Where is God?"

Perhaps it is because we have not been satisfied to be created in the image of God, but have tried to create God in our own image. If we were God, we are inclined to say, we would never have allowed the world to fall into its current state. We would not let evil flourish and the good seem to flounder. We would not sit back in the wings and seem to do nothing. We would not have been born into an obscure Jewish family, relying on lowly shepherds to spread the word. We would not, after only a few years of public ministry, die a humiliating death on the cross. We would not make people rely on the testimony of others as the basis of their belief. We would not make people wonder, "Where is God?"

In the midst of our struggles and our pain and our gloom, we look for a God who will wipe it all away, who will bring order out of the chaos, who will do what we expect to be done. But in doing so, we miss the God who is already here in the midst of the agony and the confusion, who accompanies us in our suffering, and who brings new life out of our dying.

The message of the Christmas story is not that God will come to us someday, if we are good enough, and rescue us from all that ails us. Rather, the Gospel proclaims that God is already here, in both the joys and sufferings of our lives. That is the Good News which makes life worth living.

A story related by Ralph Whitlock a year ago in the *Manchester Guardian* brings that mystery to life in a wonderful way. He described a nativity play which he attended in East Africa in a village around an old mission compound, miles out in the bush, with a seasoned companion.

> The church was packed. The noise exceeded that of a proverbial magpie roost. Families struggled in, with the maximum of fuss, to settle down on benches, only to get up again a few minutes later to take junior urgently outside. Huge moths fluttered in, pursued by equally large bats.

Across one end of the building, curtains concealed a temporary stage, and from the dressing rooms behind, an equally vociferous cacophony resounded. After a time, a stately lady emerged and made her way to the harmonium, from which she pumped out carols, some of which were vaguely recognizable. The half-hours drifted on, but who could be bored with so much uninhibited entertainment going on all around?

Some years earlier a missionary had written a nativity play for the church, which had used it ever since. As the seasons passed, however, sheets of the script were lost, and now only the first five or six pages were left. In no way deterred, the producer and cast used those.

We sang a carol which I presently identified as "O come all ye faithful." ... Came a roll of drums, and the curtains parted. The Angel Gabriel strode in to announce to Mary, who sat quietly on a stool, that she was to have a baby.

In succession we were treated to a parade of the shepherds, the Wise Men and King Herod, each visitation being introduced by another carol. The audience was entranced. Then came a hiatus. The curtain was pulled along, and the building was unduly quiet.

"What's happening?" I whispered. "Oh, this is where they've come to the end of the script, and now they have to decide what happens next," said my companion.

As he spoke voices were raised behind the curtain. The audience listened enchanted as the arguments grew louder and more heated. "They're having the usual argument," my companion advised me. "They never think of working it out beforehand."

A child in the front row got up and peeped through the join in the curtain. After a moment he shouted something and beckoned to his mother, who went to look. Others followed her, and as there was evidently something worth seeing, they had soon pulled the curtains wide open. There, making his way from a corner of the stage, crawled a chubby black baby, nearly naked.

Delighted to see so many beaming faces, he made his way to the center of the stage, like an old professional, and there sat down, with a beatific smile on his face. The audience shouted their appreciation.

Suddenly there arose a greater commotion from the dressing rooms, where evidently consternation prevailed. "Hey! Where's that baby? Where's baby Jesus?"

The audience told them with a roar of delight, "He's here! He's here already!"

"He's here already!" What a wonderful expression of the good news of Christmas! What a powerful statement of the Christian faith that has been given to us! What a consoling reminder in the midst of life's difficulties!

Emmanuel — "God with us" — that is the proclamation of Christmas. That is to be the basis of our joy, of our hope, of our love for one another. That is the mystery which stretches us beyond our own narrow limits and vision, past those realities which oppress us, to the God who is always present with us.

As we go forth from this service tonight into the imperfect world that does not meet our expectations, let our faith and our consolation and our challenge be caught up by those words: "He's here already!"

John 1:1-14

Christmas: A Time of Excess
Christmas Eve and Christmas Day 1993

Christmas is a time of excess!

There are many senses to that word, I suppose, not all of them positive. We can eat or drink or sleep or watch television to excess, and that is simply self-indulgence. I mean that Christmas is a time of wonderful extravagance, of there being far more of things than usual, far more than is strictly necessary.

That is the pattern that God set. When mankind disobeyed and turned against God, God made a lavish promise — of a Savior who would set things right and bring unending life for all. God fulfilled that promise extravagantly by sending, in the fullness of time, not just a holy man, not just an ambassador for the Divine, but his very own Son. How extravagant and excessive! How much more than required! John Donne said, "Twas much, that man was made like God before. But, that God should be made man, much more."

The signs that announced this lavish action continued the pattern of extravagance. While much has rightly been made of the simplicity of Jesus' birth — to humble parents, with a manger for a bed and insignificant shepherds as greeters and witnesses — it was an angel, the very essence of extravagance, who appeared to the shepherds and caused the glory of the Lord to shine around them. And if that were not enough, "suddenly there was with the angel a multitude of the heavenly host praising God and saying, 'Glory to God in the highest.'" Add to this the mysterious "wise men from the East" and a bright, moving star that guided them, and gifts of gold and frankincense and myrrh, and what wonderful excess there was to that first Christmas!

That is why our extravagance at Christmas is altogether fitting. In response to God's lavishness, it is right that we should do much more than necessary in decorating our homes, that we should spend too much time baking cookies for our neighbors or delivering packages to our friends, that we should give away way too much money to those in need. It is appropriate that we bring out the best vestments, and that the Altar Guild spend more hours than they have adorning the church with greens and flowering plants, and that we worship at odd hours the God who "so loved the world that he gave his only-begotten Son."

My favorite form of extravagance at Christmas is the music, especially the carols. All music is extravagance, of course; music is not sparse or frugal. But perhaps more than any other music, the joyful carols of Christmas help us all to be extravagant, to open up our hearts, to give more of ourselves than we might otherwise.

The *Oxford Book of Carols* describes carols as "songs with a religious impulse that are simple, hilarious, popular, and modern. ... The word 'carol' has a dancing origin, and once meant to dance in a ring." Those of you at Lessons and Carols last Sunday may immediately think of "My Dancing Day" that the Junior Choir sang: Jesus sings in the first person and describes his birth as his chance "to call my true love to my dance." Dance is another wonderful form of extravagance.

"The typical carol, the book goes on, gives voice to the common emotions of healthy people in language that can be understood and music that can be shared by all. Because it is popular it is therefore genial as well as simple; it dances because it is so Christian, echoing St. Paul's conception of the fruits of the Spirit in its challenge to be merry — 'Love and joy come to you.' Indeed, to take life with real seriousness is to take it joyfully, for seriousness is only sad when it is superficial; the carol is thus all the nearer to the ultimate truth because it is jolly."

To take but one example, think of "Angels we have heard on high," which we will sing at Communion. It is a paradigm of hilarity and extravagance. The images are of angel voices bouncing off the mountains and of shepherds who cannot contain themselves. The melody exudes joy, and the rhythm virtually compels you to dance. But most remarkable of all is the chorus, which proclaims the angel's song, "Gloria in excelsis Deo — Glory to God in the highest." The word "Gloria" alone is allotted 18 notes! Wonderful extravagance! Sometimes I get so carried away, it is hard not to sing "Glo-ho-ho-ho-ho-ria!" And then we repeat the whole line!

But is this all just a bit of fluff, an escape from harsh reality, a momentary flight from Sarajevo, from cancer, from poverty, from all-too-common violence, from loneliness? Christian joy is not a denial of human suffering, but an affirmation of hope in the midst of it. While fully acknowledging life's difficulties, it proclaims a belief in a God who loves us extravagantly and who never abandons us in our distress.

Writing in his diary in 1918, Sir Henry Rider Haggard reflected on the Christmas Day just past that both heartened and saddened him:

> This morning was typical Christmas weather, a white frost and a brilliant sky. I have been to a children's party at Dolly's where we played games. It was happy and sad to an old man. One remembers many Christmas parties as far back as fifty years and more ago and oh! Where are the children that played at them? There is a tall clock ticking away at the end of this room; the man who cleaned it the other day said it was the oldest he had ever handled. It has seen many more Christmases than I have, four or five times the number, and still it ticks unconcernedly, marking the passage of the hours and the years. Doubtless it sounded the moment of my birth as it will do that of my death. Remorselessly it ticks on, counting the tale of the fleeting moments from Yule to Yule. Yes, Christmas is a sad feast for the old, and yet — thanks be to God who giveth us the victory — one is full of hope.

The extravagance of the first Christmas did not obliterate the pain of childbirth nor the wails of the parents of the Holy Innocents slaughtered by Herod nor the uncertainty of what lay ahead. It did express an overflowing Divine love that would never again be completely repressed.

Our liturgy tonight, our proclamation of Good News and our singing of hilarious carols and our participation in another manifestation of Divine excess — the Eucharist, and indeed all of our magnanimous activities during this season, are our extravagant response to this Divine love. With the jubilant shepherds, let us

> "Come to Bethlehem and see him whose birth the angels sing;
> Come adore on bended knee, Christ the Lord, the newborn King.
> Gloria in excelsis Deo. Gloria in excelsis Deo."

The Word Became Flesh
Christmas Eve and Christmas Day, 2004

And the Word became flesh and dwelt among us.

Perhaps you saw the front page story in the paper earlier this week. The 50-year-old picture shows two young men, looking remarkably alike, one in a hospital bed, the other standing by his side. Their mouths are open in song, presumably singing along to the portable 45 rpm record player on the hospital stand, loaded with a stack of records ready to fall to the turntable, one after another. Likely this was Christmas music, since the story of these twin brothers on the day before Christmas Eve in 1954 is a Christmas story, not only in its calendar proximity to this feast, but also in the illumination of its mystery.

Before transplants became commonplace, 23-three-year-old Richard Herrick was dying of chronic nephritis, an inflammation of the kidneys. Although in all other previous transplant attempts to that point, the receiver's body had rejected the new organ, Ronald Herrick offered to give up his kidney if it would bring new life to his brother. Since they were identical twins, the doctors thought the chances for success in this case were much higher. On that historic occasion in Boston 50 years ago this week, they did indeed succeed, paving the way for hundreds of thousands of kidney transplants and eventually for liver and heart transplants as well. Richard did die eight years later from causes unrelated to his surgery, but not before he married the charge nurse assigned to him in his recovery; they had two daughters, one of whom became a teacher and the other a nurse in a kidney dialysis unit. Ronald and his wife now live near his brother's widow, and in his retirement, he promotes and encourages organ donation.

This remarkable event qualifies as a Christmas story on many levels. It is, of course, a story of selfless giving, of one risking his own health and life and giving "of his substance" to another out of great love and generosity. It is also an inspiring dramatization of new life coming out of suffering and adversity, not only for the recipient, but also for his new family, which came into being out of this crucible and flourished and became fruitful. Beyond the immediate characters, this episode literally brought new life to hundreds of thousands of others: those who have received transplants and their families and the people whose lives they have affected. In a significant way it has changed human history.

But the unique reason this account links us to the Christmas story is its flesh connection. The gift received by this needful human being, who was powerless to help himself, was clothed in living, human flesh. This was not an external gift of some thing, but that which became part of his earthly body, integral to his vibrant, fragile, transitory, mundane, wonderful human existence. Flesh in part defines us as human beings. Isaiah describes both its beauty and its fragility in saying, "All flesh is grass, and all its beauty is like the flower of the field. The grass withers, the flower fades..." (40:6). It is this flesh which Jesus took on himself, becoming human and living among us. He "did not count equality with God a thing to be grasped," scripture tells us, "but emptied himself ... being born in the likeness of men" (Phil. 2:6-7). "And the Word became flesh and dwelt among us."

How difficult it is for us to grasp the enormity of that reality! The One through whom all things were made became human, a living, breathing, fleshly man, dependent upon bones and blood and organs like kidneys and lungs and a heart for his earthly existence. In so doing he sanctified even more the divinely created dignity and worth of each human person, and he made possible our ultimate freedom from the chains of sin and death. Far above any other human history-changing event, Jesus becoming flesh and dwelling among us set the stage at the end of his earthly life for radically transforming reality itself and restoring all of creation to its right relationship with God.

Perhaps this 50-year-old account of the Herrick brothers, although it completely pales in comparison to the unique event of the Incarnation, can shed some small light on the reality of the mystery of Christmas. The engaging story of frail but vital human beings struggling to live and to love and to give and to be fruitful reminds us that Jesus engaged in that same human struggle, subject to the same limitations and joys and challenges that all human beings experience. The gift of life 50 years

97

ago through fleshly exchange points us to the much deeper mystery of Jesus, the Son of God, becoming real flesh and dwelling among us. The inspiration of these ordinary people whom adversity made ready to give and receive so fully urges us to open ourselves to the call of Christmas, that we too might receive and give back to others all that God bestows on us.

We are not told in the caption of the newspaper's photograph what song the Herrick twins are singing together in this captured moment which still in some sense lives on. Let it be for them and let it now be for us:

"Joy to the world! The Lord is come: let earth receive her King; let every heart prepare him room, and heaven and nature sing, and heaven and nature sing, and heaven, and heaven and nature sing."

The Word of Love
Christmas Eve 2006

In many and various ways God spoke of old to our fathers by
the prophets; but in these last days he has spoken to us by a Son
(Hebrews 1:1).

These opening words from the Letter to the Hebrews focus for us the amazing mystery and the deep Good News we celebrate this night. They proclaim that the God who created the universe, who set the moon and the stars in their courses, who formed man and woman out of the earth and made them "but little lower than the angels" (Psalm 8), even in the face of continued human resistance and hostility, took the final step. Despite our inability and unwillingness to live out our given identity as children of God, God did not condemn or destroy or abandon the human race. Rather God, who had sent numerous prophets to call his human offspring to claim their true identity as children of one Father, spoke one final irrevocable word. In a complete gift of self, God sent his Son, Jesus, to become flesh and dwell among us. God spoke the last word, the word that continues to resound throughout all creation, the word of love.

That is the great Good News of Christmas. That is why for centuries we have celebrated in song and pageantry the birth of the human but divine child. That is the underlying truth which, despite layer upon layer of increasingly suffocating consumerism, never is extinguished. God, who "in many and various ways ... spoke of old to our fathers by the prophets ... in these last days ... has spoken to us by a Son."

In these last days, these last 2,000 years, a blink of an eye in the lifetime of creation, we human beings have not heard well this word of love. As John tells us, "He was in the world, and the world was made through him, and the world knew him not. He came to his own home, and his own people received him not." In fact, it has often been those who claim to have received him, who assert that they above others have heard and understood God's word of love, who seek to impose that understanding

99

on others with anything *but* love. Human history is rife with this easy but unfaithful response, right to our present day.

In last Sunday's comic section, the strip titled ironically enough "Non Sequitur" summed up our latest version of this recurring pattern. As the little girl and the horse are trudging up the snowy hill with their sled, the horse objects, "Um … you lost me there. Explain that again?" "OK," she replies. "One group of followers willingly sacrifice themselves to blow up people who follow a different religion." "Yessh," affirms the horse. "Can't get more fanatical than that, eh?" "Well," the girl goes on, "the other group of followers are willing to commit all of their resources to launching overwhelming military strikes in retaliation."

"And how about the third group of followers?" asks the horse, as they reach the top of the hill and stare down the steep slope. "They're willing to blow up the entire planet." Beginning their descent, the horse inquires, "And why are they doing all this to each other?" The girl answers, "To prove which one is the true religion of peace." As they pick up speed, they elevate off the earth and soar through the air. Coming to rest on a limb high up in a tree, the horse reflects, "I'll never understand how you guys made it to the top of the food chain." "Well," responds the girl, "they don't call it blind faith for nothing."

If we did not laugh, we would cry.

What we act out nationally and globally, we also live personally and locally. We cannot merely point the finger at religious zealots and politicians. Our comfortable faith also blinds *us* to the far-reaching implications of the mystery we celebrate tonight. To return to the original metaphor, in many ways we do not hear and receive the word of love God speaks to us. We contribute to or tolerate the violence in our society. We hold grudges and promote divisions among us. We ignore rifts in our families and do not actively work to bring God's love to bear on our relationships, those we choose and those which are thrust upon us.

God still raises up prophets among us, of course, to call us deeper, to show us how the love of God ought to resound more vibrantly in our deafened world. The Amish community in Paradise, Pennsylvania stirred all of us this year. Rocked by the senseless shooting of five of their daughters, these committed believers refused to respond in kind. They met with the killer's family to assure them of their forgiveness and prayers and to invite them to the girls' funerals. They created a bank account to raise funds for the killer's children. They participated in his funeral. One of their members wrote in a published statement, "I wish yet to say that with God all things are possible and that in heaven the lion and the lamb shall lie down together." What a witness. What a moving embodiment of God's word of love. What a celebration of God's grace, continually and surprisingly at work in the world.

Tonight let our celebration make us attentive to God's word of love. Let the scriptures awaken in us God's invitation to let that love extend through us to others near and far. Let our joyful singing proclaim our hope in the power and the resilience of God's life-giving grace.

Some of you may have seen a front page article in Wednesday's *Chapel Hill News*. It described our monthly Monday night service here in the church, an amazing opportunity to worship with our neighbors and friends with developmental disabilities. This month's service was the traditional free-wheeling Christmas pageant in which everyone gets a costume and a rhythm instrument for making a joyful noise to the Lord. "Not So Silent Night" was the headline! One of our student leaders, who regularly tells a scripture story at these services and talks about what it means for the participants, was quoted in the article as saying, "Honestly, every single lesson boils down to 'God loves us, and we all love each other.'" Our celebration tonight proclaims the same lesson, that same deep mystery: "In many and various ways God spoke of old to our fathers by the prophets; but in these last days he has spoken to us by a Son."

Hebrews 1:1- 12; John 1:1-14

Jesus, the Unifying Bridge
Christmas Eve, 2008

At the beginning of this month, a great crowd gathered a few miles from here for the official opening of the new Durham Performing Arts Center. Approaching a religious service, the program culminated in the unveiling of an engaging light sculpture entitled "Sleep No More" by its Spanish artist, Jaume Plensa. After a children's chorus sang "This little light of mine, Durham's gonna let it shine," a narrow beam of bright white light was unleashed, which now shines straight up into the heavens further than the human eye can see. Indeed, Plensa intends his creation to be a bridge, "connecting heaven and earth, connecting body and soul." Acknowledging the unfulfilled longing in this finite world, the artist expressed his vision that "We will love to look up and walk up to the heavens."

For thousands of years, human beings have felt this chasm between the earth and the heavens, between the temporal and the infinite, between the human and the divine. Knowing that there is more to existence than what immediately presents itself to our senses, we have lifted our eyes and our hearts upward, seeking something more. Sensing that our temporality and finitude put us on shaky ground, we have searched for something more solid in which to put our trust. Realizing that we continually dig ourselves individually and communally into deeper and deeper holes through our bad decisions and self-seeking actions, we have longed for more profound wisdom and reconciling, life-sustaining grace. Consciously or not, we earthly mortals have sought a bridge "connecting heaven and earth," something to link us beyond ourselves, some larger entity to unify us with the deeper mysteries and powers of existence.

Christmas is the announcement of that bridge, the proclamation of that restoring link, the celebration of that ineffable gift which restores us and brings us life and lifts us up to union with all that is, created and uncreated. For in a specific time and place, in the birth of a child named Jesus, God bridged the gap between the earth and the heavens, the temporal and the infinite, the human and the divine. This one person was not only the human child, born of Mary, but also, according to John, the Word, the Logos (in Greek), God's articulation of himself as Love. "The Word was with God, and the Word was God; he was in the beginning with God." But he was also in Israel, 2,000 years ago, subject to hunger and cold and rejection, capable of great compassion and self-giving and sacrifice. In Jesus of Nazareth, God overcame the gap between the temporary and the eternal, between the deserved consequences of our actions and God's mercy, between death and eternal life.

God's gift of Jesus as a unifying bridge did not merely benefit human beings. All of creation was restored through the fruit of the death and resurrection of Jesus, already implicitly contained in his birth (Adrian Nocent, O.S.B. in *The Liturgical Year: Advent, Christmas and Epiphany*, Liturgical Press, 1977). Paul makes clear in his writing to the early Christians in Ephesus that God's purpose "which he set forth in Christ ... [was] to unite all things in him, things in heaven and things on earth" (Ephesians 1:9-10). As part of those earthly things, we are united then, through the gift of Jesus, with the entire cosmos and with its Creator. That is why we will proclaim in celebratory song to end tonight's service, repeating several times for emphasis, "let ... heaven and nature sing."

We sing tonight then, not only out of custom, but in thanksgiving for this incredible gift of God's incarnation, which has restored and transformed all of creation. We sing not in simple nostalgic memory of Christmases past, but in hope and expectation for God's continued saving grace in a sinful and broken world. We sing, not holding on to our fears and cynicism of what the future may bring, but celebrating the unconquerable power of God's love and grace, made manifest in Jesus: Jesus, the link between the temporal and the infinite, Jesus, the embodiment of unending life and grace, Jesus, the light of Durham and Chapel Hill and Honduras and Botswana and Iraq and Afghanistan and Zimbabwe and Washington, D.C., Jesus, the unifying bridge, "connecting heaven and earth." While we share the vision of Plensa, the light sculptor, of loving "to look up ... to the heavens," we know that we do not need literally "to walk up to the heavens" because the heavens have already come to us.

John 1:1-14

The Wise Men and the Star
The Epiphany of Our Lord Jesus Christ
January 6, 2007

Today is a unique feast of the liturgical calendar. That we are here on a Saturday morning is unusual right away, and it tells us that The Epiphany ranks right up there with Christmas as having its own special day, January 6, which is not transferred to a Sunday. I thought I would observe the special nature of The Epiphany by preaching, not from the pulpit, but from among you. I hope you will find that engaging, not just odd!

What makes this feast especially unusual are the wise men — these mysterious strangers who show up in today's Gospel story and then are never heard from again in scripture. Who are these guys and why do we think they were important?

We sang a special hymn about them right before the Gospel: "We Three Kings." That mysterious melody so intrigued us when I was growing up that we had an alternate version — not a very grammatical one, but we loved it! "We three kings of Orient are, tried to smoke a rubber cigar. It was loaded and exploded … bang!" "We two kings of Orient are..." and so on. After we got down to one king and then the third and final "bang!" we would sing, "Silent night…"

Actually that hymn (when sung the right and reverent way!) reflects a lot of tradition that grew up in the Church over the centuries, adding details that are not found in Matthew's story. The Gospel writer tells us that there were "wise men from the East" who came to Jesus in response to the star. He mentions three gifts, gold and frankincense and myrhh, so presumably they were a trio, but we don't know for sure. We have come to call them kings (as in today's psalm), but Matthew just says "wise men" ("magoi" in Greek, meaning "sages," from which we derive the word "magi"). Presumably they were astrologers, educated men who studied the stars — scholars — and that raises an interesting point. While scripture is certainly explicit about the importance of loving

God with our whole *mind,* along with our heart and soul, the Bible provides us very few specific models of those who made a career out of it, so to speak. Most of these examples come from post-scriptural times, e.g. Augustine, Thomas Aquinas, Teilhard de Chardin. In this parish and on this campus, it is a grace for us to see that the magi affirm the importance of academic pursuits as a pathway to God. Through their diligent studies, they came to recognize and to worship the Divine presence among us. Although the Gentile representatives could have come from any walk of life, e.g. Simon the Cyrene, who later helped Jesus carry his cross, or the Roman centurion, it is notable that these first witnesses were scholars.

Being witnesses was the important thing, of course, and the wise men *from the east* are in special contrast to the shepherds. You see in the crèche here the shepherds on the left and the wise men on the right. Or if it is easier for you to see them in the stained glass window over the back door, they are reversed: shepherds on the right and wise men on the left. The shepherds represent the Jews, God's chosen people, who were awaiting a Messiah. The wise men represent all the rest of us and are Matthew's way of saying that Jesus came for everyone, even those who were not taught by the Jewish faith to believe in the one true God. Even though the magi were not of the house of Israel, they still were led by God's grace to worship Jesus as king. They were the fulfillment of the Psalmist's proclamation today: "All kings shall bow down before him, and all the nations do him service" (Ps. 72:11). That is the Good News of The Epiphany, a word which means manifestation or showing. The Epiphany is the showing of God's wondrous glory to *all* people. As personified in the wise men from the East, "All the ends of the earth have seen the salvation of our God."

There is another key role in this Epiphany story, mentioned in the Collect for today: "O God, *by the leading of a star* you manifested your only Son to the peoples of the earth..." The star serves as another model for us. Think about what a star is. It is not the sun. It does not shine of itself, but reflects the light that shines upon it. It shines not for itself, but to point others to a far more important reality beyond itself. It shines not from its own will and desire, but as part of the Divine plan to manifest God's Word to all people.

Pope Leo the Great, preaching on this day in the fifth century, declared: "The obedience of the star calls us to imitate its humble service: to be servants, as best we can, of the grace that invites all men to find Christ." Each of us in our own way and all of us together are to shine with the Divine light that is given to us that, like the magi, others may come to see our Lord Jesus Christ and to fall down and worship him. We are to let our light so shine before others "that they may see [our] good works and give glory to [our] Father in heaven" (Mt. 5:16).

Ephesians 3:1-12; Matthew 2:1-12

Baptism: Identity and Mission
The First Sunday after The Epiphany: The Baptism of Our Lord Jesus
Christ
January 9, 2005

The feast we celebrate today, The Baptism of Our Lord Jesus Christ, has never captured the public imagination like Christmas has or Easter or even the Epiphany. Yet it is a very significant liturgical occasion, one of four days recommended by the Prayer Book for the celebration of Baptism along with Easter, All Saints, and Pentecost. Pretty good company! That is why we are celebrating Baptism at the 11:15 service today and renewing our Baptismal Covenant at the other services.

Over the years I have come to appreciate more and more this lesser-recognized feast. Despite the jar of the 30-year Gospel leap from Jesus' infancy three days ago on the Epiphany to his mature adulthood today, this liturgy proclaims to us who Jesus really is and therefore who we are as his followers. The Church purposefully places this feast at the end of the Christmas season and at the beginning of our approach to Lent — which this year begins just a month from today! It answers the question for us, "Who is this who was born in a stable and is on his way to the cross?"

In today's reading from the Acts of the Apostles, Peter declares that "God anointed Jesus of Nazareth with the Holy Spirit and with power." In the Gospel, Matthew describes that anointing as connected to Jesus' baptism: "The heavens were opened, and he saw the Spirit of God descending like a dove and alighting on him; and lo, a voice from heaven, saying, this is my beloved Son, with whom I am well pleased."

Jesus is not just a holy man. He is not merely a great prophet. He is the Son of God, beloved by the Father. He was filled with the Holy Spirit to bring about the reconciliation of the Divine with the human, to carry out God's redemption on earth. At Jesus' baptism, that identity was declared, and out of that identity his ministry was established. His journey to the cross was now begun.

We who follow Jesus also have our identity established at our baptism. We are named, and therefore claimed, "in the Name of the Father, and of the Son, and of the Holy Spirit." We are "sealed by the Holy Spirit in Baptism and marked as Christ's own for ever." That is who we are, children of God. We are, as it were, branded with the cross, so that we and all the world may know that we belong to God's beloved Son. What a heritage! What a destiny! What Good News!

It is said that every morning Martin Luther would remind himself, "Martin, you are baptized." Not only did those words serve as an assurance, a comfort, but also as a call, a challenge to live out that identity. For Jesus, for Martin Luther, for us, what we do with our lives stems from who we are. Ministry flows out of identity.

That is why the Baptismal Covenant, which you will find if you will turn to pages 304 and 305 and which we will all renew shortly, deals with both identity and mission. The first three questions establish who we are: those who believe in God the Father, Jesus Christ, the Son of God, and God the Holy Spirit. We are the community of the faithful who have received the Good News of God's creative, redemptive, and unifying work as told to us in scripture and articulated in these words of the Apostles' Creed.

The next five questions define the direction our lives are to take, given this identity. They reveal what our attitudes and actions, which comprise our ministry, are to be.

In the first question, words taken from the second chapter of the Acts of the Apostles, which describe the early Christians, tell us how we are to carry on the continuity of the Christian faith. We are to learn and preserve the teachings about Jesus, to participate truly and fully in the fellowship of the Church, (the current phrase for that is "radical hospitality"), to take part regularly in the Holy Eucharist, and to pray faithfully. For 2,000 years, Christians have done these things because of their Baptism.

In the second question, we acknowledge that we are sinners, that we often fall far short of living fully our identity as God's children. We promise never to let that separate us permanently from God, but to keep asking for God's forgiveness and God's help.

In the third question, we declare that the gift of our faith is not a private gift, simply between ourselves and God. Rather, the Gospel, the Good News, is given for everyone. To the extent that we can, we are to make it available to others: to friends, co-workers, students here on campus, the needy, all those who in different ways hunger for the presence of God in their lives. Our deeds and also our words, i.e. our invitations to church, our promise of prayers, our not being ashamed of who we are, can be the means of God's grace for others, just as, if you think about it, others' word and example have been for each of us.

In the fourth question, we embrace the presence of God in all (not some!) of our neighbors. No matter how difficult or undeserving we may think others to be, we aspire to look on them as loved by God and to emulate that Divine love. We pledge ourselves not to return evil for evil, not to put ourselves above others by judging them, not to begrudge others our forgiveness, not to use other people for our own purposes. Rather, "with God's help" (as in all these promises), we endeavor to make love our primary motive.

In the final question, we commit ourselves, not just to individuals we may encounter, but to all races and nations. We align ourselves with the forces of love and compassion and understanding, not of hate and judgment and ignorance. We acknowledge with Peter in the second lesson that "God shows no partiality," or as the stained glass window above the left of the altar depicting this scriptural scene has it, "God is no respecter of persons."

When we renew our Baptismal Covenant, which articulates our identity and mission, we do not do so simply as individuals who happen to be in the same room. We do so as part of Christ's body, the Church. We join ourselves not only with other members of this congregation, nor merely with other members of the Chapel of the Cross, nor simply with other members of our diocese, nor even just with other Episcopalians and members of the Anglican Communion. As we declare at the beginning of the baptismal service, "There is one Lord, one Faith, one Baptism, one God and Father of all." Baptism is a communal and community-making sacrament. It joins us to others, living and dead, who are far beyond our experience. It stretches us to be more than we can be simply by ourselves.

On this powerful feast of The Baptism of Our Lord Jesus Christ then, let us stand, and at the bottom of page 292, renew our Baptismal Covenant.

Acts 10:34-38
Matthew 3:13-17

We Have No Wine
The Second Sunday after The Epiphany
January 18, 2004

What an amazing Gospel story this is! At the beginning of his public ministry, according to John, the Word who had become flesh, the only Son of the Father, the Lamb of God who takes away the sin of the world, accomplished "the first of his signs ... and manifested his glory; and his disciples believed in him." And what sign did he do for this momentous occasion? Did he topple Herod from his throne? Did he obliterate famine? Did he put a stop to all crime and punish evildoers? He used six large stone water jars to provide about 150 gallons of fine wine for a sagging wedding reception!

Can you imagine?! That is enough wine for a modest crowd of, say, 300 people to have 10 glasses apiece! Even for a celebration which customarily spread out over a number of days, since this one had already been going for a while, it was either a huge wedding reception — or a huge success! Nobody ever forgot it! A good time was had by all. Apparently Jesus would have agreed with Shakespeare, who wrote, a millennium and a half later, "Come, come good wine is a good familiar creature if it be well used; exclaim no more against it."

You may think I am being sacrilegious, but scripture makes it clear that Jesus and his followers were no ascetics. In Luke's Gospel (7:34), Jesus confronts fickle human demands by saying, "For John the Baptist has come eating no bread and drinking no wine; and you say, 'He has a demon.' The Son of man has come eating and drinking; and you say, 'Behold, a glutton and a drunkard, a friend of tax collectors and sinners!'" Obviously, by his own admission, Jesus knew how to enjoy the gifts of creation and how to celebrate with others. One commentator on this passage imagined him "full of laughter, dancing with the bride, wine dripping down his beard and mutton chop in hand"! Not our culturally fashioned image of Jesus, but not incompatible with scripture either.

In fact, if you think about it, that Jesus should have radiated joy makes a lot of sense. He was at home in his Father's creation, even if "his own received him not." People were drawn to him and followed him, even leaving their homes and livelihoods to be wherever he was. Children flocked to him and loved to be in his arms. A pensive, uptight loner does not elicit that wholehearted response.

But the amazing nature of this Gospel story is not revealed simply in its widening of our vision of the joyful and life-affirming personality of Jesus, God's Word made flesh among us. This first of Jesus' signs speaks to us even more broadly of the generosity and the power of God.

I spoke several months ago in connection with the widow's mite about the lavish magnanimity of God. That divine liberality is reflected in the extravagance of creation, which Dom Helder Camara called "wasteful" — a positive term for him. "Fruits never equal the seedlings' abundance," he wrote. "Springs scatter water. The sun gives out enormous light." The recent pictures from Mars graphically remind us of the vast reaches and mysteries of space, which dwarf our tiny planet the Prayer Book calls "our island home." Another of its prayers proclaims that God "made the universe with all its marvelous order, its atoms, worlds, and galaxies, and the infinite complexity of living creatures" (p. 827).

Several weeks ago on a family trip to Key West, we visited the Butterfly and Nature Conservatory, a solarium where well over 1,000 multi-colored butterflies of all the earth's continents fluttered around us and feasted on various flowers and fruits. The beauty and variety of just this one of "the infinite complexity of living creatures" reflect the incomprehensible imagination and generativity and loving munificence of our Creator. God always provides excessively more than enough, "infinitely more than we can ask or imagine," even at a wedding celebration in Cana of Galilee, which of course is a foretaste of the heavenly banquet that awaits us.

If our Gospel story proclaims the liberality of God, it also reveals in a striking way God's efficacious power. Ordinary water, set aside for simple purification purposes, was transformed by the divine intention into fine wine. Something commonplace and good became something extraordinary and excellent. The celebration which was about to end prematurely went on to glorious fulfillment.

We are called to faith in that loving power. Too often our vision is limited to our seemingly hopeless situation and inadequate resources. Our focus, like that of the hosts and guests at Cana, picked up on by Mary, is expressed in the mantra, "We have no wine." Later on a hillside in the wilderness, it became, "We have no bread." We easily make our focal point what we do not have. "We have no wine."

Mary, however, takes that human, self-pitying, inward focus outward. She turns to her son, believing in his efficacious love. Even when he does not immediately respond, she readies the servants for action. She envisions new possibilities, and she places her trust in God, doing what she can to cooperate with any divine initiative.

Her faith is rewarded far more than she might have hoped. Not only in quantity does Jesus respond, but in quality. The situation moves from no wine to an abundance of the best wine. Jesus' glory and power is manifested in an amazing way.

This Gospel story should not only expand our grasp of the magnetic, dynamic Jesus. It should also stir hope and faith in us of God's powerful generosity and faithful providence. When we are tempted to view only the limitations of our lives, to grumble and lament that "we have no wine," may we, like Mary, both take action and lift up our and others' needs to God. For God will act in ways that we cannot imagine, transforming what we already have into what we need.

John 2:1-11

Most Loved Servants
The Presentation of Our Lord Jesus Christ in the Temple
February 2, 2005

Turn with me, if you will, to the top of page 66 in the Prayer Book, titled "The Song of Simeon," words which we just heard in the Gospel. Omitting the last two lines, a doxology which is added to the scriptural words, let us read this familiar canticle together.

"Lord, now lettest thou thy servant depart in peace, according to thy word; for mine eyes have seen thy salvation, which thou hast prepared before the face of all people, to be a light to lighten the Gentiles, and to be the glory of thy people Israel."

What gracious, powerful, poignant words! Among the most well known and the best loved in all of scripture, these words of Simeon form this ancient canticle, the Nunc Dimittis, named with the first two words of the Latin version. This familiar canticle is used at Morning Prayer, is especially appropriate at Evening Prayer, and is sometimes sung at funerals.

These words, therefore, carry significant associations for many of us: reverent chanting, worshipping God in the beauty of holiness, being surrounded and upheld by other believers, commending to God friends who have died.

But the most significant association is that of Simeon himself, one of the most noble, endearing, grace-filled figures in the Bible, even though he appears only this one time. Luke characterizes him as "...righteous and devout, looking for the consolation of Israel, and the Holy Spirit was upon him. And it had been revealed to him by the Holy Spirit that he should not see death before he had seen the Lord's Christ. And inspired by the Spirit he came into the temple; and when the parents brought in the child Jesus, to do for him according to the custom of the law, he took him up in his arms and blessed God and said, "Lord, now lettest thou thy servant depart in peace, according to thy word."

There is so much communicated by these words: the intimate, yet reverential relationship between Simeon and God — the relationship of a servant to a well-loved and trusted Master, a servant who has been promised something great by his Lord and has now received it, a servant who feels respected and secure enough to ask that his term of service now end.

That relationship of Simeon to God should be ours also, one in which we know and joyfully accept precisely who we are: not the master, not the one in authority, not the one ultimately responsible, but also not the rejected, not the abandoned, not the unwanted. We are the most loved servants, the ones given a place, the ones to whom a promise has been made that will unfailingly be kept.

Simeon's promise was that "he should not see death before he had seen the Lord's Christ," i.e. the anointed one, the Messiah. Our promise is Jesus himself, the Way, the Truth, and the Life, who is with us always, "even to the close of the age." No matter what may befall us, no matter what sufferings may dampen our hope, no matter how our patience may be tried, we can, like Simeon, without bitterness and without fear, depend on God's faithfulness, even in the midst of death.

Without bitterness and without fear. … Those are very hard traps for us to avoid in our lives. Too often "the slings and arrows of outrageous fortune" leave us scarred and resentful. Life is not what we expected it to be. Catastrophes happen; difficulties overwhelm us; those we love die. We blame others; we blame ourselves; we blame God. We protect ourselves from disappointment by refusing to hope in anything beyond our limited power, our limited vision, our limited love. We fear that we will not measure up to present and future challenges, that evil will overcome, that we will be left alone.

But bitterness and fear are not to characterize us as most loved servants of God. Like Simeon, we are to be patient, to believe in the Lord's promise, to know God's faithfulness. How difficult it must have been for Simeon to feel his life ebbing away and not to sense any fulfillment of the Holy Spirit's revelation to him that he was yet to see the Messiah. Day after day went by, and life went on as usual; no sign of redemption in sight. The promise must have seemed impossible. But Simeon persevered; he waited; he believed. And he was rewarded.

We, too, can find it difficult to trust God's promise. We are made for God, but we cannot see God. Life's unexpected wounds tempt us to believe that God is not there and may never be. Unless life goes as we plan, we think we are abandoned.

Accepting ourselves as servants, however, leads us to revise our expectations, to know that we are not the master, not the one in charge. And it convinces us that neither are we abandoned and alone. Rather we are most loved servants, the ones who are looked after, to whom a promise has been made that will be unfailingly kept.

Whenever we pray these words of the Nunc Dimittis, may they remind us, like Simeon, to bear with courage and patience what is asked of us in this life. May they encourage us with faith and trust to hold fast to God's unfailing promise to us. And when the time comes for us to view our Messiah face to face, may we as treasured and most loved servants, to whom a promise will now have been kept, make ours this prayer of Simeon, "Lord, now lettest thou thy servant depart in peace, according to thy word."

Luke 2:22-40

Salt and Light
The Fifth Sunday after The Epiphany
February 6, 2011

This week I received a copy of an email a new parishioner had written to an Episcopal cathedral in Europe, asking to transfer her membership here. The dean "replied to all" and graciously included in his response to her, "The Chapel of the Cross has a wonderful reputation in the Church as a healthy, vibrant, committed community and I rejoice that you've found such a community." When I finished smiling broadly — several minutes later! — I began to think, "That is a lot to live up to! How can we grow as that vibrant, committed community that others perceive us to be?"

You might recall the story Tammy Lee told in her sermon last week of the young doctoral student whom her African-American congregation persisted in addressing as "Doctor." When she protested to her pastor that she had not yet earned that honorific title, he clarified for her, "We call you, not what you presently are, but what we know you are becoming."

Jesus does the same for us in today's Gospel. "You are the salt of the earth. ... You are the light of the world." He is giving us our identity and mission, the amazing role that we are to grow into.

As metaphors, salt and light may have much less meaning for us today than they did for Jesus' first followers. In the days long before refrigeration, they knew the critical importance of salt in preserving meat and in making decaying food palatable. In fact Roman soldiers were paid with a ration of salt or in Latin *salarium*, from which we derive the word *salary*. Without this commodity, life was threatened and its vibrancy dampened. This week in contrast, we saw the report that for most of us today, our health is imperiled by far too much salt in our diet. Light too is cheap and plentiful these days and as easy as the flip of a switch or the setting of a timer. The importance of light for safety and clarity is something we easily take for granted, but its crucial role was not lost on these pre-electricity early followers of Jesus.

Even if these metaphors have over time lost their taste, to quote today's Gospel, we can still appreciate the most critical dimension of what Jesus meant in using them: Salt and light do not exist for themselves. Salt is only good if it enhances the flavor of food or restores a needed element to a living body or, apropos to this time of year, keeps the ice underfoot from being so dangerous. Light is only valuable if it illumines the reality in front of us and reveals goodness and infuses something with beauty. Neither exists for its own sake but to enhance and to bring life to, to serve if you will, other creatures around them. That is when salt and light most fulfill their God-given identity and mission.

The same is true for us. We do not exist for ourselves. As individuals and as a part of the Church, we are most fulfilling our God-given purpose and mission, when we are being salt and light, when we are serving others. Never think, for example, that whether or not you come to church and participate in the communal worship of God each week is just a private decision, to be based primarily on what you think you get out of it. Your presence in the worshipping community is so much more than that. When you are strengthening the body of the faithful by your participation, when you are helping to proclaim the Gospel in word and in hymn, when you are praying for the Church and for the world, when you are approaching the table of the Lord not "for solace only [but] for strength," when you are sent out "to love and serve the Lord," you are living into the identity of salt and light that Jesus calls forth in us.

And not only in church. When you go forth "in the name of Christ," when you pursue your studies or faithfully perform your work or devote yourselves to loving your families, when you serve those in need, when you stand up against injustice and "respect the dignity of very human being," when you consistently give back to God a generous part of what you have been given, when you care for your "families, friends, and neighbors, and for those who are alone," you are living into the identity of salt and light that Jesus calls forth in us.

In our corporate ministry, when we serve God and others with our full resources as this "healthy, vibrant, committed community" we aspire to be, we are deeply and truly fulfilling our mission. When we open our doors for students and visitors and people seeking the Divine to "worship God in the beauty of holiness," to experience welcome and fellowship among us, to meet free of charge in our buildings for support and instruction and being equipped to serve, we are living into the identity of salt and light that Jesus calls forth in us.

When we go as a community to where the need is: to feed the hungry, to cut wood for those needing heat, to build houses for those without adequate homes, to support those suffering from AIDS and those in prison, to build relationships with those in other countries and other cultures, we are living into the identity of salt and light that Jesus calls forth in us.

When as a parish we give away a significant part of our financial resources to ministries and organizations struggling to serve others and to make God's compassion and mercy present in our world, we are living into the identity of salt and light that Jesus calls forth in us.

And yes, when we are stretching ourselves farther than this parish has ever yet been able to stretch itself, not only in the range and scope of our annual operations and ministries, but also in caring for our aging buildings and in doing all that we possibly can to increase and to renovate the space with which we can welcome and support and educate and equip and send forth others, when we join together truly to be "a light on the hill" and those who are boldly building to serve, then also we are living into the identity of salt and light that Jesus calls forth in us.

"You are the salt of the earth. … You are the light of the world. A city set on a hill cannot be hid." We do not exist for our own sake. We are here to be salt and light for others. We do not come to church, we do not serve others, we do not open up our doors, we do not give away our money, we do not build more space for our own satisfaction or to earn the praise of others. Our motivation is not to become known as "a healthy, vibrant, committed community" for our own glory. Rather we seek to love and serve the Lord who loves us and calls us to be salt and light for others. "Let your light so shine before men, that they may see your good works and give glory to your Father who is in heaven."

Matthew 5:13-20

The Theology of Abundance
The Fifth Sunday after The Epiphany
February 8, 2004

You may know that who preaches at each service is the decision of the rector. At the Chapel of the Cross, I assign all the clergy liturgical roles three months at a time. I try to spread the assignments around, giving the Holy Spirit a chance to work through different preaching voices, yet maintaining some continuity. I resist the temptation to look at all the lectionary scripture passages ahead of time and to assign myself the ones that I would prefer to preach on! That would not only be unfair to the other clergy, it would deprive me of the chance to struggle with God's word, even when it is not at first appealing.

I say all that as a disclaimer today, because I want you to understand that I did not knowingly assign myself to preach on yet another Gospel reading which dramatically reveals God's magnanimous generosity! Three weeks ago I drew the story of the wedding at Cana with six gigantic stone jars filled with 25 gallons or so each of transformed fine wine, and in that sermon I built on an earlier one on the widow's mite, entitled "The Lavish Magnanimity of God." Now in today's Gospel, through the power of Jesus, Simon Peter and his partners catch "a great shoal of fish," which threatens to break not only their nets, but both their boats as well. Imagine how many that would be! Another inviting opportunity to talk about the theology of abundance! Just so you know that I am not carefully choosing the "few" bible stories that illustrate the abundant life which we spoke of in today's collect. In fact, there is an ample supply of such passages — the medium is the message!

There is an ample supply — an abundance — of *whatever* is needed; more than we thought, more than we could have hoped for. That is part of God's revelation to us in the Gospel. There is more fish, more wine, more bread, more of the wonderful gifts of all creation, but also more forgiveness, more mercy, more love, more compassion, more rejoicing over one sinner who repents than we could have ever imagined.

And there is more than enough of everything possible, not by accident, but because the very nature of God is one of overflowing generosity, of magnanimous vitality, of lavish creativity. Goodness and kindness and dynamic love flow out from God like warmth and light from the sun, like water from a cascading cataract, like seedlings from a mighty tree. That is what we mean by a theology of abundance. God does not skimp. God does not hold back. God does not refuse us because we do not deserve the abundance of divinely created life. "The Father ... makes his sun rise on the evil and on the good and sends rain on the just and the unjust" (Mt. 5:45).

God invites us as children of God to imitate the generosity of our Father. Rather than hoarding what we have, material or otherwise, we are to share what has been freely given to us. Rather than treating what we have and produce as simply our own, we are to make it available as part of God's generous love to others. Rather than living out of a theology of scarcity, we are to embrace a theology of abundance. Imagine if we all were concerned about getting enough oxygen, so we all took a huge breath and held onto it — until it began to hurt! Or if we began to gulp air as fast as we possibly could — until we hyperventilated. Instead we are to breathe both in and out, using what we need but also giving back so that God can use what flows through us in a life-giving way. Receiving and giving, taking in and giving back, that is the dynamic of life and health and love.

That applies not only to all the material gifts of creation, but also to the spiritual gifts as well. The kindness, the compassion, the love, the forgiveness that God has graced us with are also to be passed on to others. "Judge not," Jesus says, "and you will not be judged; condemn not, and you will not be condemned; forgive, and you will be forgiven; give, and it will be given to you; good measure, pressed down, shaken together, running over, will be put into your lap." (Luke 6:37-38)

"Good measure, pressed down, shaken together, running over" is constantly being put into our lap. We are to acknowledge it all as gift and give thanks to God in word and in deed, especially by imitating God's generosity and compassion.

How do we do that concretely? Let us take two examples: our forgiveness of others and our money. It is a great temptation to be stingy with both, and interestingly, our degree of generosity in one is inexorably tied to our generosity in the other.

We are to imitate God's generous forgiveness. How far does that go? It is best for each of us to consider how patient God has had to be with us and how many times we have needed the grace of forgiveness. There is nothing like that intimate, discomforting knowledge to convince us how generously we ought to forgive. But since we are often selfishly blind to that reality, consider this sentence from today's second lesson. Paul writes to the people of Corinth that "Christ died for our sins in accordance with the scriptures, that he was buried, that he was raised on the third day in accordance with the scriptures, and that he appeared to Cephas (Aramaic for "Peter"), then to the twelve."

The implication of that last word never struck me until recently — "the twelve." Jesus' resurrection appearance was, of course, after Judas betrayed him but before the selection of Mathias to fill out the 12, but Paul does not say "to the eleven." So Paul seems to be telling us here that Jesus, after he arose, appeared to Judas! Doing so can only have been to show his love for this man whose name has become synonymous with "traitor" and to urge him to accept forgiveness. Since Judas shortly afterward hung himself in despair, we can only presume that he was unable to receive that loving gift, but we do not judge. Suffice it for us to grasp that we are not to begrudge any others our forgiveness, even though their sin approach that of Judas.

Nor are we to be stingy with our financial resources. Although we are to be prudent stewards of our money, I strongly suspect that none of us are in danger of losing our souls by giving away more than we should! "I have good news and bad news," said the preacher. "The good news is that we have more than enough money to cover this year's budget and even to increase substantially our outreach giving and our building endowment. The bad news is that it is still in your wallets!" This is a difficult issue for many of us to address, but we need to understand it as an integral part of our individual and communal response in faith to the God of generosity and love.

For it is God who creates us and not we ourselves. It is God who gives us infinitely more than we can ask or imagine. It is God who calls us to be generous as our heavenly Father is generous. To God be the honor and the glory now and forever. Amen.

I Corinthians 15:1-11
Luke 5:1-11

More Than an Individual Decision
The Fifth Sunday after The Epiphany
February 8, 2009

A line from a newspaper column jumped out at me this week. It said simply, "This is more than an individual decision." It could have been referring to many recent news stories. One could easily say that of Bernard Madoff's alleged decision to create a fraudulent investment pool, bilking clients of $50 billion. Thousands of investors, from the very wealthy to average citizens to benevolent foundations and those they serve, suffered great losses and drastic consequences from this one, catastrophic individual decision. This statement could have been made about various public officials who, we learned recently, have not paid their share of income tax, leaving others to shoulder that burden and discouraging the rest of us by their example. "This is more than an individual decision."

That statement could even have been made from a different perspective about Captain Sully Sullenberger's heroic landing of his plane on the Hudson River. His entire focus was not on himself or his reputation or preserving the plane for the airlines, but on the safety of his passengers. He knew that his action "was more than an individual decision." This week Elwin Wilson of Rock Hill, South Carolina flew to Washington to apologize to Congressman John Lewis for his racist attitudes and behavior. Forty-eight years ago, when Lewis came to Rock Hill as one of the freedom riders of Martin Luther King Jr. and tried to enter a "Whites Only" waiting room, a young Elwin Wilson beat him up. He had been working up to his public anger by keeping at his home a black baby doll hanging from a noose. But gradually over the years remorse began to eat away at him, and he has now apologized not only to Representative Lewis, but also to the entire town of Rock Hill. "I want to love people," he said, "regardless of what color." He knows what damage he caused others, and now he hopes that his example might strengthen others to do what is right. Both his actions in May of 1961 and his recent taking responsibility for them and making amends to those affected were more than individual decisions. For good or for ill, what we do, public or private, affects us all.

The story commented on by the newspaper columnist was none of these, although it could have been about any of them. It was referring to a mother of six children's decision to have further "infertility" treatment, resulting in her giving birth to octuplets. The female columnist rightly bewailed the complete lack of regulation of fertility technology — parents wanting to adopt go through much more scrutiny — and drew attention to the enormous financial price tag being run up in that neonatal unit. This mother's desire for further children and the cooperation of her fertility specialist in the face of all common sense should have been much "more than an individual decision." What we do, for good or ill, affects us all, and inherent to our identity as human beings is the communal dimension of all that we do.

Frederick Buechner writes in *The Magnificent Defeat*: "Your life and my life flow into each other as wave flows into wave, and unless there is peace and joy and freedom for you, there can be no real peace or joy or freedom for me. To see reality — not as we expect it to be but as it is — is to see that unless we live for each other and in and through each other, we do not really live very satisfactorily; that there can really be life only when there really is, in just this sense, love."

Today's scripture readings reinforce that mystery. Paul lives out his commission to preach the Gospel, not with a "one size fits all" approach, but tailoring his message to his listeners so that God's word can find them where they are. Jesus spends his time, out of compassion, with those who are sick or possessed with demons, freeing them from their afflictions. Also out of love, he goes to a lonely place and prays, not out of mere self-interest, but to be in union with his Father that he might better serve others. It is interesting to note that the Evangelist makes a special point of saying that after Jesus took Peter's mother-in-law "by the hand and lifted her up, and the fever left her ... she served them." Healing and new life and energy are not just individual gifts, but ones for the whole community. We also are given our lives and our health and our resources that we might serve.

In some ways, in our society we have been growing in our grasp of this communal dimension of our identity and existence. Racial justice, while still far from complete, has been a manifestation of our growing awareness that in John Donne's words, "no man is an island" and that we do not lead isolated lives. Even the banning of second-hand smoke and the requirement to wear seat belts are a result of increased awareness that so much of what we do "is more than an individual decision." The major struggle of the environmental movement is to help us learn that our lifestyles and our consumer decisions affect not just those around us, but those on the other side of the world and those far into the future. Perhaps one positive outcome of the current economic crisis is to instill more deeply in us how much our lives depend on one another and that we cannot be satisfied simply to make sure that our own economic needs are met, but that in Buechner's words, "our lives do flow into each other as wave flows into wave."

Some years ago Garrison Keillor read "A Letter from Jim" on his weekend radio show, "A Prairie Home Companion." In that letter, his friend Jim confesses to him that he had been planning to take a trip to a conference with a female co-worker for the purpose of entering into an adulterous relationship. He had already kissed his unsuspecting wife and children goodbye and had gone outside to wait for his friend to pick him up, when he began to have second thoughts:

"As I sat on the lawn, looking down the street, I saw that we all depend on each other. I saw that, although I thought my sins could be kept secret, they would be no more secret than an earthquake. All these houses and all these families, my infidelity will somehow shake them. It will pollute the drinking water. It will make noxious gases come out of the ventilators in the elementary school. When we scream in senseless anger, blocks away a little girl we do not know spills a bowl of gravy all over a white tablecloth. If I go to Chicago with this woman who is not my wife, somehow the school patrol will forget to guard an intersection and someone's child may be injured. A sixth-grade teacher will think, "What the hell" and eliminate South America from geography. Our minister will decide, "What the hell — I'm not going to give that sermon on the poor." Somehow my infidelity will cause the man in the grocery store to say, "To hell with the Health Department. This sausage was good yesterday; it certainly can't be any worse today."

Jim concludes, "I just leave the story there. Anything more I could tell you would be self-serving, except to say that we depend on each other more than we ever know."

I Corinthians 9:16-23; Mark 1:29-39

Listen in Silence
The Last Sunday after The Epiphany
February 9, 1986

How fallibly human was Peter's response to the awesome epiphany which we have just heard proclaimed. The divinity of Jesus shone dazzlingly through his humanity, and he was revealed talking with Moses and Elijah about his impending death. That was all too much for Peter. Whether he could not comprehend or accept the fact of Jesus' passion and death (which the beginning of our Gospel reading tells us Jesus first predicted eight days earlier), or whether Peter simply could not quietly take in all that was happening, he blurted out some nonsense about making shelters for the glorified trio — not knowing what he said, as Luke tells us.

That was the wrong response, obviously. Not only does Luke seem to reprimand him (the same Luke who earlier in his Gospel holds up to us Mary, Jesus' mother, who "kept all these things in her heart"), but God the Father himself interrupted Peter to say "This is my Son, my Chosen. Listen to him!"

"Listen to him. Do not block out what is fearful. Do not fill up the space with inanities. Be silent. Listen. Take in."

When God the Father talks, especially from a cloud, everyone listens! Peter and James and John got the point. After the voice had spoken and Jesus was found alone, Luke tells us, "They kept silence and told no one in those days anything of what they had seen." Peter's is not an untypical reaction. Most of us have as much trouble handling silence as did he. We are constantly surrounded by noise: traffic, TV sets, radios — even Walkmans now to take noise wherever we go — machines of all sorts, Muzak, watches that beep to let us know that another hour has gone by! And that is only the external noise.

Underneath all that is a whole level of interior noise which comes rushing at us the second the external noises quiet down, when we have finished our busy tasks and have a moment to ourselves. Past disappointments, resentments, hurt feelings, fears, guilt, failures, loneliness, all mix into a confused jumble of feelings that oppresses and deadens us, urging us to retreat back to a world of noise and distraction that can drown out what we do not want to face.

It is little wonder, then, that when God on occasion leads us up the mountain to let his divinity shine through our ordinary experience, when God wakes us from our sluggish sleep to overwhelm and dazzle us, either with beauty or joy or pain, we do not know how to respond. We have not learned to listen to reverence.

At a Shabbat service at a synagogue a few weeks ago I found this reflection in the Jewish prayer book:

Judaism begins with the commandment:

Hear, O Israel!
But what does it really mean to hear?

The person who attends a concert
With his mind on business,
Hears — but does not really hear.

The person who walks amid the songs of birds
And thinks only of what he will have for dinner,
Hears — but does not really hear.

The man who listens to the words of his friend,
Or his wife, or his child,
And does not catch the note of urgency:
"Notice me, help me, care about me,"
Hears — but does not really hear.

The man who listens to the news
And thinks only of how it will affect business,
Hears — but does not really hear.

The person who stifles the sound of his conscience
And tells himself he has done enough already,
Hears — but does not really hear.

The person who hears the Hazzan pray
And does not feel the call to join with him,
Hears — but does not really hear.

(And my favorite!)

The person who listens to the rabbi's sermon
And thinks that someone else is being addressed,
Hears — but does not really hear.

"Hear, O Israel." "Listen to him." Silence is as important to hearing as space is to seeing. Without it there is no depth, no possibility of true perception. Yet silence, like space, is not particularly good in itself, but only because it allows something beautiful to form and take shape within it.

Silence can be a negation, to remain silent in the face of injustice, for example, or to give someone "the silent treatment." But to seek silence, both external and internal, that seeing we might perceive, and hearing we might understand, is an affirmation of the richness and the depth and the mystery of life as God has given it to us.

We need to beware of constantly surrounding ourselves with noise and distraction. We need to consciously create for ourselves times when we are not only free of outside noise, but also willing to listen patiently and attentively to our inner struggles. We need to look for God not only in the earthquake and the wind and the fire, but also in the still, small voice.

The last few months we have begun at Chapel of the Cross to make more room for silence in our worship. After the readings and the sermon, we have a chance to listen and reflect before we move on. I encourage us all to treasure and make use of those precious times for listening, for digesting. Let us not be too quick to reach for the bulletin to find out the next page number. Even when the reading or the sermon seems not to speak to us, our very action speaks of our reverence for God's Word, and it can instill in us a love for, and a recognition of our need for, silence in our lives.

Let those communal times of silence encourage us to work at providing ourselves individual, daily silent space as well. We do not always have to play the radio or turn on the television or busy ourselves with whatever distracts us from being quietly attentive. If we never take the time to listen to what is going on inside ourselves and to how God might be revealing himself to us, let us begin. If we do from time to time slow down and try to listen, let us be encouraged and increase our efforts.

Any time, of course, is a good time to let the role of silence deepen in our lives. But this week as we move from Epiphany season into Lent, it is especially appropriate. That one season follows the other is no accident. During Epiphany we have, through the readings, celebrated God's manifestation of himself to us. From the story of the wise men, to the baptism of Jesus, to the first miracle at a wedding in Cana of Galilee, to Jesus' declaration in the synagogue at Nazareth, "Today this scripture been fulfilled in your hearing," the awesome, transcendent God has revealed himself to us, incarnate. During Lent, we, like Peter after the miraculous catch of fish, fall on our knees and say, "Depart from us for we are sinful people, O Lord." In light of the glory of God revealed, we see ourselves in all of our smallness and finitude and selfishness. And in our repentance, we are led with Jesus in Holy Week to suffering and death and thereby to resurrection and new life.

But we cannot make that journey if we are not attentive, if we are not listening, if we are not silent enough to hear God at work in us and in the world around us, calling us to die that we might live.

The reflection from the Jewish prayer book ends with this prayer:

On this Shabbat, O Lord,
Sharpen our ability to hear.

May we hear the music of the world,
And the infant's cry, and the lover's sigh.

May we hear the call for help of the lonely soul,
And the sound of the breaking heart.

May we hear the words of our friends,
And also their unspoken pleas and dreams.

May we hear within ourselves the yearnings
That are struggling for expression.

May we hear You, O God.

Amen.

Luke 9:28-36

Seek My Face
The Last Sunday after The Epiphany
February 13, 1994

*You speak in my heart and say, "Seek my face." Your face, Lord,
will I seek.*

These words from today's psalm, Psalm 27, touch us in the depth of
our souls. For they speak of our inmost desire to know God, the one
in whose image we are created, the one who knit us together in our
mothers' wombs, the one about whom we confess, "Our souls are
restless until they rest in thee, O God."

This psalm gives voice to our longing for God, yet it also acknowledges
that that yearning itself is there by God's initiative, that we seek God
because God first sought us. "You speak in my heart and say, 'Seek
my face.' The desire I feel inside me for God is God's whisper echoing
deep within me, 'Seek my face … Seek my face.' In response, then, do
I declare, Your face, Lord, will I seek."

It should fill us with awe and give us great comfort that these words
are thousands of years old, that human beings have been praying these
words for many centuries, that God's whisper has echoed in countless
generations of human hearts before us.

Elijah heard it. He obeyed its summons to "stand upon the mount
before the Lord." He looked for the Lord in a great, strong wind and
in an earthquake, and in a fire, in all the spectacular events around him,
but the Lord was not in any of these, but in "a still, small voice."

Peter and James and John heard it on a high mountain; in fact they
literally saw the face of the Lord. The human Jesus they knew, whose
tears they had witnessed, whose smile was so familiar to them, whose
countenance they had seen strained in anger and peaceful in sleep,
was so transformed before them that, as one evangelist tells us, "his
face shone like the sun." His divinity, usually hidden from them "as

through a glass darkly," was now revealed to them "face to face." What an indescribable experience that must have been.

Their response was similar to ours whenever we have a mountaintop experience: They wanted to stay, to make it last. Peter said, "Master, it is well that we are here; let us make three booths, one for you and one for Moses and one for Elijah." But that was not to be. Jesus' face ceased to shine; the divine glimpse they had been given faded; their search for the face of God took them back down the mountain again.

Each of us catches a flash of the divine presence from time to time. Whether in a still, small voice like Elijah, or in a more radiant epiphany like the three disciples. The ordinary existence around us is abruptly transfused with the light of God's divinity, and we suddenly grasp that that is the reality and our ordinary vision the illusion. But in this life, that realization is short-lived. Most of our lives are spent seeking, rather than finding.

Friday morning I awoke to a much brighter world than usual. So much ice and sleet had accumulated through the night, that even through the blinds, the outdoors (in the words of today's Gospel) "became glistening, intensely white." As I lay pondering this, I became aware that what was most startling was the profound quiet: no cars were in the streets; no one was moving about. The utter, unexpected stillness filled me with a sense of God's life flowing through, charging all of creation. Then I heard still, small voices in my ear, "Hey Dad! No school today; let's go sledding!"

While that was not exactly what I had in mind to do, my sons and I did go and we did have fun — mostly. I got anxious that one of them might hit a tree at the bottom of the hill, and then I got cross and yelled at them when they got too competitive about which one could sled farther. It was, literally I suppose, a 'going back down the mountain' experience as the earlier sense of God's glory faded.

But thinking back on it that night, I was grateful for that brief glimpse of God's energy, of God's grace alive around me, whether in the beauty and stillness of creation transformed by winter or in the energy of two young boys, enchanted to be alive and looking for excitement. I realized that, whether or not I am aware of it, creation, human and otherwise, continually throbs with God's dynamism. Just as Jesus was just as much God's Son down on the plain as he was transfigured on the mountain, only less obviously so, so God is just as much at work around us in the ordinary times as he is in those "aha" experiences.

Gerard Manley Hopkins, the great Jesuit poet in the last century, wrote movingly about the vibrancy of God in creation despite man's frequent lack of recognition. I would like to close with an excerpt from his poem entitled, *God's Grandeur.*

> The world is charged with the grandeur of God.
> … There lives the dearest freshness deep down things;
> … Because the Holy Ghost over the bent
> World broods with warm breast and with ah! bright wings.

I Kings 19:9-18
Psalm 27
Mark 9:2-9

God's Forgiveness from Within
Ash Wednesday
February 25, 2004

You cannot see it very well from where you are, but a friend recently gave me this small, sealed hand wipe. It is marketed as the "Wash Away Your Sins Towelette," containing "anti-bacterial formula" which "kills sins on contact." The package hypes this product as not only "handy" and "reliable," but even "heavenly scented"! "Right your wrongs with a swipe," it declares on the back. It offers these six-step directions:

> Remove moist towelette.
> Devoutly wipe away wrong-doing.
> Spot check for stubborn guilt.
> Wipe again as needed.
> Discard sins in waste receptacle.
> Go forth purified and moisturized.

Of course this is a tongue-in-cheek novelty product, not a serious one; but its quick and easy, "do-it-yourself" mentality does help us to see some fallacies in our own habitual approach to repentance. Too often, for example, we regard sin and guilt as something outside of us, as external accretions which can be removed with the correct intentions and actions. We might feel some uneasy responsibility and discomfort about certain ways we have behaved, but it wasn't really us who did that. As Flip Wilson's Reverend Leroy used to say, "The devil made me do it!" So we do something unusually nice for someone or we give away some extra money or we say a special prayer, and then we feel better. We have wiped away our sins and guilt. Or so we think.

The trouble is that sin is more than external to us. While we are created in the image of God and therefore good, and while we are much more than the sum of our thoughts and actions, still our identity and our character are informed and infused by our decisions, some of which are sinful. By sinful, I mean that which goes against our identity and mission as children of God and therefore as brothers and sisters of one

137

another. Any actions and consciously-agreed-to thoughts which do not reflect our love of God and of our neighbor infect us from the inside, not just the outside, and they separate us from God and one another. We cannot just wipe them away as if they never happened.

We cannot, but God can. Unlike the suggestion of the "Wash Away Your Sins Towelette," we cannot absolve ourselves. Only God, whom we have offended by our lack of love, can forgive us. Because God has created us, only God is in a position to reach inside us, so to speak, and to forgive us, to recreate us and give us new life. God can restore us to ourselves and in relationship to others. God, our Creator and Redeemer, can continually give us new life.

God can and does. Not because we say the right words or perform the right actions. Not because we wipe ourselves with the right heavenly scented ointment. Not because we somehow manipulate or force that forgiveness. God forgives us even before we ask, and by our asking we accept that precious and unmerited gift.

"Return to me with all your heart," says the Lord. "Acknowledge your true identity as children of God. Repent of what separates you from me and from my other children. Ask forgiveness and you will receive it: 'good measure, pressed down, shaken together, running over, will be put into your [hearts].' I will never fail you. I will never reject you. 'Behold, I make all things new.'"

The Lenten Desert
The First Sunday in Lent
February 17, 2013

Some 35 years ago, I had the privilege of helping to lead a pilgrimage to Israel. Our five weeks there included a trip into the Sinai Desert. Bouncing along in a jeep for hours through rocky terrain (not sand) where there were no roads, we neophytes felt very dependent on our guide. Nothing familiar comforted us — no road signs, no other traffic, no signs of other human beings at all, just dry, arid landscape promising nothing ahead beyond the next outcropping. We found it eerily beautiful in some ways, but fearful and abhorrent in others.

Lent is our time in the desert. Like it or not, the Spirit drives us along with Jesus into the wilderness where nothing is familiar, where our usual coping mechanisms are insufficient, where we quickly find that we are not in charge. We are not the first, of course. Not only did Jesus precede us, just after his divine Sonship was revealed at his baptism. The Israelites themselves, after being delivered from slavery to Pharaoh, wrestled in the desert with their identity as God's people, fully accepting the mysteries of that demanding reality before finally being brought into the Promised Land. Any true schooling in God's ways seems to lead through the desert. That is where, in the words of today's psalm, God "teaches sinners in his way." There God "guides the humble in doing right and teaches his way to the lowly."

On our desert excursion, I remember suddenly coming across two young men trying to walk their way through this wilderness. They gratefully accepted a ride after draining almost to the bottom the canteen of water we offered them. Our guide was barely restrained in his contempt for their arrogance in thinking they could conquer the desert on their own with little help or resources to call on. He lectured them as if they were his own children, as well he should. Their very lives were at stake.

It is one thing to be driven into the desert by the Spirit, to learn by humbling experience that you are not self-sufficient but that you receive all that you have from the hand of God. It is quite another to tempt fate, to think that rules do not apply to you, that your own strength is enough to take on any challenge that offers itself. Desert experiences come along often enough without seeking them out. Someone dear to us dies. We lose our job. Someone cherished by us betrays us. We fail in a major responsibility. We find our life altered by our or another's addiction. Our economic security becomes shaky. Loneliness threatens to drown us. Our health is no longer dependable as it once was. When the Spirit seems to drive us into the wilderness, as it did Jesus, we learn to let go of control and to seek God's presence and grace. In the midst of the wild beasts, we allow the angels to minister to us.

Our goal in daring the bleak hospitality of the desert was to stay at a Bedouin oasis, rising at 3 a.m. to climb the two hours to the top of Mount Sinai, where Moses is said to have received the ten commandments, and to hike back down to be out of the dehydrating sun well before noon. Later we toured the centuries-old St. Catherine's monastery there, carved into the side of the mountain. I vividly recall an ancient room piled high with the skulls of hundreds of monks who had lived there. Because of the pervasiveness of rock, they had to reuse over and over shallow graves for those who died, collecting and preserving their bones when a grave was again needed.

Our times in the desert remind us of our mortality. It is simply a given. As we heard on Ash Wednesday, we are dust and to dust we shall return. When all is good and abundant and we live as in a garden, that context fades. But the stark reality of the desert, where nothing is easy and all is hard, deepens the awareness of that undeniable mystery within us. Death does pervade life.

But ultimately it does not overcome it. Our Christian faith teaches us that no matter how many deserts we pass through, life overcomes death. No matter how arid our landscapes might get, God's bountiful life is the ultimate reality. Even on a Lenten Sunday, with its focus on the desert and on temptation, our ultimate proclamation is of Jesus' triumph, of God's covenant with us, of the nurturing waters of baptism, which assuredly bring life and prosperity and resurrection to God's people.

The evening we returned to Jerusalem from the Sinai Desert all those years ago, I wrote in my journal, "I am glad to be out of the desert. It was beautiful in many ways, but so stark and so barren. It would be choking to try and live there."

When we find ourselves in the desert, facing the wild beasts and aspects of life we would rather be free of, it is good to remember that life is more than the desert. Time there always comes to an end. God is with us and angels minister to us, and the Spirit will drive us back out of the desert once again.

Will You Not Surrender to This God?
The Second Sunday in Lent
March 8, 1998

Lent is a time of dramatic images which recall for us the reality of the Christian story. Beginning with Jesus' temptation by Satan in the desert and ending with Jesus' brutal death on the cross as a common criminal, Lent reminds us of God's constant overflowing love for humanity and of humanity's constant refusal to respond. "Remember what God has done for you," the scriptures cry out to us. "Will you not surrender to this God?"

The readings today present us with several dramatic images of God. In the first lesson God assures Abram of his faithful love, "Fear not, Abram, I am your shield; your reward shall be very great." In the darkness Abram falls into a sleep-like trance, and a smoking fire pot and a flaming torch move between the carcasses of animals which have been cut in half. For someone to walk between halves of animals while making a promise meant, "May this happen to me if I break this covenant." So God, represented by the fire, makes a total, unbreakable commitment to his servant and ultimately to the Jewish people and to us.

Notice that it is only God, not Abram, who "cut a covenant," who bound himself by moving between the cut animals. God unconditionally binds himself in love, first to the chosen people and then to all his human creation. By offering this story today, the Lenten lectionary asks us, "Will you not surrender to this God?"

The Gospel also confronts us with a powerful image of God's inviting, boundless love: "O Jerusalem, Jerusalem. … How often would I have gathered your children together as a hen gathers her brood under her wings." What a poignant picture of the faithful, forgiving love of God, especially to anyone who has actually watched a "broody hen" gather her newly hatched chicks to her breast. How tenderly she nudges each little stray back to her bosom; how gently her wings enfold the baby chicks! Jesus chooses this compassionate image to portray the divine love.

Some years ago, I recall reading through the curriculum for the three-year-old Church School class which my wife, Betsy, was teaching that year. Based on the lectionary scripture readings, the lesson for this Sunday suggested using a game. The children mill around the room like little chicks, pretending to peck and saying, "Cheep, cheep!" The teacher stands in the middle, holding a blanket about, in this case, her shoulders and over her arms. When she opens her arms and says, "Cluck, cluck," the chicks run under her wings and press in on her as quickly and as closely as possible! (Don't you wish you signed up to teach Church School?!) Experientially, then cognitively, the point is made that God's love is as welcoming and as encompassing and as compelling. Will you not surrender to this God?

For the truth is that we resist this love. Like a child who runs away from home, thinking its own way is better, we prefer our ways, our thoughts, to God's ways, God's thoughts. "O Jerusalem, Jerusalem ... how often would I have gathered your children ... and you would not." "O Chapel Hill, Chapel Hill. ..." "O Chapel of the Cross, Chapel of the Cross. ..." "O Stephen, Stephen. ..." Hear your own name. "How often I would have gathered your children together as a hen gathers her brood under her wings, and you would not!"

Life is not about winning. Life is not about having our own way. Life is about surrender, surrendering to the God who binds himself to us, who constantly beckons to us, who loved the world so much that he gave his only-begotten son.

Lent serves as one more of God's attempts to gather us in as closely as possible. The Lenten liturgy recalls for us God's unceasing but unrequited love. In the depths of our being, we hear God calling our name, encouraging us to return with all our heart, inviting us to live as children of the covenant, urging us to let God gather us and enfold us and embrace us.

Will you not surrender to this God?

To Err Is Human; To Forgive, Divine
The Fourth Sunday in Lent
March 14, 2010

"To err is human; to forgive, divine." Alexander Pope's words take on a profound meaning in light of today's powerful gospel story of the man who had two sons. Each of the sons embodies for us the human condition of constantly erring. Each is self-centered in his own way. They represent us! The younger son is irresponsible, inconsiderate, demanding. He lives for the moment and for himself. The good of others and how his actions affect them are not on his radar scope. Even when he repents and returns home, it is out of hunger and desperation, not out of concern or affection for his family.

The older son is much more dutiful and upright, obedient to his father, shouldering his responsibilities. But his hard work and staying within the lines have not increased his love for others and ennobled his soul. Rather he has become self-righteous, bitter, resentful, judgmental, unforgiving — a true idol for all of us regular church-goers! Both of these sons illustrate for us ways that we humans err.

Their father, on the other hand, perhaps softened and strengthened by his life's experiences and by his transforming vocation of being a parent, embodies for us the awesome mystery of divine forgiveness. Even though his younger son has selfishly turned his back on his family and squandered his legacy, bringing shame on them all, the father exhibits divine compassion and keeps looking for his return. Spotting him at a great distance, he runs out and embraces him and kisses him. He demands no explanations or even apology. Before his son can even speak, he freely and generously expresses his love and forgiveness in his heartfelt embrace and kiss. With no inclination whatever to treat his son as a hired servant, he organizes a lavish celebration to make clear his joy and jubilation.

When the elder son returns and refuses to join the party, his loving father also goes out to *him* and urges him to come in. He assures him of his constant love and devotion and tries to help him move past his resentment and jealousy. As his younger son has been dead and now is alive, the father fervently wishes his elder son also to move from deadness into new life.

"To err is human; to forgive, divine." In this story, Jesus wants us to see past our human projections of God and to be stunned and surprised by God's loving and bountiful forgiveness. We do not earn that compassion. We do not even unleash it by saying or doing the right thing. It is good for us to apologize, to acknowledge our sinfulness, just as the younger son did — *after* his father kissed and embraced him. As Robert Farrar Capon notes, "Confession is not something you do in order to get forgiveness. It's something you do in order to celebrate the forgiveness you [already] got for nothing." That is not a reality we can reason to. That is a mind-boggling mystery revealed to us by God in scripture and especially in the person of Jesus, who forgave his executers from the cross and told us this story and exhorted us to forgive others from our hearts 70 times seven times. That is why when we hear the revelations of scripture, which far surpass all our understanding, we exclaim, "Thanks be to God." God's bountiful love and compassion are not something we fabricate, hoping that is the case. They are revealed to us through our faith, and they call us from death to life.

For in this story, Jesus also wants us to emulate the father, to move beyond the separateness of living as sinful sons and to let ourselves be drawn into union with our Father by absorbing more and more of the One in whose image we are made. "To err is human," and we are human and should know that we often fail and are often in need of our Father's unearned but lavishly given forgiveness. But to forgive is divine, and since we are made in the image of the divine and baptized with the Holy Spirit, we are also to aspire to grow into forgiving others as we have been forgiven. That is a difficult thing to do, as hard as it was for the elder son. But in our best moments we know that is who we are called to be: to let go of our claim of requital, of our demand for satisfaction, of our need to punish others, and to let the divine life in us call us to forgive. To refuse to do so is spiritual death and can even lead to physical death, as evidenced by the all too frequent occurrences of disgruntled employees who open fire on fellow workers and eventually on themselves. Such extremes show us the foolishness of beginning down that path of refusing forgiveness.

The story is told of an old Cherokee who explained to his grandson about a battle that goes on inside people. He said, "My son, the battle is between two wolves inside us all. One is Evil. It is anger, envy, jealousy, sorrow, regret, greed, arrogance, self-pity, guilt, resentment, inferiority, lies, false pride, superiority, and ego. The other is Good. It is joy, peace, love, hope, serenity, humility, kindness, benevolence, empathy, generosity, truth, compassion and faith." The grandson thought about it for a minute and then asked, "Which wolf wins?" The old Cherokee simply replied, "The one you feed."

Every day we have chances to feed one wolf or the other, to nourish our human death-seeking tendencies or to respond to the divine life within us. We can justify our anger and our sense of being wronged or we can ask God to help us let that go and move on, to let the overpowering love of the Father flow through us to all those also made in the image of God. "To err is human; to forgive, divine." May the God who reveals the depth of the Divine mercy and compassion to us give us the grace to accept joyfully the Father's forgiveness and to nourish the divine spark within us by living faithfully in the household of God.

Luke 15:11-32

Easter Sunday 2015

We Wish To See Jesus
The Fifth Sunday in Lent
April 6, 2003

At a very important point in John's Gospel, which we just heard, some Greeks come to Jerusalem for Passover. They make contact with one of the disciples who had the Greek name of Philip and poignantly declare, "Sir, we wish to see Jesus." Up until then, according to John, Jesus has insisted several times, "My hour has not yet come." But at this sign that his light is beginning to extend even to the Gentiles, Jesus understands and declares, "The hour has come for the Son of man to be glorified." He knows that like a grain of wheat, he must now die to be fruitful. Although his soul is troubled, he embraces the purpose for which he has come into the world, leading us liturgically into the events of Holy Week, beginning next Sunday. "Now shall the ruler of this world be cast out," Jesus proclaims; "and I, when I am lifted up from the earth, will draw all men to myself."

Perhaps most of us can identify with the deep desire of those Greeks: "Sir, we wish to see Jesus." Especially at this time when our souls are troubled, when our country is involved in a controversial war that is both far off and as close as our living rooms, we want to perceive Jesus. In the bifurcation of breathing in both the springtime beauty of Chapel Hill and the sights and sounds from the battlefields in Iraq, we long to find Jesus. In our sorrow and helplessness at all the violence and killing, "we wish to see Jesus."

I and, I am sure, you have been struggling with that these last weeks. Where is Jesus in all this? What are we to think and feel? How do we respond as American Christians to what is being done in our name?

No matter what our stance on the necessity of this war, it seems to me that as human beings and as Christians, we are called first of all to let ourselves grieve for those who are suffering. Soldiers on both sides of the conflict, their families, and children and adults surrounded by war, are dying or living with the terror of death so nearby or being wounded in body and in spirit. Our souls should be troubled. Our temptation — and I certainly find it in myself — is to deny our grief by ignoring it or by distancing ourselves from it by angrily denouncing those whom we hold responsible for its cause. Soren Kierkegaard reminds us, "It takes moral courage to grieve. It takes religious courage to rejoice." I am not suggesting that anger is necessarily inappropriate here, but it should not be a substitute for our grief. If we do not grieve, we will not be able to rejoice. Those at our Sunday night Compline service, for example, who have been praying each week for Jessica Lynch and other POWs by name were able to rejoice much more at her rescue than those of us who have kept things at arm's length.

Something that will help us more honestly grieve will be to express our confused thoughts and feelings to others, especially in the context of Christian community. Too often we do not share our vulnerability with one another, not wanting others to know we do not have all the answers or seemingly right responses. I certainly find myself doing that in this confusing and unsettling time, and I hope that one positive outcome of this conflict will be to help us live more true and honest Christian community. Like Jesus, we are to acknowledge to one another that our souls are troubled and to grieve together.

In addition to allowing ourselves to suffer with those who suffer — the definition of true compassion — and to do that within some significant communal dimension, we are to find ways to respond in action. Several weeks ago, we heard our North Carolina Episcopal bishops ask us to do things "which will give flesh to God's abiding love for all the children of this earth, even those we look upon as our enemies. We encourage you," they wrote, "to use your imagination and energies toward creative and loving ends." I see evidence of that all around, from the prayers at Compline and other services to the Vestry writing letters to soldiers connected with this parish, to the offering we are taking this morning for those who suffer. It is important that individually and communally we continue to find ways to put our grief and our faith into action.

"We wish to see Jesus." I believe that Jesus is there in the midst of those who suffer and in the midst of our confusion and pain. "If anyone serves me," Jesus says in today's Gospel, "he must follow me; and where I am, there shall my servant be also." Jesus is in the midst of the suffering, and if we want to follow him, we will be there as well. "Now is the judgment of this world," he asserts, "now shall the ruler of this world be cast out." But how does Jesus overthrow and conquer? Not by force or violence or destruction but by love and by drawing all men to himself. One long-range danger of war is that it unconsciously reinforces in us the notion that force is what accomplishes things. Power over others is what is most desirable. But Jesus teaches and lives and encourages us to another way. Die to yourself, Jesus proclaims, and live for others. Like the grain of wheat, fall into the ground and die and bear much fruit. Do not love your life first and foremost and therefore lose it. Follow me in the way of love, which does not flinch from suffering, and find your life with me there in the midst of it.

As we move ahead to Palm Sunday and Good Friday and Easter Day, we do so with a deeper understanding of the suffering of this world and of Jesus' place within it. The liturgy and the scripture and our common grief help us to unite ourselves with him and to follow where he leads — to the cross and to the tomb and to new, unlimited life. We have a unique opportunity to satisfy the desire within us expressed so long ago by some Gentile predecessors, "Sir, we wish to see Jesus."

John 12:20-33

The Engaging Story of Lazarus
The Fifth Sunday in Lent
April 6, 2014

All through Lent, we have been treated to some of John the Evangelist's most engaging stories about Jesus, all long, detailed encounters with specific individuals. We heard about Nicodemus, a seeker, who came to Jesus by night because he was not yet ready to risk the insecurity and danger of following Jesus. Then Jesus interacted with a different sort of seeker, the Samaritan woman at the well, who was alienated from herself and from her community. She became a believer, and many of her village with her. Last week Jesus healed the man born blind, who slowly gained spiritual sight along with his physical vision, while the Pharisees became even more obdurate in their blindness about Jesus. Finally today, John introduces us, not to potential followers or to those ostracized by society, but very interestingly to Jesus' closest friends, Martha and Mary and Lazarus.

We may not think of Jesus, the Messiah, as having time for, or interest in, intimate friends, but these siblings were not part of the inner circle of the 12 or even of the further 72. Jesus was not preparing them to go out and preach the Gospel and spread the kingdom. They would not later have to fulfill any significant responsibilities, such as writing down the Gospels or being martyred or founding new churches. No roles interfered here; they could just be close friends and care unreservedly for each other.

Mary showed her love for Jesus, John tells us, by anointing his feet with oil and wiping them with her hair, a dramatic image of their affection for each other. When Lazarus got sick, his sisters sent word to Jesus, "Lord, he whom you love is ill." They did not even use his name, knowing Jesus would know "he whom you love" referred to Lazarus. And they did not even say, "so come heal him," because they knew they could count on their close friend Jesus to respond.

But how did he respond? John tells us, "Now Jesus loved Martha and her sister and Lazarus. So when he heard that he was ill, he stayed two days longer in the place where he was." That is not what they — or we — expected. Love seems to demand Jesus' dropping everything to rush to his friend's side. But think of how Lazarus' life was changed by later being raised from the dead. What a difference that must have made in him! Jesus guarded that opportunity for the one whom he loved, something for us all to consider the next time we are tempted to rescue others from what may be significant redemptive pain for them. Sometimes at least, loving like Jesus means staying in the place where we are.

Eventually he did go, of course, and again we see the depth of his feelings for these friends. When Jesus talked with Martha and Mary and saw their tears, John tells us "he was deeply moved in spirit and troubled." In fact he started crying as well. Even though he seemed to know what was coming, their pain was his own pain. He wept so much, others said, "See how much he loved him." And at that point, at the climax of the story, he had the stone rolled away and gave Lazarus back to his sisters.

In its framework, then, this is a story about deep friendship and shows us a moving, human side of Jesus that we can easily miss. This unique human/divine person really is like us in all things except sin, including the intense joy and wrenching heartbreak of intimate friendship.

Out of the context of these illuminating friendships, this Gospel story dramatically proclaims the stunning power of God manifest in Jesus. Last week, we heard that "Never since the world began has it been heard that anyone opened the eyes of a man born blind. If this man were not from God, he could do nothing." Now we see that this unprecedented divine power in Jesus extended to raising to life one who had been dead and buried. Nothing is outside the realm of God's power as revealed in Jesus. Every obstacle can be overcome and every enemy conquered, including the enemy of death. When we are tempted like Martha and Mary to say, "Lord, if you had been here, this would not have happened," we are to remember the incredible grace and power of God as revealed in Jesus, which ultimately always triumphs.

This powerful story is getting us ready for Easter. John's use of shared imagery tells us that: the cave, the stone rolled away from the door of the tomb, the linen discarded. Does all that ring a bell? That prepares us for the ultimate story, the Father's raising Jesus from the dead, and that not for earthly life only, but for eternal life. The raising of Lazarus was a resuscitation; it was temporary; he would die again. But it points us toward the permanent resurrection of Jesus from the dead. He does not die again, and his triumph over death is one that we all share. That is the basis of our faith and our deep joy.

First, however, Jesus must endure his Passion, and that is what we will celebrate liturgically next week. On Palm Sunday (and again on Good Friday), we will hear another long, moving Gospel story about Jesus, this time about his betrayal and trial and suffering and death. In all of these stories, handed on to us by his devoted followers, we are privileged to encounter for ourselves the amazing, redemptive, unconquerable grace of God at work in Jesus of Nazareth.

John 11:1-45

Maundy Thursday — A Different Night
Maundy Thursday
April 8, 2004

"Why is this night different from all other nights?" So begins the Seder, the Passover meal, celebrated this week by Jews throughout the world, as it has been for thousands of years. The foundation of the feast is found in tonight's first reading from Exodus. In preparation for their liberation, brought on by the angel of death passing over their houses because of the blood of the lamb on their doorposts, Moses and his people were to eat this ceremonial meal. In time it became an annual remembrance of God's saving power in delivering the Jews from the bonds of slavery.

As Christians we can ask the same question on Maundy Thursday, "Why is this night different from all other nights?" Tonight we commemorate Jesus' transformation of the Passover meal, according to Matthew, Mark, and Luke, by taking and blessing and breaking the unleavened bread and giving it and the cup of blessing to his followers, declaring it to be his body and blood. The early Christians continued in this breaking of the bread, understanding it not only as a defining ritual, but as a life-giving mystery in which they encountered God's saving presence. This repeated action connected them with the living Jesus and with one another. It made present again the incarnate reality of the transcendent God and Jesus' liberating them from sin and death. As Paul instructed the early Christians in Corinth, in tonight's second reading, "As often as you eat this bread and drink the cup, you proclaim the Lord's death until he comes" (I. Cor 11:26).

The gift of the Eucharist has come down to us through countless generations of Christians. It strengthens us and draws us into the Divine presence and sustains us for service in God's name. To celebrate Eucharist is much more than to recite some ancient words and to eat a fragment of bread and to sip from the cup of wine and then to go away unaffected. The Eucharist is rooted in the mystery of the Incarnation, God becoming present among us in the person of Jesus, a man of flesh and blood. Unlike his heavenly Father, people could and did touch Jesus.

They reached out to him to be healed, to feel his blessing, to hold him, to wash his feet with tears of repentance. They also, of course, as we will hear tomorrow, betrayed him with a kiss, whipped him, spit on him, crucified him. While in a very real sense, after Jesus' ascension to the Father, that tangible presence has been no longer available to us to love or to reject; in a sacramental sense, it is available. Through our faithful obedience to Jesus' command, through the physical, earthly, human act of eating and drinking his body broken for us and his blood poured out for us, we are drawn into the spiritual, heavenly, divine realm of life and union with God.

We may not be any more at ease with partaking of the Eucharist than we are with obeying Jesus' other command on this special night, found in our Gospel reading, to imitate him by washing each other's feet. We may find it all unsettling. Or if we do regularly participate in communion, we may do so mainly out of habit or social pressure, unwilling to attach the same importance and meaning that Jesus gave it. We are not always comfortable in grounding our faith in the physical realm. We prefer to intellectualize or spiritualize our belief, focusing on abstract religious truths. "One of the blunders religious people are particularly fond of making," says Frederick Buechner, "is the attempt to be more spiritual than God." But God's primary spiritual acts are all expressed in the physical realm: creation, the incarnation, the crucifixion, the resurrection, the Eucharist. God's love is manifest in the material and temporal, and through that physical realm, we as God's creatures are connected to the spiritual and eternal.

"He who eats my flesh and drinks my blood abides in me, and I in him," Jesus instructed his disciples. Jesus abides in us. Just as the blessed bread and wine enter into us and become part of us so that they can no longer be distinguished from us, so too does Jesus enter into us and become part of us. What an amazing thought! "Abide" means to dwell in, to remain with, to find a home with. Jesus lives continually in us. What a difference that should make in our lives, in the way we treat others, in our patience with ourselves, in our hope in the midst of difficulty.

And we abide in Jesus. In the incarnational sacrament of the Eucharist, in eating and drinking "the Body of Christ, the bread of heaven" and "the Blood of Christ, the cup of salvation," we are, if you will, swallowed up into the Body of Christ, where, in the words of the Prayer Book, we "are united one to another, and the living to the dead." We become part of something much larger than ourselves, something that far transcends all our limitations, all our sins, all our petty faults and self-preoccupation. We abide in Jesus Christ and become part of his Body, physically and sacramentally connected with the saving Jesus and with one another.

"What makes this night different from all other nights?" Tonight Jesus gives us the gift of himself, the expression and means of continuing life, a foretaste of the heavenly banquet. Jesus, who became flesh for us, nourishes us corporeal beings with his own physical and mystical presence, unites us to his victory over the slavery of sin and death, and promises to raise us up at the last day. As often as we eat this bread and drink the cup, we proclaim the Lord's death until he comes again.

Exodus 112:1-14a
I Corinthians 11:23-26
John 13:1-15

Good Friday
Good Friday
March 29, 2013

Good Friday is a threat to our human Gospels of self-fulfillment. It calls into question our assumptions that life should be manageable, that all things should be fair and just, that everything should turn out the way that we want it to. It gives the lie to our expectations that we lead charmed lives, that we control our own destiny, that we can at least keep suffering at arms' length. It shatters our illusions that life revolves around us.

Drawing us here to this annual commemoration, Good Friday calls us to hear the story of Jesus' suffering and death, to see the wooden cross that will soon be brought in before us, to accept, and not to turn away from, the reality that, in the words of the Prayer Book, "the way of the cross is the way of life."

We are all painfully aware of the suffering in our lives: the deaths of those close to us, the unrealized hopes, the shattered relationships, the health problems, the financial struggles, the agonies of self-doubt and insecurity, the inescapable loneliness, the limitations and selfishness of others, our failures to be and to achieve what we ought. And, except for death, we do not know what yet lies ahead of us.

We struggle against such suffering, and in one sense it is only right that we should do so. We do all that we can to eliminate pain, to work against injustice, to ease the suffering of others. But in another sense, we must accept affliction in our lives as inevitable, as that which shapes and molds us, as that where we most encounter God.

Good Friday confronts us, not only with the intimidating reality and inevitability of suffering — if this is true for the master, it will also be true for the servants — but also with the mystery that somehow this suffering is integral to realizing our identity as those created in the likeness of God. Just as it was true for Jesus that his full identity as God's Son could not shine through until he had embraced the cross, so it is for us that we cannot be fully revealed as God's children until we have yielded to the suffering that molds and shapes us.

Thomas Merton in *New Seeds of Contemplation* writes:

> Souls are like wax waiting for a seal. By themselves they have no special identity. Their destiny is to be softened and prepared in this life, by God's will, to receive, at their death, the seal of their own degree of likeness to God in Christ. And that is what it means, among other things, to be judged by Christ.

> The wax that has melted in God's will can easily receive the stamp of its identity, the truth of what it was meant to be. But the wax that is hard and dry and brittle and without love will not take the seal: for the hard seal, descending upon it, grinds it to powder.

> Therefore if you spend your life trying to escape from the heat of the fire that is meant to soften and prepare you to become your true self, and if you try to keep your substance from melting in the fire — as if your true identity were to be hard wax — the seal will fall upon you at last and crush you. You will not be able to take your own true name and countenance, and you will be destroyed by the event that was meant to be your fulfillment.

Jesus is the model for us. Although his passion repulsed him so much that he begged his Father to take this cup from him, he "became obedient unto death, even death on a cross." Because he did, because of his loving obedience, "God has highly exalted him and bestowed on him the name which is above every name."

If we, too, can regard with new eyes and with a more loving heart and with more receptive arms, the suffering in our lives, we, too, will emerge triumphant, will be stamped with the likeness of Christ, will reflect our full identity as children of God.

That is the message of hope that Good Friday holds up to us; and yet its radical proclamation, which both shatters our illusions and restores our hope, goes even deeper than that. For beyond its call to us to look upon our suffering in a new way, the crucifixion and death of Jesus also proclaims to us that it is not how *we* handle suffering that makes the ultimate difference. The Good News of Good Friday is that Jesus, God's very Son, took upon himself the sins and sufferings of us all. Through the cross, he procured for us the ultimate conquest of all that opposes us, even death. Robert Capon put it this way: "The whole slop-closet full of mildewed performances (which is all you have to offer) is simply your death; it is Jesus who is your life. ... You can fail utterly, therefore, and still live the life of grace. ... Because at the very worst, all you can be is dead — and for him who is the Resurrection and the Life, that just makes you his cup of tea." (*Between Noon and Three: Romance, Law, and the Outrage of Grace*)

Good Friday rescues us from our suffocating self-preoccupation, from the notion that we must save ourselves, from the presumption that *we* must rescue the world. It holds up to us, rather, the One upon whom our gaze is to be fixed, Jesus, our Savior.

It is he whom we have come to behold on this Good Friday. It is he upon whom we focus in hearing the story and in looking upon the cross. It is he who burns away our human Gospels of self-fulfillment and immerses us in the Holy Gospel of our Lord Jesus Christ. Amen.

Forgiveness Is Never Going To Be Easy
Good Friday at St. Paul AME
April 21, 2000

Sister Helen Prejean, in her book *Dead Man Walking*, familiar to many
of us as a movie, includes this passage:

"Lloyd LeBlanc has told me that he would have been content with
imprisonment for Patrick Sonnier. He went to the execution, he says,
not for revenge, but hoping for an apology. Patrick Sonnier had not
disappointed him. Before sitting in the electric chair, he had said,
'Mr. LeBlanc, I want to ask your forgiveness for what me and Eddie
done,' and Lloyd LeBlanc had nodded his head, signaling a forgiveness
he had already given. He says that when he arrived at the sheriff's
deputies there in the cane field to identify his son, he had knelt by
his boy — 'laying down there with his two little eyes sticking out like
bullets' — and prayed the Our Father.

"And when he came to the words: 'Forgive us our trespasses as we
forgive those who trespass against us,' he had not halted or equivocated,
and he said: 'Whoever did this, I forgive them.' But he acknowledges
that it's a struggle to overcome the feelings of bitterness and revenge
that well up, especially as he remembers David's birthday year after year
and loses him all over again: David at 20, David at 25, David getting
married, David standing at the back door with his little ones clustered
around his knees, grownup David, a man like himself, whom he will
never know. Forgiveness is never going to be easy. Each day it must be
prayed for and struggled for and won."

Most of us have not had a child brutally murdered, like Lloyd LeBlanc
did. We have not had to forgive a human being who had sunk as low
as Patrick Sonnier. But we have all experienced deep pain, caused or at
least partially caused by another. We have been betrayed by one whom
we trusted. We have been deprived of what we counted on as ours.
We have been deliberately misled. We have been wrongfully accused.

Our intentions have been misunderstood. We have had to work harder because of the thoughtlessness of others.

We are wronged daily, sometimes deeply, sometimes much less so. But no less than Lloyd LeBlanc we are called to forgive, to relinquish claim of requital, to let go of blame and resentment and bitterness. Sister Prejean's concluding words are just as true for us: "Forgiveness is never going to be easy. Each day it must be prayed for and struggled for and won."

Today's scripture readings focus on the significance of forgiveness. Jesus exhorts us in the Gospel to forgive without limit, as often as someone wrongs us. This is no perfunctory exercise, but one which affects us at our deepest level. We are to forgive our brother from our heart. Who can do that? How can we truly let go of resentment even once, let alone time after time?

Perhaps we need to step back for a moment and come at this from another way. After all, Jesus' parable is in two parts, and the first part tells us about God's forgiveness of us. We are the servant who owes 10,000 talents and cannot pay. Everything we have has been given us by the king, and yet we are often ungrateful, selfish, and unproductive. When we are held accountable, we are the ones, or should be, who beg for mercy and compassion and forgiveness. And most of all, we are those referred to in this parable whom the king magnanimously absolves and releases, forgiving all our debt. Our life and our freedom and our opportunities are precious, undeserved gifts from God, who as today's Psalm tells us, "is full of compassion and mercy, slow to anger and of great kindness. ... He has not dealt with us according to our sins, nor rewarded us according to our wickedness. For as the heavens are high above the earth [an infinite quantity], so is his mercy great upon those who fear him."

And how do we fear him? How do we reverence and pay homage to and live in awe of this God who graces us with so much, especially loving, unconditional forgiveness? The second part of the parable illustrates that or rather shows us how *not* to do that.

Again we are the servant, who now does not extend the same generous forgiveness he has received. Having been released from the debt of 10,000 talents, he refuses to forgive his fellow servant who owes him only 100 denarii. (Such is the difference between what we owe God and what others owe us.) He casts him into prison, which is what we try to do to those from whom we withhold forgiveness: we confine them in an enclosed space within us. The truth is, however, that as in the parable, it is we who end up imprisoned and unfree — not simply because our master holds us accountable, but because locking others within us and holding in our resentment costs us the love and freedom and peace which sustain us and allow us to flourish.

Stephen Crane paints this graphic picture of such self-destruction using another analogy:

In the desert
I saw a creature, naked, bestial,
Who, squatting upon the ground,
Held his heart in his hands,
And ate of it.
I said, "Is it good, friend?"
"It is bitter — bitter," he answered.
"But I like it
Because it is bitter,
And because it is my heart."

It is not only for others' good that Jesus calls us to forgive, but for our own good as well. True forgiveness is a precious gift to a fellow servant, a liberation for ourselves, and an act of gratitude and obedience to God.

"Forgiveness is never going to be easy," however, as Sister Prejean notes. "Each day it must be prayed for and struggled for and won." Praying for the gift of forgiveness is something we do too little of. While forgiveness is a decision, as it was for Lloyd LeBlanc, we need God's saving grace both to make that act of the will and to persevere in it. Part of our daily prayer ought to be for help in forgiving, not only for those daily annoyances that afflict our existence, but also for those deep-harbored resentments that we buried long ago. Consciously or unconsciously we have all said, "I will never forgive so-and-so. That painful memory is unpardonable. I cannot forgive."

Yes, you can. With God's grace you can. As God has forgiven you 10,000 talents, so you can forgive 100 denarii, no matter how large it seems to you. Ask God for the grace of forgiveness; that is the first step. But make it a genuine prayer. If you do not want to forgive, spiritual writers tell us, ask for the grace to want to forgive. If you cannot authentically make that request, ask for the grace to want to want to forgive! Go back as far as you have to in order to start on solid ground.

Keep on asking daily; that is the second step. Sometimes immediately, but more often eventually, your prayer will be answered. Cooperate with that grace; that is the third step. Struggle with it; win it. True forgiveness is at the core of your spiritual journey, at the heart of the Christian life. Do not back away from it. Be encouraged by the God who forgives you, who "is full of compassion and mercy, slow to anger and of great kindness." Let that God work in you, who bids you forgive your brother from your heart.

Psalm 103
Matthew 18:21-35

With The Rev. Thomas Nixon, senior pastor of St. Paul AME

In the Midst of Death We Are In Life
Easter Day
March 27, 2005

Yesterday morning about this same time, the day after the solemn tolling of the bell 33 times on Good Friday to mark Jesus' death and the day before this joyful Easter celebration, 20 or so of us gathered quietly in the chapel. We were marking, as the Prayer Book allows, Holy Saturday, a time of mourning and waiting, a time of quiet and listening. We recited together an anthem from the burial office, which begins "In the midst of life we are in death; of whom may we seek for succor, but of thee, O Lord?"

"In the midst of life we are in death," a continual truth about our lives. Death fills our front pages and news programs, whether suicide bombings or removing feeding tubes or abducted children or high school shooting sprees or the not-so-long-ago tsunami. Death has touched many of us this year, claiming family members or friends. This month alone will see five funerals here at the Chapel of the Cross. In the midst of life we are surrounded by death.

But today it is fitting that hundreds of us gather, as do millions around the world, to proclaim on Easter that the corollary is also true: "In the midst of death we are in life." Death is not the end. Jesus' words from the cross, "It is finished," refer only to his earthly life and to his mission of reconciling us with the Father. They mean not the loss of hope, but the extension of hope. They signify that now life is changed, not ended. At death, *we* are not finished. Because the Father raised Jesus from the dead, God will also give life to our mortal bodies. Despite the pain and loss we experience at the death of others and despite the fear and incomprehension with which we look on our own deaths, death has no lasting victory; death carries no ultimate sting. In the midst of death we are in life.

That is true, of course, not because of some innate human capacity, but because of the power and love of God. Easter is not the triumph of the human spirit, but the victory of the Divine authority and compassion, which rules even over evil and death. We celebrate Easter, not because we have somehow accomplished it, but because it has been freely given to us, unearned and undeserved. As proud human beings, we do not easily receive what we have somehow not produced, even though we did not bring ourselves into existence, let alone give ourselves the oxygen, temperature range, nourishment, upbringing, education, friends, challenges, and all that we need to lead productive lives! Even so, we like to think of ourselves as somehow self-made and self-sustaining, as getting along nicely without God. Why do we even need Easter? The Rev. Barbara Brown Taylor puts it this way: "The power of God is now and has always been the power to raise us from the dead. Period. It is not about us. It is about God. Our only role is to stick our feet straight up in the air and admit that without God we might as well be put to bed with a shovel." She concludes: "Now that is a message that can empty out a church fast." (*God in Pain*)!

Seeing no one is leaving, however, I am emboldened to continue! If we then trust the power of God and believe in life beyond death, does that mean that we are not to be concerned with the deaths that surround us? Does that faith become a convenient protection from our own fears and the pains of others? Does it absolve us from striving against the forces of death and respecting the dignity of every human being? No! Jesus' resurrection to eternal life in no way denigrates this earthly, transitory life. On the contrary, it calls us to engage more fully in its challenges and opportunities, its celebrations and disappointments, its paradoxes and simplicities, just as Jesus did. The more abundant life that Jesus came to bring all of us does not begin only at death; it has already begun at our baptism. Our faith would have us embrace that life, especially through our compassion for others and through our dedication to justice and peace for all people, not through simply contenting ourselves with the assurance that things will be better in the next life. As Teilhard de Chardin observed, "Christianity does not ask us to live in the shadow of the cross, but in the fire of its creative action."

Perhaps in a different way than she meant, Barbara Brown Taylor is right: The message of our dependence on a God who opens to us the free gift of eternal life and calls us to witness to and to serve others in light of that ennobling gift should empty out our church fast! It should send us eagerly into a world in need of that hope and that compassion. It should send us to the homeless and the hungry, the refugees and the prisoners, the sick and the disabled, the lonely and the desolate. It should send us to one another, especially in our times of need. And it should bring us back into church regularly and often, to sustain us and nourish us for service and to remind us of God's great gift to us.

Easter is an earth-shaking feast. It is no accident that at Jesus' death and resurrection the earth quaked and the curtain of the temple was torn in two. The former things were changed and the old was made new. Through the gift of Jesus, the Father reconciled us to himself and called us to help bring that love and reconciliation to all people. As Karl Adams has written in his book, *Son of God*, "We confess him no less sincerely than did the disciples in days gone by. For the truth is that every genuine Christian life proclaims, with ever new voice in ringing tones, the fact to which the Apostles once testified with their blood: 'He is risen from the dead, of which we are witnesses.'" "Alleluia. Christ is risen. The Lord is risen indeed. Alleluia."

An Easter Limerick
Easter Sunday
April 4, 1999

Please repeat after me, line by line:

Thank God for the mystery of Easter
Which allows me to live as a Feaster.
No failure or loss
Is exempt from the cross:
Good News when I fall on my kiester!

Starting an Easter sermon with such a communal chorus of an original limerick certainly borders on the irreverent and, some may think, falls completely into it! I don't know what's gotten into me — I hope the grace of God! For this verse is not meant to take the mystery of Easter lightly, but to celebrate joyfully its profound reality. I hope you will not mind if I use these few lines as a framework for this morning's sermon.

"Thank God for the mystery of Easter." What a gift Easter is to us and how different our lives would be without it! Our hope would be taken away. Not only would we be more alone in our lives, more left to fend for ourselves, more defenseless against the "changes and chances of this life," but we would have no hope for the next life. Each loss would be irrevocable; each death would be the end, including our own.

Jesus' resurrection — not resuscitation, not like Lazarus, revived for a few more years; but resurrection, rising to a new, boundless life, never to die again — changed that hopelessness forever. "O death, where is thy victory? O death where is thy sting?" That is the amazing mystery of Easter which changed our world eternally, and for which we pull out all the stops this morning to give God thanks. An Easter gift, like life, simply handed to us out of love.

"Which allows me to live as a Feaster." Here I ran into the limits of language! I wanted to say "which allows us to live as Feasters," but that appropriate addition of the more complete communal dimension not only ruined the rhythm, it lessened the rhyme. Such are the limitations of art!

A Feaster, of course, is one who feasts, one who celebrates, one who sees life as abundance to be shared, not scarcity to be hoarded. A Feaster accepts all the gracious gifts that are given, knowing they are unearned, but, unlike the older brother of the Prodigal Son, ready to join in anyway. A Feaster sees life as a banquet where all are invited to the table, where all God's children are welcomed and loved. The reality of Easter — the power of God — allows us, although not without stumbling, to live as Feasters.

You may think that "feaster" is not a real word, and I suppose in our everyday language it is not; but I did find it used with a capital letter (as I have) by no less an Anglican luminary than George Herbert, who meant by it, one coming to the sacramental feast of the Lord's table. Hopefully in a few moments, we will all be Feasters, those who come with open hands to receive physical and spiritual nurture at Holy Communion. In so doing, we not only express sacramentally our lives as Feasters, i.e. those who continually receive freely and undeservedly the gifts of God and therefore God himself, but we also participate in a foretaste of the heavenly banquet and declare our Easter belief that "Christ has died, Christ is risen, Christ will come again." Each time we celebrate the Eucharist, it is an Easter feast.

"No failure or loss is exempt from the cross." Jesus' resurrection not only conquered death but sin. Sin no more has the power to separate irrevocably human beings from God. Nor do the effects of sin — our own or others — hold ultimate sway. Nothing that human beings do is the bottom line; no sin that we commit cannot be forgiven; nothing that happens to us is beyond redemption because of Jesus' death and resurrection.

Mary McDermott Shideler in *Creed for a Christian Skeptic* wrote:

"Essentially, the doctrine [of the resurrection] answers the question, 'Do we live in a world where the tree lies as it fell, where the past is beyond redemption, where the Omnipotence can be defeated?' Certainly this is the world of the crucifixion, and by and large the world of our daily lives. In it, evil overcomes good and man overcomes God, not in appearance only but in dreadful fact. The child has died and cannot be restored to life. We have sinned and the effects of our sin will persist forever. Youth is gone and we shall never get it back. The ultimate outrage has happened; we knew that it could not, but it has. But the doctrine of the resurrection says of them all: they are not lost; they will be restored; they can be redeemed."

Given all the burdens that weigh us down in our lives, it is easy to become cynical. It is hard to maintain our faith in an active, dynamic, God, whose redeeming grace is at work in the world. I offer you one story which happened here this week, a small Easter happening. It is not a very long story because we only know the result and nothing of what led up to it. Palm Sunday evening a parishioner discovered a paper bag left on the steps of the church. Inside were the taken-apart pieces of two brass candlesticks inscribed with the words "Chapel of the Cross," which had been stolen from the chapel some time ago. Also included was a hand-scrawled note with the words, "I am deeply sorry. I don't know what got into me. Praise Jesus," and a small cross drawn underneath. Whatever got into this person originally, it was God's grace that ultimately prevailed. "No failure or loss is exempt from the cross." Many times we do not see the fruit of redemption in this life; in this case we did.

And that brings us to the last irreverent line of this Easter limerick: "Good News when I fall on my kiester!" This slang term is not much used anymore (I am not even sure how to spell it!), but it refers to that part of the body best designed to absorb the blow of a fall! Some people have more capacity than others! No matter how much padding we have, however, a hard physical fall stuns and devastates us, and so do mental, emotional, and spiritual falls. They wound us, isolate us, color our approach to life. That is when we must hold fast to the Good News, to the Gospel reality that we are not alone, that sin and suffering and death have no ultimate power, that Jesus is risen indeed and has conquered far greater foes than we will ever face.

That is the Good News of Easter. That is the faith that gives meaning to our lives. That is the mystery for which we give God thanks this joyous Easter morning. In a variant of the blessing from last night's Great Vigil, "May Almighty God, who has redeemed us and made us his children through the resurrection of his Son our Lord, bestow upon you the riches of his blessing" and help you all to live faithfully as Easter Feasters.

What Do We Hold Onto?
Easter Day
April 20, 2014

Sometimes we are not sure what to hold onto. From our childhood we are taught to hold onto our mother's hand when we cross the street. We are urged to hold onto the railing of a flight of stairs. We are encouraged to hold on when the footing or the bicycle path or the boat ride becomes a little rough. "Hold on tight; stay steady; don't fall."

As we mature, we are exhorted to hold onto our values, to remember and hold onto who we are, to hold onto our priorities and the example of those who have gone before us. All these things can keep us stable in the face of life's many choices and in the midst of disturbance and confusion. They can help us keep our bearings and reassure us and keep us on a steady course.

And most often they do work for us. We know what to hold onto, and life is fulfilling and meaningful, and it seems like it always will be.

But storms come, and we get knocked off our feet, perhaps even totally turned upside down. A devastating physical or mental illness hits us or someone we love; we lose our job or we don't get the one we needed or wanted; someone very close to us betrays us; death separates us from one around whom our life has revolved. We feel lost and directionless and alone. We do not know what to hold onto.

Even when our personal lives are relatively stable, the violence and the hatred and the destruction all around us can be disorienting and disconcerting. The school shootings and knifings, the intractable wars and incessant bombings and constant acts of terrorism all over the world, the hate crimes in our own country, even the destructive forces of nature unleashed by tornadoes and mudslides and avalanches, the busloads and ferry loads of students whose promising lives suddenly come to an end. The enormity of it all weighs us down, and we look for some hope and some constancy. We do not know what to hold onto.

Our temptation is to grab and hold onto the wrong thing. We want that sense of security and wellbeing, so we bury ourselves in our work or consume our lives in the unquenchable thirst to make more and more money or lose ourselves in whatever is handy to distract us. We hold onto our handheld devices or cling to our standing in the community or latch onto one more person who might make us whole and keep us happy.

Mary Magdalene found herself in that disorienting situation in this morning's well-known Gospel story. She had finally found someone to give meaning and wholeness to her life and had dedicated everything to following him. Now suddenly Jesus was snatched away from her by the authorities and put to a cruel death. Her world had crumpled. She could think of nothing else to do but go to his tomb as soon as Passover was finished and complete the burial ministrations that had been cut short. When she saw the stone was moved away from the opening to the tomb, she presumed the worst. Her sorrow turned to frenzy, and she ran back crying to tell the others the bad news that even Jesus' body had now been taken. Returning to the tomb (where else was she to go?), her tears and her loss and her anguish so blinded her that she did not perceive that angels were speaking to her or even recognize Jesus when she first saw him. But hearing him speak her name instantly and completely changed all that. Her despair was turned to elation, and she immediately threw her arms around the fulfilling one she thought was lost to her.

Jesus' reaction to her spontaneous gesture may surprise us. This was the happy, friendly resurrected Jesus, who later invited his disciples to "handle me and see" that it was really him in the flesh. This was the playful resurrected Jesus who was here disguised as a gardener and later appeared in and disappeared from locked rooms! We might expect him to sashay Mary around the garden in a little victory dance, and maybe he did! Maybe John just left that out! But whether he did or not, what John does tell us is that he said to Mary, "Do not hold me." What? Surely Mary deserves to be able to hold onto Jesus, whom she had so mourned and to whom she was so devoted. Is not that what we are supposed to do — to hold onto Jesus?

But here is the most surprising thing. Mary was not upset! She was all by herself again, but now she believed. She did not get to hold onto him, but now she held onto her faith in Jesus and the work he had given her to do. She went to his brethren and fed their faith with her own. "She told them that he had said these things to her."

Life almost never turns out to be what we thought it would. Life always surprises us, sometimes delightfully but also sometimes devastatingly. In both situations, we do not know how to respond. In the midst of giddy joy or of agonizing desolation, we do not know what to hold onto.

The message of Easter is that no devastation in this life, even the devastation of death, is the end. No matter how our hopes have crumbled, no matter how our sense of security may have been destroyed, there is yet life ahead of us. In the midst of that death and of that life ahead is the risen Jesus. Because he has overcome death and sin, because he has died once for all and remains risen from the dead, we are part of that irrevocable victory. While, like Mary Magdalene, we are not to hold onto Jesus and cling to him for security and to try to stay forever with him in our private garden, we are like her to hold onto our faith in the resurrected Jesus and to go to our brothers and sisters in witness to that faith, and to live our lives in light of that faith in the service of God and others.

That Easter faith is to ground us and to guide us and to focus our attitude toward and our very definition of life and its meaning.

Not all share that perspective, of course. This past season on Downton Abbey, the striking character of Violet (played engagingly by Maggie Smith) was consoling Edith, her granddaughter, in her despair. "My dear," she counseled, "all life is a series of problems, which we must try and solve, first one, then the next and the next, until at last we die"! While we can appreciate the positive attitude and the lack of self-pity in Violet's advice, her fatalism certainly falls short of the Good News of God in Christ proclaimed in the ever vibrant and ever new feast of Easter.

What do we hold onto? Not our fantasy of what our lives should be, not our suffocating self-preoccupation, not our cynicism, not our lack of vision and hope, not on any of the false choices with which we try to fill the emptiness in our lives. We are to hold onto our faith in the risen Jesus, who will never abandon us and will always call us past whatever death we face to the fuller life beyond it. We are to hold onto our unity with and our service to all the other children of God. We are to hold onto the generous and unearned gift God gives us of never-ending life and love and forgiveness. "Alleluia. Christ is risen. The Lord is risen indeed. Alleluia!"

To Bind Up the Brokenhearted
Easter Day
April 5, 2015

Easter is for the brokenhearted.

Mary Magdalene, the epitome of the brokenhearted, represents all of us in today's moving Gospel reading. Her world has been shattered. The one who has transformed her life, the one whom she has loved much, the one in whom she has placed all her hope, has been suddenly and cruelly executed. Her heart has been rent terribly asunder. She knows nothing else to do but to go to the tomb that morning after the Sabbath, at least to be near the place where she last saw him, as painful as that memory will be.

Even after she finds the stone taken away and runs to tell the others, she remains inconsolable. After Peter and John leave her and go home, she stands weeping outside the tomb, still longing just to glimpse the lifeless body of the one she mourns. It is in that deep despair that Jesus and the overpowering joy of Easter find her. "Mary," Jesus exclaims. "Rabboni," Mary cries in recognition. In that transforming moment, her world is not only put back together, but elevated to a whole new dimension. She now sees with the eyes of faith, and her heart is completely healed and restored and beating with a new energy. She returns to the disciples and shares the good news. Easter is for the brokenhearted.

Remember this is what Jesus came to do. Early in his ministry, he read in the synagogue from the Book of Isaiah: "The spirit of the Lord is upon me, because the Lord has anointed me; he has sent me to bring Good News to the oppressed, to bind up the brokenhearted." (61:1) Even before that first Easter, Jesus cared for the brokenhearted. He healed lepers and restored them to society. He cast out demons and restored those so afflicted to themselves again. He brought back children from the threshold of death and restored them to their parents. He raised his dear friend Lazarus from the dead amidst his own tears and restored him to his sisters.

Now, having been raised himself from the dead by his Father, never to die again — not a resuscitation like Lazarus, but a true resurrection to unending life — Jesus once for all binds up the brokenhearted for all time. No matter what loss we may endure, no matter what suffering, no matter what disappointment, even the irrevocable separation of death itself, that is not the last word. "O death, where is thy victory?" exults Paul. "O death, where is thy sting?" (I. Cor. 15:55) "Hail thee, festival day," we sang to open our service; "day whereon Christ arose, breaking the kingdom of death." Death has lost its ultimate power. Easter is truly for the brokenhearted, and that includes all of us.

For we have all lost in death those whom we love — a grandparent, a parent, a spouse, a friend, even for some of us, a child. We have groaned inwardly at the senseless killings of others, here in our community and across the world. We have all felt our hearts break. Our world is turned upside down, and what seemed so sure and secure no longer seems so. The wind is taken out of our sails. We feel lost. We stand weeping outside the tomb, not knowing what to do or where to go.

Easter speaks to us in our despair. It does not deny our pain or loss. That is all too real, as it was for Jesus himself and for Mary Magdalene and the others. But it does transform it and at least eventually heal it and give us hope in the midst of it. The glorious mystery of Jesus' triumph over sin and death overwhelms every other reality. It is the ultimate and final word. It binds up our hearts and makes them whole.

But why do we have to go through that painful journey? Why does God ask us to experience that pain in the first place? Would it not be better if we protected our hearts more closely and did not love so much, so that our hearts would not break in the first place and not need binding up?

Contrary to what you might think, your heart is not created to be sheltered and kept from harm. Your heart is meant to flourish and to grow in its capacity to love. That can only happen if it is broken. Just like an athlete, through weightlifting, actually tears the body's muscles so that they can heal and grow bigger and stronger, so through opening yourself to the changes and chances of this life, you must endure heartbreak so that your heart can mend and grow to a fuller capacity. Jesus did urge us not to let our hearts be troubled (John 14:1); we are to draw on the grace and love of God in finding peace. But Jesus did not say, "Do not let your hearts be broken." In fact he modeled for us the very opposite, and in so doing, in opening himself to the pain of the world, he grew in wisdom and age and grace before God and man.

If we follow Jesus in opening our hearts to others, we will also grow in our capacity to love, not only in this life, but in the life to come. We may think of life after death as at best stagnant, as "rising above" any need for change or growth. But remember that at a funeral we pray to God for the one who has died that, "increasing in knowledge and love of thee, she may go from strength to strength in the life of perfect service in thy heavenly kingdom." (BCP, p. 481) In the womb, you developed many capacities you were unaware of and for which there seemed no purpose at the time — for example sight, speech, taste, dexterity, mobility. So too in this life, you are developing capabilities for the next stage which you can only dimly understand, as through a glass darkly. But they are real nonetheless and seemed to be fully acquired only through embracing the inevitable heartbreak of this world.

Easter is for the brokenhearted. It is the Good News Jesus came not only to proclaim to us, but to procure for us and for the whole world. Easter is the ultimate reality, the gift that can never be taken away. "Alleluia. Christ is risen! The Lord is risen indeed. Alleluia!"

John 20:1-18

The Touch of God
The Third Sunday of Easter
April 17, 1988

As a preacher, I have always envied the luck of newspaper columnists, who every so often get away with rerunning old columns. "While Mr. Royko is on vacation," the editor's note says, "we are printing for your enjoyment some of his past columns." Preachers don't get away with that.

However, I am going to work a variation on a theme this morning. About three years ago, I preached a sermon called "The Sacramentality of Touch." When today's readings began to suggest some of the same ideas to me, I went back and reread it. I decided, since some of those ideas bore repeating, that I would not "rerun" the sermon, but reuse some of the premises, presenting them in a different fashion and adding some further reflections. All this I offer to you in the spirit of "truth in advertising" and of "honesty in packaging."

Among other things, the Gospel accounts of Jesus' resurrection appearances are notable for the prevalence of physical touch. In today's Gospel, Jesus tells his incredulous disciples, "See my hands and my feet, that it is I myself; handle me and see." Last Sunday we heard Jesus' words to Thomas, "Put your finger here ... and put out your hand, and place it in my side." Mary Magdalene clung to her risen Lord with such relief and joy that he had to ask her not to.

The occurrence of touch is not restricted to resurrection appearances, but is observable in many earlier Gospel accounts as well. The Greek word "haptesthai," which connotes not incidental contact but a sense of holding, even for a time, is used often of Jesus himself. That sense of grasping is the meaning of "touch" in these passages: "And they were bringing children to him that he might touch them ... and he took them in his arms and blessed them, laying his hands upon them." (Mark 10:13,16) And not just with children, but even with lepers: "And he stretched out his hand and touched him saying, 'I will; be clean.'

And immediately his leprosy was cleansed." (Matthew 8:3) When Peter, James and John were cowering down in fear at the sight of Jesus tranfigured on Mount Tabor, "Jesus came and touched them [grasped them], saying, 'Rise, and have no fear.'" (Matthew 7:17) That picture of Jesus, as a warm affectionate person, may surprise us.

We may think of Jesus simply as the Word of God, as a reserved, though authoritative, teacher who relied primarily on verbal discourse as a medium of communication. But, of course, Jesus is the Word made flesh, who communicated God's love not only through his words, but through his whole corporeality, including his touch. He washed the feet of his disciples; he touched the blind man's eyes; he reached out his hands to the lepers; he embraced the children. Even after his resurrection, as the evangelists take pains to point out, he ministers to his followers, not as a disembodied spirit, but in the flesh. "See my hands and my feet," Jesus says in today's Gospel, "that it is I myself; handle me and see; for a spirit has not flesh and bones as you see that I have."

Jesus, the self-revealing Word of God to us [and that Word can variously be translated love, forgiveness, faithfulness, justice, mystery, embrace] was made flesh and lived among us in the flesh. He is the one referred to in the First Letter of John, which we heard just this morning, "which was from the beginning, which we have heard, which we have seen with our eyes, which we have looked on and touched with our hands."

We, too, who are his witnesses, are corporeal. We, too, are to mediate God's love to one another in the flesh, partly through touch. The arms outstretched in forgiveness, the encouraging pat on the back, the reassuring hand on the arm, the warm and friendly greeting, the sexual intimacy of a faithful couple, are all powerful mediations to one another of a God who reveals himself to us, who constantly cares for us, who delights in us as part of his creation.

Of course, we cannot touch another without being touched. To do so physically is impossible; to do so metaphorically is to make the other into an object. Touching others, both physically and metaphorically, is both giving and receiving. In our "can do" Western culture, we need to remind ourselves regularly of the importance of receiving.

At wedding rehearsals, when we reach the point where the couple, each in turn, take the right hand of the other and say the vows committing themselves to each other for life, I encourage the one receiving the vows not to think that this is now the other's turn, but to be as attentive to receiving the touch and the vows from the other as they are to being the initiator. So, too, in touching others, we are to receive others' touch of us.

The truth is that as physical beings we are greatly in need of others' touch. The television program, "Nova," a few years ago revealed some very interesting studies on the phenomenon of touch. One experiment with baby monkeys separated them from their mothers at birth by a glass wall. The wall had perforations such that they could still hear and smell and, of course, see their mothers, but not touch them. When later joined with the pack, they exhibited marked antisocial behavior, and subsequent autopsies revealed that even certain parts of their brains had failed to develop because of this lack of touch.

A study with human beings involved leaving some change in a phone booth, which the typical subsequent user pocketed. Each person who did so, on leaving, was asked by the same "bystander" if he or she had noticed that person's change left on the counter. The words, the tone of voice, the facial expression used by the "bystander" were exactly the same for everyone, but half of those asked received a slight touch on the arm with the question. The percentage of that group which returned the money was markedly higher than of those who were not touched, suggesting that touch establishes human connections much more basically than do other forms of communication.

Another study utilized a librarian who, on checking out books, used the same few words and the same non-commital expression with each person. With some of the people, she briefly touched their hands in returning their library cards. Outside, each person was interviewed about the adequacy of the service they had received and the friendliness of the librarian. The response of those who had been touched was substantially more positive than that of those who had not.

Physical touch seems to bridge the gap between human beings, perhaps even calling forth chemical responses within our bodies. Whatever the phenomenon, touch comforts and assures us and relates us to one another. When we are distressed, "a shoulder to cry on" or "an arm to lean on" may be our literal need. Effective hospital chaplains know how important touch can be for those feeling the isolation of a hospital bed.

Historically, the Church, in her liturgy, has recognized the importance of physical touch: the joining of hands in marriage, the scriptural laying on of hands which became an essential part of Confirmation and Ordination and Unction (the anointing of the sick). More recently the Peace, an ancient practice, has been restored to the Celebration of Holy Eucharist. While we perhaps still have a long way to go in appreciating the deep significance of the Peace and its implications for our lives, still it has transformed our liturgical consciousness and practice by giving us a fuller experience of ourselves at worship as the Body of Christ.

In all of this discussion of the importance and the sacredness of touch, we would be remiss and naive if we did not recognize that touch can be used for evil as well. Touch can be possessive or violent and abusive or inappropriate. It is easy to be self-serving and unloving in our use of physical touch. However, recognizing our own sinfulness through unloving touch and accepting the necessity of resisting in love the touch of others who would abuse us or possess us or manipulate us, still at this Easter season we rejoice in our corporeality, which we share with Jesus, our Savior and brother. We look forward to communicating the love of God within us to others in a tangible way. And, we are attentive to receiving the caring, forgiving, nourishing touch of others, which points us to the loving, embracing God. Amen.

Acts 4:5-12
I John 1:1-2:2
Luke 24:36b-48

The Cost of Loving
The Fifth Sunday of Easter
May 3, 2015

What beautiful, inspiring words John writes to us in today's second reading: "Beloved, let us love one another, for love is of God, and he who loves is born of God and knows God. He who does not love does not know God; for God is love. ... Beloved, if God so loved us, we also ought to love one another."

On our good days, these words have power to stir all of us, to lift up our hearts, and to move us beyond our plodding preoccupation with ourselves. Even on our bad days, we know that these words ought to move us, that at the heart of genuine life is receiving God's love and returning that love to others. Love, we know, is the answer.

And we intend to start living that answer soon: As soon as I get by this current crisis, as soon as I catch up on all that I have to do, as soon as so-and-so stops causing me so much grief, as soon as people become more loveable, as soon as love's demands are not so great, as soon as things calm down.

I know that God wants me to abide in the Divine love and that God calls me to love others, but how can I do that when life is such a hassle and when people around me keep making a mess of things, making it difficult, if not impossible, for me to love them? I could do a lot better if God would just give me better people to love!

We have this funny idea that love is supposed to be easy and natural, almost effortless. Somehow, we are not prepared for the great cost of love: the wounds we absorb, the dying to self, the constant effort and energy love requires. If we are patient and kind and do not keep track of wrongs only when it is easy, that is not love at all; that is self-indulgence. Love, as Paul described it, bears *all* things, endures *all* things, not just the easy things, but especially the most difficult things, the hurtful things. That is when we are most called to love, when we begin to learn from the inside, what love really is.

We tend to view others' eccentricities and mistakes and offenses as deviations from the way life should be, as intolerable burdens to bear, as unjust suffering that weighs us down. Our lives would be so much better without them! While there is some truth to that perspective, it is also true that it is in these very struggles that God's invitation to love most strikes home. It is only when there is some cost to us that we are learning to love. The inevitable suffering that comes to us from others then, rather than being detrimental to our lives, may be exactly what we need to be schooled in love.

St. Francis de Sales encouraged his people 400 years ago, "You learn to study by studying, to play the lute by playing, to dance by dancing, to swim by swimming; and just so you learn to love God and your neighbor by loving. All those who think they can love in any other way, deceive themselves."

Frederick Buechner put it another way, "What's friendship, when all's done," he asked, "but the giving and taking of wounds?" Wounds are not what we must ultimately fear; they are part of life. What is most deadly to us is avoiding wounds by refusing to love. That is isolation. That is sterility. That is defeat. "Unless the grain of wheat falls into the ground and dies, it remains alone..."

Jesus uses another agrarian metaphor in today's Gospel. "I am the true vine, and my Father is the vinegrower. ... Every branch that bears fruit he prunes to make it bear more fruit." We understand that image. The vine grower, the one devoted to making the vine fruitful — in our case the Father, does what is best for the vine to make it fully alive and fruitful. The rose bushes on either side of the yard in front of the chapel were carefully and lovingly trimmed back last fall so that new roses would bloom, usually by Mother's Day, which is next week. So too does our vine grower tend to us and prune us to bear more fruit.

It is not that we can claim that all the difficult things that happen to us are directly sent to us by God. We cannot know the mind of God.

But the changes and chances of this life which confront us, the people who at least at times call for our deepest reserves of loving, even our own limitations, which discourage us and make us feel like failures, all these burdens and demands, and even ones which balloon into catastrophes, are not extraneous to the abundant life God gives us, but integral to it. They are the very means of grace that allow us to respond to John's scriptural exhortation to love one another as God has loved us. Whether or not God directly intends these hardships in our lives, God accompanies us in them and transforms us through them to become the children of God we are born to be.

Jesus says in today's Gospel, "I am the vine, you are the branches." What a powerful image! Notice he does not say, "I am the *stalk*, and you are all connected to me." That would be incredible enough. But no, Jesus says, "I am the vine," the whole thing, and "you are the branches," part of the vine, part of me! So even though God is transcendent and wholly other than us, still through the mystery of the Incarnation, Jesus become flesh, we are raised up to the Divine level and in some real sense abide in God and are part of God! "I am the vine, you are the branches." "Abide in me as I in you." We are not separate, not isolated, but part of, to use another scriptural metaphor, the Body of Christ.

That is why we are to love one another. Because to love others is to love God — and in fact it is to love ourselves since we are all bound together! To love others is to love the vine with all its branches, including ourselves. To love others is to love God and the whole Body of Christ. "Beloved, let us love one another, for love is of God, and he who loves is born of God and knows God. He who does not love does not know God; for God is love. ... Beloved, if God so loved us, we also ought to love one another."

I John 4:7-21
John 15:1-8

Loving God In All Things
The Sixth Sunday of Easter
May 9, 1999

O God, you have prepared for those who love you such
good things as surpass our understanding: Pour into our
hearts such love towards you, that we, loving you in all
things and above all things, may obtain your promises,
which exceed all that we can desire. (Collect for today)

"Pour into our hearts such love toward you, that we, loving you in all things." While that commendable prayer sounds sweet and harmless, be careful of praying it. It is a costly prayer. To want deeply to be filled with God's love and to love God in *all* things means that we have to be prepared to give up all that is not loving in us: all the resentment and bitterness, all the non-forgiveness, all the condemnation and judgment of others, all the pride and exaggerated sense of self-importance, all that keeps us from the love of God.

Do you want to give all that up? At my deepest level I know that I do, although with great fear and trembling. I know that that is what I am created for. I know that love is ultimately stronger and more life-giving than hate. I know that when confronted with injustice and hatred, either aimed at me or at others, that is when I most need to let the love of God pour through me and displace my resentment and my need to punish and my drive to return evil for evil. At my deepest level I want to be filled with God's love that I may love God in all things, but I do not often live there.

At a much shallower, daily life level, I find those instincts to refuse forgiveness or to punish those who have the gall or the bad sense or the stupidity to offend me or to threaten back when I am threatened very strong, a part of my identity that I cling to in relating to the world. But it is the part of the old self to which we are to die, beginning with our baptism. It is the sin in us that we are to let Jesus redeem. It is what we are to let God empty in us that we might be filled with divine love and love God in all things.

Last Sunday morning Bishop Johnson was here and preached a strong sermon that encouraged us to treasure and to live and to share our Christian faith, but also to respect other world religions and other pathways to God. Without falling into the trap of relativism, he encouraged us to respect the dignity of every human being and not to allocate to ourselves the responsibility of deciding who is to be saved and who is not. "It is one thing," he declared, "for Jesus to say, 'I am the way and the truth and the life,' and quite another for Christians to say, 'We are the way, the truth and the life.'" That triumphal attitude, he said, leads to crusades and inquisitions and holocausts and ethnic cleansings.

I deeply appreciated the Bishop's sermon, and I am sorry to say that I have been unable to convince him to have it printed and copied for wider distribution. To tell you the truth, however, my temptation to judge others and to respond to their convictions with hostility is much more exacerbated by other Christians than it is by non-Christians! Yet Peter exhorts us in today's epistle, "All of you, have unity of spirit, sympathy, love of the brethren, a tender heart and a humble mind. Do not return evil for evil or reviling for reviling; but on the contrary bless, for to this you have been called, that you may obtain a blessing."

This week, I found this inspirational charge put to a severe test twice. The first was when I received a copy of a letter sent by a local citizen to Jose Campos, who was abruptly deported six months ago to El Salvador after living here for over 15 years, leaving behind Daisy Diaz and their five children. Fortunately, thanks to the generous efforts of many people, including some from this parish, Jose is now back; and now that he and Daisy can legally do so, they will be joyfully married in this church this Saturday.

The letter, after congratulating Jose on his return to his family, then asks him:

"Are you a Christian? Are you a Catholic? Let me be very direct. I read that your wedding is to be May 15th at the Chapel of the Cross. This "church" is not Catholic or Christian. They have priestesses on their staff. If you are married there, your wedding will be legal but *not* the Holy Sacrament of Matrimony. An Episcopalian (sic) minister cannot give God's Blessing validly. The Episcopal Church is an Apostate body. It is *not* a true Christian Church. ...

"If you are married at the Chapel of the Cross, you will gravely offend SENOR JESUCRISTO and LA SENORA DE GUADALUPE. Please do not do this. ... The welfare of your soul is at stake. I wish you well. May Jesus Christ be praised!"

I take great exception to that letter! It is one thing to have an opinion about the nature of a religious body, although I find it expressed without any of the elements encouraged by Peter in his letter: "unity of spirit, sympathy, love of the brethren, a tender heart, and a humble mind." It is quite another to impose that opinion on another and to try to manipulate him with threats of Divine disapproval and damnation. I felt like calling this man and asking him how dare he intrude on such a sacred moment in a man's life and claim to speak for God with whom he obviously has only a passing acquaintance! No one would have been the better for it, however, including me. "Do not return evil for evil or reviling for reviling; but on the contrary bless." I am working on that!

My second temptation of returning evil for evil this week came in reading in the newspaper about the group from Kansas that has announced they will be in Chapel Hill next Sunday to picket at the University's graduation ceremony and at Binkley Baptist Church "in religious protest for touting gay sin." UNC is targeted because it was the first college campus in the South 25 years ago to recognize a gay student group. Binkley was chosen because last month it allowed two area local ministers to bless a same-sex union there.

I observed this group, known as Westboro Baptist Church, at General Convention in Philadelphia in 1997. It was a sad and disturbing sight. Men, women, and children, apparently mostly the children and grandchildren of one man, held graphic signs both depicting and denouncing gay sex in words and pictures. They also picketed and shouted hateful slogans at the funeral of Matthew Shepherd, the young gay man who was so brutally murdered in Wyoming. Their website is www.godhatesfags.com, which they declare to be "a profound theological statement, which America needs more than it needs oxygen or bread."

"Pour into our hearts such love towards you that we may love you in all things." Not an easy prayer to pray in this situation. How are we to love in the face of such hatred, especially promulgated under the guise of virtuous faith? While righteous anger, which I certainly feel, is appropriate, returning evil for evil or reviling for reviling is not. Apparently flyers circulating on Franklin Street this week have been urging a counter protest, using ugly and violent language. We should certainly speak out in the face of such vicious bigotry; in fact we cannot keep silent. But we are to do so not out of our selfishness and need to punish, but out of our love of God and our love for others.

Let us pray for all those involved next Sunday, both those being picketed and those picketing. Let us pray for our students and faculty that the joy of their celebration may not be diminished. Let us pray for the people of Binkley Baptist Church that they may feel the support and the protection of our community. Let us pray for those protesting and counter-protesting that they may not be consumed with hatred but may respect the dignity of every human being. And let us pray now for ourselves in the words of today's collect:

O God, you have prepared for those who love you such good things as surpass our understanding: Pour into our hearts such love towards you, that we loving you in all things and above all things, may obtain your promises, which exceed all that we can desire; through Jesus Christ our Lord. Amen.

That They May All Be One
The Seventh Sunday of Easter
May 11, 1986

"I do not pray for these only, but also for those who believe in me through their word, that they may all be one." (John 1:20-21)

Jesus was talking about us in that prayer, those of us who make up the Church in the post-Apostolic times; that includes us and those who have preceded us in the faith and those who because of us will believe and be the Church after we are gone.

Jesus prays for us as part of the entire Church, with all its denominational forms, as part of the Episcopal Church with its connection with other Anglican communions, and as members of this particular worshipping body of Christians, the Chapel of the Cross.

And his prayer, which may surprise us, is not that we be successful and flourish, not that we be safe and secure, not even that we be happy. Jesus prays that we may all be one. Why would he pray for that? Because Jesus goes on to say, if we are one in the Father and the Son, even as they are in each other, then the world will believe in Jesus as the manifestation of his father. By experiencing our unity, the world will be led beyond us to the union of Father and Son, which is both the Church's model and its principle. In other words, unless the Church — and that includes us at Chapel of the Cross — lives out its unity, it cannot perform its essential mission in the world. That is why Jesus prays that we may all be one.

What does it mean to be one? What can we say about it?

First of all we can say that being one is not simply a passive trait, a privation, i.e., a lack of division. If that were so, any group who agreed never to disagree would exemplify oneness, even though they might not have anything to do with each other. No, oneness implies a more active unity, a working together, a significant interaction, a deep harmony, a real cohesiveness.

Nor does being one imply uniformity, as if all of us were to be exactly the same. On the contrary, Paul tells us in his First Letter to the Corinthians that we are a body, which consists, not of one uniform member, but of many. If the foot should say, "Because I am not a hand, I do not belong to the body," that would not make it any less a part of the body. And if the ear should say, "Because I am not an eye, I do not belong to the body," that would not make it any less a part of the body. If the whole body were an eye, where would be the hearing? If the whole body were an ear, where would be the sense of smell? ... If all were a single organ, where would the body be? As it is, there are many parts, yet one body. (I Corinthians 14-20)

One of the best dramatizations I have ever seen of the mystery involved here was a short movie which showed two hand puppets arguing with one another. Each was a mixture of contempt and fear of the other. And suddenly, in the midst of the bickering, the camera pulled back to show that the puppets were each on a different hand of the same puppeteer, revealing in a flash of insight that they were in reality one, not only because they were given life and voice by the same creator, but also because they were part of one body, who was that very creator.

The suggestion here, by both Paul and the maker of the movie, is that the unity for which Jesus prays for us is not something we have to create for ourselves. It is simply given to us as children of God and members of the Body of Christ. Our task is not to forge our unity, to manufacture it, but to discover it, to manifest it, to live it out. That is no easy task, and that is why Jesus prays that we may be what we are, that we may be one.

If we are to be one here at the Chapel of the Cross, as this particular manifestation of the Body of Christ, what is that to look like? What elements are to be involved in living that out? There are many, but I would like to focus on three. It seems to me that the first element must be mutual respect of the various parts of the Body for one another, the young and the old, the "cradle Episcopalians" and the newly confirmed, the high church and the low church, etc.

Rather than be threatened by or distanced from one another because of our differences, we need to welcome the diversity that makes up a healthy body. Secondly, we must genuinely care about and care for one another. Just as the hands must wash the body and the lips protect the mouth and the fingers massage the tired neck, so must we take care of one another as members of the same Body. To neglect that care, which frequently calls for great sacrifice, is to neglect our very selves.

A third element, and one in which perhaps we need to grow more than in any other, is a regular interchange on the difficult issues facing us today. The human tendency is to maintain a semblance of unity by avoiding any real meeting, especially on the most controversial questions. It takes significant effort to work against that tendency. The old joke is that the two things you cannot talk about in the Episcopal Church are politics and religion. We must work that that line does not become more than caricature. It is not necessary, or probable, that we would all come to consensus on every issue; but for any real sense of unity, we need to support one another in struggling to respond out of our faith to the serious issues of our time.

An example of one such issue which has been surfacing all around us is the use of divestment as leverage to dismantle apartheid in South Africa. It is not only University trustees who have to face this complicated issue. We also as individuals with investments, as members of institutions with portfolios, including this parish and this diocese, as voters with moral responsibilities, need to face squarely this issue and be prepared to take significant action.

On Friday, I was privileged to attend in Durham a press conference with Bishop Tutu, who was here to give the commencement address at North Carolina Central University. He told us first of the story going around Pretoria that Prime Minister Botha has given up playing chess because he cannot control his black bishop!

But then he went on to tell us of the nearly 1,500 people killed in the last 18 months, mostly by the security forces of South Africa, of the very little progress that has been made in the overall structure of things, of his conviction that the evil of apartheid as a system is that it leads people to doubt that they are children of God, loved equally by God, and of his conclusion that the only possible way to avert a violent, bloody revolution is for the international community to bring the strongest possible economic sanctions against South Africa, which include total divestment.

He was asked about the common position being taken that total divestment only hurts the blacks more, that it is better to support companies that were trying to stay and make the situation better. He replied that the blacks did not want apartheid improved; they wanted it dismantled. "Improving the situation," he said, "is like saying 'We will make your chains more comfortable.'"

This is one significant moral issue facing us as individuals and as a parish; there are many others. We may certainly not agree, especially in the beginning, about the ways that we should respond and the actions that we should take. But we should not let that stop us from trying to foster and manifest a deeper sense of unity by facing in formal and informal ways the hard questions together.

That is not political activism. That is simply trying to acknowledge and live out our unity with one another and with all children of God. That is being the Church as Jesus prays for us to be in today's Gospel reading. That is to reflect the oneness of the Father with Jesus and the love with which God loves us, that the world may believe and know that same love.

As Jesus prayed for us: "I do not pray for these only, but also for those who believe in me through their word, that they may all be one; even as thou, Father, art in me, and I in thee, that they also may be in us, so that the world may believe that thou has sent me." Amen.

John 17:20-26

The Mystery of the Ascension
The Seventh Sunday of Easter
May 24, 2009

Today is a transition Sunday. Coming in the midst of three principal liturgical feasts, it forms the bridge between Ascension Day, which we celebrated on Thursday, Pentecost a week from today, and Trinity Sunday one week later. If we imagine the seven weeks of the Easter season as an extended display of celebratory fireworks, these three major feasts form the final intense barrage of pyrotechnics, which signal the completion of the joyous celebration. These are the final, intense Easter season high points from the Church's theological and liturgical storehouse.

Pentecost and Trinity Sunday, we are more acquainted with, occurring each year on a Sunday and occupying a more familiar niche in the awareness of most Episcopalians. We will be hearing more about them the next two weeks. But what about the Ascension? Since it is the only one of the seven principal feasts of the Church year which never occurs on a Sunday, we are much less exposed to this key part of the Christian faith. Besides that, it involves a curious story about Jesus in front of his disciples being "lifted up and a cloud [taking] him out of their sight." As Dr. Joyner reminded those of us here on Thursday night, a famous stained glass window at King's College, Cambridge, shows the disciples looking up above their heads, seeing only Jesus' feet disappearing into a cloud at the top of the window. Are we to take this scriptural account that literally; and if we cannot, does it have any essential meaning for us as followers of Jesus?

The Good News that we proclaim through the mystery of the Ascension is not that Jesus' glorified body elevated before the apostles' very eyes until he was just a dot, too small to be seen. The Church does not insist that Jesus' body kept relentlessly rising until he finally reached the extra-terrestrial throne of his Father, as yet undiscovered by the astronauts or the newly revived Hubble space telescope! To use the jargon of a current popular movie prequel, the Ascension is not a "beam me up" story. In fact the hymn that we just sang before the Gospel questions that literalism: "And have the bright immensities received our risen Lord, where light-years frame the Pleiades and point Orion's sword? Do flaming suns his footsteps trace through corridors sublime, the Lord of interstellar space and conqueror of time?"

That last phrase, beginning with "Lord," hints at the real meaning of the mystery of the Ascension. When we say Jesus ascended, we mean it in the same sense as "the king ascended to the throne." We mean that, just as the Father raised Jesus from the dead, so too did he elevate him to dominion over heaven and earth. When the Letter to the Ephesians, from the liturgy for the Ascension, declares that God made Jesus "sit at his right hand in the heavenly places," it means, as it goes on to say, that Jesus is "above all rule and authority and power and dominion, and above every name that is named, not only in this age but also in that which is to come." Jesus is Lord, this intriguing mystery of the Ascension reveals to us — not any Herods or Caesars or any of their distant successors. Jesus is Lord, not only of interstellar space, but of all his Father's creation, a truth which is to be both an assurance and a reminder for us, as well as a call to believe and an invitation to yield to its demands on our lives. "Jesus is Lord over all" lies at the heart of our Baptismal Covenant, and we are to live each day in the light of that mystery.

In addition to proclaiming Jesus' universal Lordship, the Ascension also declares (in close connection) Jesus' omni-presence. Rather than affirming that Jesus has left, not only the building, but the earth and the cosmos itself, leaving us desolate and adrift, the Ascension asserts the reality that in Jesus' words, he is "with [us] always, to the close of the age." Although Jesus no longer appears in bodily form as he did to his first followers for a time after his resurrection, since Jesus is one with the Father, he is universally present throughout creation, just as his Father is. And not only in creation. Jesus is present to us through the Gospels, through the sacraments and liturgy of the Church, through the gift of the Holy Spirit, through "the least of these my brethren," indeed, "wherever two or three are gathered together" in his name. Our hymn answers in the second verse its own question about where the ascended Jesus is present: "The heaven that hides him from our sight knows neither near nor far; an altar candle sheds its light as surely as a star: and where his loving people meet to share the gift divine, there stands he with unhurrying feet; there heavenly splendors shine." Jesus' presence is not limited to distant galaxies, but is real and continuous all around us. The Lord of Lords is "with [us] always, to the close of the age."

Today, then, we acknowledge the mystery of the Ascension, and we look forward to celebrating the unleashing of the Holy Spirit at Pentecost and the rich but impenetrable mystery of the Holy Trinity. As we proclaim Jesus' lordship and declare his omni-presence and his dominion over all things, let our prayer be that of the feast of the Ascension:

Almighty God, whose blessed Son our Savior Jesus Christ ascended far above all heavens that he might fill all things: Mercifully give us faith to perceive that, according to his promise, he abides with his Church on earth, even to the end of the ages; through Jesus Christ our Lord. Amen.

Being the Nurturing Community — Watered by Grace
Pentecost Sunday
June 8, 2014

This morning on the feast of Pentecost, we will baptize 10 children. Five Sundays ago we baptized eight infants when our Bishop Suffragan was here. Before that, we baptized an adolescent at the Easter Vigil and a week later two more babies, a total of 20 baptisms in the Easter season! But it is not the numbers that should astonish us, but what really happens at Baptism. In this foundational Christian sacrament, these children are "sealed by the Holy Spirit in Baptism and marked as Christ's own forever." They are, according to the Catechism in the Prayer Book, adopted as God's children and made "members of Christ's Body, the Church" (p. 858).

Like the disciples on Pentecost in our first reading, they are "filled with the Holy Spirit"; but they do not usually begin "to speak in tongues, as the Spirit gives them utterance" (although, as you know, some do put forth an utterance or two from time to time!). Nor do we hear "a sound … from heaven like the rush of a mighty wind," nor see "tongues as of fire, distributed and resting on each one of them."

But while none of the dramatic external signs of the first Pentecost may accompany these baptisms, these children are just as surely filled with the Holy Spirit, and we just as surely witness the beginning of a radical transformation. It is easy to look at these children after their Baptism and to think that nothing has changed, but it has. The signs are not as apparent for us as they were for the bewildered multitude in Jerusalem: disciples telling in many tongues the mighty works of God. But the Holy Spirit does come upon them, and the transforming work of God in them is begun.

A bishop once told of a dream:

"The dreamer entered a spacious store in which the gifts of God were kept, and behind the counter was an angel. In his dream the would-be purchaser said, 'I have run out of the fruits of the Spirit. Can you restock me?' When the angel seemed about to refuse, the dreamer angrily burst out, 'In place of war, injustice, lying, hate, tyranny, I want love, joy, peace, integrity. ... Without these I shall be lost.' But the angel behind the counter replied, 'We do not stock fruits. We only keep seed.'"

While the gift of the Holy Spirit to these children in Baptism is complete, the development and the manifestation of God's grace in their lives is not. That needs to be nurtured and nourished and encouraged to grow.

That is where we come in. The environment in which the seed planted in these children comes to fruition is the Christian community. Their Baptism not only connects them with God, it makes them members of the Church, where they are to develop and flourish, in the words of the baptismal liturgy, "to grow into the full stature of Christ." As this particular manifestation of the Church, we at the Chapel of the Cross are to be the place where the seed of the Holy Spirit in them grows into the fruits of the Holy Spirit. We are not to provide the place; we are to *be* the place.

The environment in which the seed planted in these children comes to fruition is the Christian community, but we are not simply to *provide* them that community — like the owners of a baseball team provide a minor league system where their players' talents can develop, or even like a university provides opportunities where students can learn — we are to *be* that community. We do not simply hire a Christian education director and a youth minister and youth and children's choir directors, as important as it is to do that, and turn the formational task over to them. We are to be the Body of Christ where the grace of God flourishes, where the members love the Lord their God with all their heart and mind and strength and their neighbor as themselves, where people strive for justice and peace and respect the dignity of every human being, where believers forgive one another from their hearts 70 times seven times, where participants give generously of their time and money and energy to carry on our common ministry, where our unity in the Spirit is cherished and manifested more than any theological or moral or liturgical or political differences.

At Baptism we promise to "do all in [our] power to support these persons in their life in Christ." That means providing them worship services and roles in them and Church School classes and Vacation Church School and EYC and mission trips. That means even more importantly, staffing these programs and volunteering to help and encouraging and supporting their efforts and events. That means supplying them with new space of their own, a youth room and classrooms and a playground, where they can be nurtured and supported as they "grow into the full stature of Christ." But it means, most importantly of all, being the community where our children and youth experience the grace of God at work, where they learn what it means to worship the transcendent God, where they are nourished by the commitment and the love and the unity that they find on every side. These children have parents and godparents and even grandparents to look after them, but they are all our children. We have just promised to do all in our power to support them in their life in Christ, and that is a commitment we should take very seriously, and endeavor to "show forth ... not only with our lips, but in our lives."

That may seem like a daunting task, one which we do not feel up to. And of course, left to ourselves it is. We are no model community; we are no paragons of virtue; we are all too fallible and even sometimes give bad example. But it is, as first the parents and godparents and then all of us answer at Baptism, "with God's help" that we can respond to the challenge and be who we are called to be.

Irenaeus, Bishop of Lyons in the late second century, wrote about our need for God's grace. He compared it to the water of Baptism with its life-giving properties:

"Like dry flour, which cannot become one lump of dough, one loaf of bread, without moisture, we who are many could not become one in Christ Jesus without the water that comes down from heaven. And like parched ground, which yields no harvest unless it receives moisture, we who were once like a waterless tree could never have lived and borne fruit without this abundant rainfall from above. ... If we are not to be scorched and made unfruitful, we need the dew [the grace, the baptism] of God."

As with water given to us by God, we will baptize those children whom God generously lends to us. Let us also receive the water of grace that God pours on us, that we may be the fruitful community that God intends for them to have and for us to be.

Acts 2:1-21

The Mystery of the Trinity
Trinity Sunday
June 7, 1998

With the passing of the feast of Pentecost last Sunday, we are finishing the liturgical cycle which began with Advent. We have celebrated the great events of salvation history: the birth of Jesus, his death and resurrection, his Ascension and sending of the Spirit. Now we settle into what is sometimes referred to liturgically as "Ordinary Time," i.e. worshipping in the context of all of salvation history, not focusing on any one particular event.

The feast which takes us into this "Ordinary Time" — a term which carries no connotation of being lackluster, but only of constituting ongoing, everyday life — is, appropriately enough, Trinity Sunday. For every Sunday we worship the One God in Three Persons. Each Eucharist we join with the seraphim, about whom we heard in our first reading, who "with all the company of heaven ... laud and magnify th(e) glorious Name," singing "Holy, holy, holy, Lord God of Hosts: Heaven and earth are full of thy glory."

Still, while every Sunday is in some sense Trinity Sunday, the readings, the prayers, and the music of this feast — one of seven principal feasts listed in the Prayer Book — focus us in a special way upon this central doctrine of the Christian faith. What can we say to glimpse a bit more of the mystery of the Trinity?

"To glimpse a bit more of the mystery" are purposefully chosen words. We cannot fully grasp nor understand God in this life. Rather we "see through a glass darkly" and know God very imperfectly. In *Wishful Thinking, A Theological ABC*, Frederick Buechner defines theology as "the study of God and his ways." But he offers this disclaimer: "For all we know, dung beetles may study man and his ways and call it humanology. If so, we would be more touched and amused than irritated. One hopes that God feels likewise."

We do well to heed the legend about Augustine, who, earnestly trying to comprehend the workings of the Trinity, wandered down to the seashore. He noticed a child making numerous trips from the water's edge up to the beach, emptying each time a shell which he had dipped into the ocean. When the saint asked him about his activity, the child replied, "I am emptying the sea into the sand." When Augustine expressed incredulity at this futile exercise, the child declared, "But I'll drain the sea before you understand the Trinity."

The doctrine of the Trinity is most directly stated in The Creed of Saint Athanasius, referred to as the "Quicunque Vult" (found on page 864 of *The Book of Common Prayer*), which dates from the fourth or fifth century. This Creed has been printed in all Anglican prayer books since 1549, except in the United States, where it appears for the first time in this 1979 edition. It says in part, beginning at the third line:

"And the Catholic Faith is this: That we worship one God in Trinity, and Trinity in Unity, neither confounding the Persons, nor dividing the Substance. For there is one Person of the Father, another of the Son, and another of the Holy Ghost. But the Godhead of the Father, of the Son, and of the Holy Ghost, is all one, the Glory equal, the Majesty co-eternal. ... (Skipping to the top of the next page) So the Father is God, the Son is God, and the Holy Ghost is God. And yet they are not three Gods, but one God. (And it concludes about 10 lines later) So that in all things ... the Unity in Trinity and Trinity in Unity is to be worshipped."

How can there be three Persons, but only one God? Although this mystery defies comprehension, let us look at examples from our human experience which can illuminate it.

Many analogies have been used throughout history which do not explain the Trinity, but which make some attempt to point us to its elusive reality. Perhaps the most famous analogy is that attributed to St. Patrick of the shamrock, three leaves joined in one stem. Another is that of water, ice and vapor, three different things, but one substance. John Wesley said, "Tell me how it is that in this room there are three candles and but one light, and I will explain to you the mode of the divine existence."

Tertullian used the horticultural explanation of "Root, Tree, and Fruit, in one plant." The Cappadocian St. Gregory of Nanzianzus spoke in the fourth century of, "The sun, its ray, and its light." Augustine used a psychological model of "amans, id quod amatur, amor," or "the one loving, the one loved, the love itself." Dorothy Sayers, in *The Mind of the Maker* in 1941, offered a modern analogy of the Trinity of Creative Idea, Creative Energy, and Creative Power.

None of these examples explain the mystery of God's Triune existence, but perhaps they lead us to three important truths about God.

The first is that God is dynamic and not static, activity and not passivity, life and not death. The interaction of the Three Divine Persons, who constitute a Unity, is an ongoing process, flowing perfectly from one to another. The analogies of the sun, of the fruit-growing tree, of the lover loving the beloved, all indicate to us the dynamic and fruitful activity of God. God indeed is life, life which teems and overflows.

The life of the Trinity overflows into creation, into "the vast expanse of interstellar space, galaxies, suns, the planets in their courses," and our own planet, Earth. The Divine life spills over into water, rock, and soil, and plants, insects, and animals. God's life flows through us, and not only biologically but also spiritually, since through Baptism, God gives us never-ending life. To be bound to the Triune God is to participate in dynamic life.

The second truth is that the very essence of God is community, a divine community of love. Although God is One, God is not solitary, alone, isolated. Rather, God is a relationship of Three Persons, each of whom love, and receive love from, and abide in the love of the other.

Since God is the Source of all that is, reality then is essentially relational, and not solitary. Despite our illusions, we human beings are not alone in our separate worlds, but connected to the God who is community, and therefore connected to one another. "That they may all be one,"

Jesus prayed in the Gospel two weeks ago, "even as thou, Father art in me and I in thee, that they also may be in us." (John 17:21)

The third important truth about God to which our belief in the Trinity leads us is that God is holy. God is so far above us, so wholly other than we, so beyond our comprehension, that we can only fall down in worship and praise and adoration. The readings this morning try to convey that holiness in dramatic images of "the Lord sitting upon a throne, high and lifted up" surrounded by six-winged seraphim and torches of fire and "living creatures full of eyes in front and behind," all of whom continually praise God. "And the foundations of the thresholds shook ... and the house was filled with smoke."

In the end, as Augustine learned from the child, we cannot understand God, especially as Trinity. Even when we catch a glimpse of the dynamic, communal, holy God, it is an elusive flash which we cannot sustain. We are left to stand in awe and reverence before this God who is both beyond us and within us, who is worthy of our complete worship. We are left to join with all the Angels and Archangels and all who surround the throne of God, and sing in the words of our final hymn,

> *Holy, holy, holy! Lord God Almighty!*
> *All thy works shall praise thy Name, in earth, and sky, and sea;*
> *Holy, holy, holy! Merciful and mighty,*
> *God in three Persons, blessed Trinity.* Amen.

Isaiah 6:1-8
Revelation 4:1-11
John 16:5-15

Batter My Heart, Three Person'd God
Trinity Sunday
June 11, 2006

To preach a sermon on Trinity Sunday is an intimidating task! Not that the doctrine of the Trinity is unfamiliar. Every Sunday we worship the Triune God; we profess our belief, for example, "in the Holy (Ghost) Spirit, the Lord, (and) the giver of Life, who proceeds from the Father and the Son; (who) with the Father and the Son (together) he is worshipped and glorified." The doctrine of the Trinity is not an unknown one, only an unfathomable one. In fact its very importance, its centrality to Christianity, along with its incomprehensibility, makes it a daunting subject for a sermon.

How does one say something about the Trinity that illuminates, even in a small way, the mystery of the unfathomable riches of God? The story is told of Brother Elric, a 12th century monk, that after botching a sermon on the Trinity, he took a vow of silence for the rest of his life! That response perhaps is not unlike that of Moses, who in our first reading "hid his face, for he was afraid to look at God."

Encouraged, however, by the words of Paul in our second reading, that we are not to think of ourselves as slaves, but as God's children, let us try to look at the mystery of God as Trinity, not only with our minds, but with our hearts.

For how else can one apprehend the reality of three Persons in one God? Reason cannot grasp it, and as Blaise Pascal wrote, "The last proceeding of reason is to recognize that there is an infinity of things which are beyond it." Reason can lead us to the mystery of God, but it is only love which can respond to it.

Nicodemus, at first, did not understand this. In our Gospel reading he tried to apprehend the mystery of Jesus through his intellect, by asking him questions: "How can a man be born when he is old? Can he enter a second time into his mother's womb and be born? ... How can this be?"

Jesus did not answer his questions directly. He persisted in pointing rather than prescribing. He stirred Nicodemus' imagination by pointing to the wind, which is invisible, yet unmistakable, impalpable, yet full of power. Then he pointed him to God's loving sacrifice of his only Son, that all might believe and have new life. Jesus wanted Nicodemus not just to know *about* God, not just to find answers to all his questions. He wanted him to *know* God, to find him in the mystery of things, to let his heart respond to the God who so loved the world that he gave his only Son.

Nicodemus, it seems, got the message. The last time he is seen in scripture, at the foot of the cross, there were no questions, no answers. He did not ponder why Jesus had to die, nor did he flee in confusion as did most of Jesus' followers. Rather with loving hands he prepared Jesus' body for burial (John 19:39-42). Listening with his heart, he performed one of the most enviable acts of love in all human history. At the grave, Nicodemus' love responded to the love of the God whom he had come to know through the person of Jesus.

The reality of God as Trinity is a proclamation of love. It is a glimpse into the very nature, the very life of God. The love of the Father overflows into the Son and the dynamic love between them is the Spirit.

God is so holy, so pure, so infinite that we must say that God is one. Yet God's oneness is so alive, so dynamic, so giving, that we cannot say that God is merely one; but rather God is like a river, overflowing its banks, bringing life wherever it touches.

Meister Eckhart used an equally vibrant image: "When God laughs at the soul and the soul laughs back at God, the persons of the Trinity are begotten. To speak in hyperbole, when the Father laughs to the Son, and the Son laughs back to the Father, that laughter gives pleasure, that pleasure gives joy, that joy gives love, and love gives the persons [of the Trinity] of which the Holy Spirit is one."

How do we hear that as Good News? How do we who feel broken, who are alone or sick or grieving, who feel no hope, how do we respond? Despite our best efforts, we seem to wall out this God. We plod along as E.E. Cummings characterized us: "earth's own clumsily striving (finding and losing and laughing and crying) children." How do we open ourselves to the dynamic Father whose love for us erupts in his Son, whose Spirit, working in us, binds us to him as his children?

We cry, as Paul tells us in the second reading, "Abba! Father!" We beg for him to overpower us. We ask, we seek, we knock.

We cannot give ourselves the life of the Trinity. We cannot through our intellects apprehend the mystery of the loving God. We cannot, even when invited, seem to respond wholeheartedly to the One who persistently and patiently pursues and forgives us. But we can ask, invite, even plead with the Triune God to break through our defenses, to overcome our resistance, to overflow unchecked into us, that we may be lost in the Divine life-giving embrace.

One who keenly grasped our deep need for surrender was the Anglican priest and poet John Donne. On this Trinity Sunday let us make ours his eloquent, pleading prayer, expressed in Sonnet 10:

> Batter my heart, three person'd God; for, you
> As yet but knocke, breathe, shine, and seeke to mend;
> That I may rise, and stand, o'erthrow mee, and bend
> Your force, to breake, blowe, burn and make me new.
> I, like an usurpt towne, to another due,
> Labour to admit you, but Oh, to no end;
> Reason your viceroy in mee, mee should defend,
> But is captiv'd, and proves weake or untrue.
> Yet dearly I love you, and would be loved faine,
> but am betroth'd unto your enemie:
> Divorce mee, untie, or breake that knot againe,
> Take me to you, imprison mee, for I
> Except you enthrall mee, never shall be free,
> Nor ever chaste, except you ravish mee.

The scriptures for today present major themes of our all-too-human lives: suffering so great as to be overwhelming, but hope in the midst of it.

Exodus 3:1-6
Romans 8:12-17
John 3:1-16

How Can God Love Every Beating Heart?
The Fourth Sunday after Pentecost
June 20, 1999

Listen again to the words of the Psalmist as the authentic anguish of a young Kosovar refugee, returning home to find her other family members have all been tortured and killed; or of a middle-aged man who has just lost his job and therefore his self-identity; or of a child whose parent has inexplicably died; or of a woman who has discovered she has a fast-growing breast cancer and must have immediate surgery:

"Save me, O God, for the waters have risen up to my neck. I am sinking in deep mire, and there is no firm ground for my feet. I have come into deep waters, and the torrent washes over me. I have grown weary with my crying; my throat is inflamed; and my eyes have failed from looking for my God."

How many of us at times, perhaps even now, have not felt that? "I am going under, and where is God?"

Jeremiah, in today's Old Testament reading, articulates the anger that often accompanies such feelings of abandonment: "O Lord, thou hast deceived me, and I was deceived; thou art stronger than I, and thou hast prevailed. I have become a laughingstock all the day; every one mocks me."

These readings belie the "prosperity theology" so fondly preached by the televangelists: "Just send for your golden 700 Club pin, and your whole life will be blessing and prosperity"; as if, if we have enough faith, nothing bad will ever happen to us.

Jesus promises us the opposite in Matthew's Gospel: "They will deliver you up to councils and flog you." He goes on to remind us, at least in retrospect, of the suffering to the point of death that befell him, saying, "A disciple is not above his teacher ... it is enough for the disciple to be like his teacher." If Jesus endured misery and anguish, we his followers can expect the same.

The inevitability of suffering, then, and the reality of our despair and anger in the midst of it, is declared clearly in our readings. It is not avoided, but that is only half the theme. Each of the readings goes on to proclaim a note of hope. Our portion of Psalm 69 ends: "But as for me, this is my prayer to you. … O Lord: In your great mercy, O God, answer me with your unfailing help. Save me from the mire; do not let me sink." Jeremiah declares, "But the Lord is with me as a dread warrior. … Sing to the Lord, praise the Lord! For he has delivered the life of the needy from the hand of evildoers." Jesus ends today's Gospel reading by assuring us, "Even the hairs of your head are all numbered. Fear not, therefore; you are of more value than many sparrows," not one of whom, he promises us, "will fall to the ground without your Father's will."

Is that too facile a faith? How can God have that intimate, caring love for each one of billions and billions of people? Does not our suffering indicate the absence of God's compassion? Or is there a powerful mystery underlying these age-old words, which can strengthen us in our fragile lives?

Another way of framing the question arises from an experience I had 25 years ago, a year before I was ordained a Jesuit priest. I was spending the summer as a chaplain-in-training in a cancer ward of a hospital in western Canada. One day a fearful nurse sent me into the room of a young woman who apparently was dealing with the indignities of cancer by keeping a gun under her pillow! As it turned out, there was no real threat. She was a forthright personality who wanted everyone to know who was in control, but she was not really dangerous — something like a female Charles Barkley! She was much more attractive than Charles, however; in fact she informed me that she was an entertainer, which I later found out meant "go-go dancer," with the professional name of "Lottie, Miss Body." I must say that title was not entirely unmerited, and it certainly suited her better than her given name, which was Ethel.

At any rate Lottie and I had a number of religious discussions; her faith to that point had been mainly superstition. Her mother had told her, for example, that if she ever took the Lord's name in vain, she would be struck by lightning. When her mother died when Lottie was still a teenager, she decided that she did not care anymore, and she flung a blasphemy up to the heavens. When nothing happened, she decided all religion was a lie.

I invited her to a prayer group that I was starting on the ward, and one night, all dressed up from a night on the town and fairly intoxicated, she burst in as we were well into our prayer. At first she sat relatively quietly; but as one of the four or five saintly grandmother types who comprised the group began to address God as one "who loves every beating heart," Lottie Miss Body snorted aloud in disbelief and demanded incredulously, "How could God love every beating heart?"

I have to tell you that that remains as one of the most memorable moments of my ordained ministry; not only because of the sheer drama of it and because of the shock that ran through the participants and the panic that engulfed me, but also because I have since pondered that question many times. In a few words, it expresses all the doubt that we are subject to. How can God love every beating heart? Of the billions and billions of people that have been and are yet to come, how can God care for and nourish and number the hairs of each one? And if that is impossible, then is all religion a lie?

You have to answer that question for yourself, of course, just as I presume Lottie Miss Body has, one way or another. A helpful reflection for me has been to consider the words of Isaiah, chapter 55: "My thoughts are not your thoughts, neither are your ways my ways, says the Lord. For as the heavens are higher than the earth, so are my ways higher than your ways and my thoughts than your thoughts." God is not a glorified human being. Our love, our vision, our focus of attention is limited. For the transcendent God, from whom emanates a cavernous universe with vast galaxies, there are no limits. While the massive numbers of people on earth are unknowable to us, we are but a tiny part of all creation. For God to nourish and to know us intimately is no more impossible than for our relatively small planet, Earth, to give birth to and sustain the infinite number of trees and plants and bushes and flowers and grasses that burst forth all over its spacious surface. Both God and Earth, quite beyond our comprehension, can fully nurture a myriad of offspring at the same time.

Whatever your own reflections on this question, and whatever deep mire you may feel yourself sinking into, let us unite ourselves with all those whose suffering is given voice by the Psalmist and pray together in faith and hope the last few verses (15-18) of today's Psalm.

"In your great mercy, O God, answer me with your unfailing help. Save me from the mire; do not let me sink; let me be rescued from those who hate me and out of the deep waters. Let not the torrents of waters wash over me, neither let the deep swallow me up; do not let the Pit shut its mouth upon me. Answer me, O Lord, for your love is kind; in your great compassion, turn to me."

Jeremiah 20:7-13
Psalm 69:1-18
Matthew 10: 16-33

Power is Made Perfect in Weakness
The Sixth Sunday after Pentecost
July 5, 2015

The rejection of Jesus by his fellow Galileans in the first part of today's Gospel foreshadows Jesus' rejection by all of Israel, culminating in the cross. "He came unto his own, and his own received him not."

Contrary to his successes in the Gospel stories of the last few Sundays, i.e. calming the storm and raising the daughter of Jairus back to life, Jesus experienced failure at his return to Nazareth. His teaching was unpersuasive and his miracles limited. The people who had watched him grow up refused to believe in him, "and he could do no deed of power there." He could do nothing except be "amazed at their unbelief" (One translation has it "[was] distressed [by].") and move on to teach in the neighboring villages.

This story should not surprise us since ultimately Jesus' three short years of public ministry were terminated by the scandalous failure of the cross. But somehow it does catch us off guard. We are not used to thinking of Jesus as inadequate to the task. After all he is our ultimate hero, and as such, we assume that, unlike us, he always succeeded at whatever he undertook. Was he not powerful, competent, in charge of whatever happened, invulnerable, uncomplaining, and accorded unwavering loyalty, like all good heroes?

No. Jesus was a profoundly different hero. He did fail, as we heard in today's Gospel. He could not "get through" to many who were closest to him. He was ultimately betrayed by one of his hand-picked followers and abandoned by the rest of them.

Such rejection stung him to the core. He wept over Jerusalem's intransigence and was deeply disappointed at his friends' inattentiveness at Gethsemane on his last night when he needed them most.

He recoiled from the death that faced him. The Letter to the Hebrews says, "Jesus offered up prayers and supplications, with loud cries and tears, to him who was able to save him from death" (5:7). Luke tells us that he begged his Father for an escape from this death, and that "his sweat became like great drops of blood, falling down upon the ground" (Lk 22:44). Eventually he came to terms with his death, but even then he faced it in silence and isolation.

In short, Jesus was much more vulnerable, more genuinely human, more profoundly weak, than our usual impression of him allows. The words addressed to Paul in today's Epistle were primarily those of the Father to Jesus, "My grace is sufficient for you, for power is made perfect in weakness." Jesus was content with weakness and vulnerability and failure that the power of God might rest upon him. His life proclaimed, in the words of Paul, "Whenever I am weak, then I am strong."

How different our lives would be if we could truly embrace that truth! How much more could God's power work in us if we could accept our weakness!

As individuals we would not spend so much time and energy proving ourselves to other people. We would not neglect to volunteer for needed tasks because of fear that we are unqualified. We would not always choose the "safe" path, but trust more in God. We would give away more of our money.

We would be more open with ourselves and others about our struggles and our doubts and our failures. We would not *demand* so much from other people, although we would risk looking for and hoping for more. We would not waste so much time and energy regretting our past, being anxious about the present and worrying about our future. Knowing our deep need for grace, we would pray constantly and insistently and humbly but expectantly for God's strength.

As a parish we would work harder to get below mere friendliness to find and to give the love and support that is truly to characterize us as Christians. We would not be concerned about our standing in the community, but only how we might better serve the community. We would not be afraid to take risks or to extend ourselves for the sake of God's kingdom. We would not worry too much about where our new leadership is to come from and how we will be able to continue to do what God asks us to do.

As a diocese, now faced with the prospect of replacing our beloved and energetic bishop, we would not be too anxious about how that will all work out. We would trust that the Holy Spirit, who has worked through our weakness up until now, will continue to strengthen and to guide us.

As a national church, just finished with General Convention, we would not be either too fearful of the challenges ahead or overconfident in our ability to handle them. We would not be too anxious about the recent outcome of legal proceedings in South Carolina. We would put our trust, not in our buildings and our earthly resources, but in God's strength and God's wisdom, which will be enough for us.

As a nation, celebrating our national holiday, we would be less sure that God is always on our side. We would be less quick to commit our military might and more ready to admit our past mistakes. We would be less obsessed with the security of our money and more concerned with those shackled by poverty and who have no real voice in our political process.

Does all that, and more that you could supply, seem impossible? It is, of course, on our own strength. But Jesus is not only our model, but more importantly our Savior and the One who sends us the Spirit. We do not save ourselves, but Jesus redeems us in our weakness and fills us with the Spirit, who is at work within us. God's words to Paul are also addressed to us as individuals, as a parish, as a diocese, as the Church trying to continue on earth the work Jesus began in the midst of inadequacy and failure, as a nation dedicated to the proposition that all human beings are created equal: "My grace is sufficient for you, for power is made perfect in weakness."

II Cor. 12:2-10
Mark 6:1-13

Take My Yoke Upon You
The Seventh Sunday after Pentecost
July 3, 2005

Take my yoke upon you, and learn from me; for I am gentle and lowly in heart, and you will find rest for your souls. For my yoke is easy, and my burden is light.

This is a special scripture verse for me, this gentle invitation from Jesus to attach ourselves to him and follow in his footsteps and learn from living in his loving presence.

It is special first of all from a very personal point of view as an ordained priest in the Body of Christ. The primary symbol of the priesthood is not the collar many of us wear, nor even the colorful chasuble, indicative specifically of the Celebrant at the Eucharist. The major symbol of being a priest is the stole, worn about the neck, evocative of the yoke of Christ. Many of us saw last month, the stole ceremoniously draped over David Frazelle's shoulders, immediately after Bishop Curry and the other priests present laid hands on him and the bishop prayed the Prayer of Consecration, ordaining him a priest in the Church of God.

Thereafter each time the priest vests for liturgical action, he or she puts it on himself or herself, as an expression of willingness to take on the yoke of Jesus and to serve others in Jesus' name. I do not know what David will choose to do, but my practice is always to kiss the stole before I put it on as a sign both of gratitude and of willing acceptance of its costs and responsibilities. To find this reading assigned in the lectionary, then, just a few days after celebrating both my 30th anniversary as a priest and my 20th anniversary as the rector at the Chapel of the Cross, makes it very special indeed. Hearing these words proclaimed again liturgically fills me with great gratitude for the privilege of serving as an ordained priest, and particularly for the gift of being able to serve so long here in this congregation, whose people and whose ministry I love and enjoy so much.

But even aside from that purely personal viewpoint, this scripture holds a cherished place for me because of its implications about our life as Christians. Far beyond its applied priestly imagery, it speaks to all of us who would live our lives in response to Jesus' coaxing invitation, "Take my yoke upon you." That is an agrarian metaphor, of course, and suggests images of beasts of burden being harnessed to the plow in order to accomplish the work of the master. Not a very appealing picture — not only because of the hard work involved, but also because of the implications of servitude. We much prefer to think of ourselves not as those in submission, but as the ones in charge. We tend to consider ourselves as under no one, not subject to *anyone's* yoke, but free.

But freedom as an absence of service and commitment is an illusion. True freedom requires limitation and submission. One cannot dance without the restrictions of gravity. A writer cannot create without yielding to the discipline and vocabulary of language. The ultimate act of human freedom remains Jesus' choosing to be nailed to the cross. Freedom involves self-giving commitment.

The question for us is not whether we will serve under a yoke, but whose yoke will it be? The important word in Jesus' invitation is not "yoke" but "my": "Take *my* yoke upon you." The implication is that we are all under some yoke, not the master as we like to imagine; but we have some choice whose yoke it will be.

What are our options? As Paul tells us in today's second reading, we can follow the law of sin and death or the law of the Spirit of life, but we will follow some law. We can set our minds on the things of the flesh or the things of the Spirit; but we will set our minds on something. We can take Jesus' yoke upon us or that of some other master, but we will serve someone or something.

We delude ourselves by thinking our freedom consists in being unconnected, neutral, without a yoke. Robert Frost has been quoted as defining freedom as "being easy in your harness," implying that by choice or not, we all have one. "Being easy in your harness" does not mean always having it easy; it means freely accepting and choosing that which both restrains you and at the same time enables you to fulfill your role, to accomplish something, to love and to serve. Your faith is part of your harness, your friendships, your relationship to another as child, as parent, as spouse. Your work, your obligations to the poor, your commitment to the Church, your loyalty to your country, whose ideals we celebrate tomorrow. All of these bonds and connections, when joyfully embraced and conscientiously lived out, can constitute taking on the yoke of Jesus and finding true freedom and thus contentment and rest for our souls.

Jesus assures us that his yoke is easy. That does not mean facile or requiring nothing of us. For some followers it has required their very lives, as it did for Jesus himself. For all of us, at one time or another, it can involve deep disappointment and loss, discipline, difficult perseverance. Jesus' yoke is easy because it fits us; we are made for it and we know that it is right for us. We know that we can be easy in the harness that Jesus, who is gentle and lowly in heart, lovingly extends to us.

Our choice then is not whether we will serve and submit to any other power throughout our lives, but whether we will accept the yoke of Jesus. Rather than "Satan and all the spiritual forces of wickedness that rebel against God," rather than "the evil powers of this world which corrupt and destroy the creatures of God," rather than our own "sinful desires that draw [us] from the love of God," we are, in the words of our Baptismal Covenant, to "turn to Jesus Christ ... and follow and obey him as [our] Lord." Whether we are priests or deacons or lay people, Jesus invites us to take his yoke upon us and learn from him. For his yoke is easy, and his burden is light.

Romans 7:21-8:6
Matthew 11:25-30

The Spirit Helps Us In Our Weakness
The Seventh Sunday after Pentecost
July 27, 2014

The Spirit helps us in our weakness; for we do not know how to pray as we ought, but the Spirit himself intercedes for us with sighs too deep for words.

What deep mystery and freeing truth and gratifying reassurance are found in these opening words of Paul in today's Epistle. They convey to us so much of the incredible grace that God fills us with and has revealed to us. Let us contemplate and absorb this richness phrase by phrase.

"The Spirit helps us in our weakness." Paul begins with a matter-of-fact acknowledgement of our weakness. That is a given, an assumption out of which a Christian operates. As human beings, we are weak.

Our weakness is a reality, however, which we all too easily deny. Even if, in our later years, for example, we are more aware of our physical limitations, we still feel the pressure at least to *seem* to others to be people who have their lives together, who can be defined by our strengths. We do not like to think of ourselves as weak, as afraid of the future, as in doubt about many things, as limited by our blind spots, as less committed than we need to be, as more self-centered and less loving than others need us to be. But we are; all of us are weak human beings.

But that is only part of the picture. Paul tells us, "The Spirit *helps* us in our weakness." The Spirit — God's active presence in the world, who brooded over the waters in creation, who led Jesus out into the wilderness to be tempted, who transformed the fearful apostles on Pentecost into bold witnesses of the Gospel — this same dynamic Spirit helps us in our weakness.

We are not simply on our own; we are not abandoned; we are not left to muddle through as best we can. God's very own Spirit, given to us at Baptism, accompanies us, assists us, in some sense accommodates us and makes up for us. What solace and encouragement we should take from that profound mystery! "The Spirit helps us in our weakness."

"For we do not know how to pray as we ought." A further elucidation of our weakness is that we do not even know how to pray, how to ask for what we need, how to present ourselves to God. When things are going well, we feel no need to pray; when things change for the worse, we feel so overwhelmed we do not know where to start. How do we convince God to ease our loneliness, to bring peace to the troubled spots of the world, to console those whom we love who are suffering?

Convince God? Even the vocabulary of our question conveys our ignorance. We do not know how to pray as we ought because we instinctively think of prayer as our initiative, as getting God's attention or currying God's favor. Rather our very desire to pray is already a grace from God, a response to God's initiating love. "No one can come to me," Jesus said "unless the Father draw him" (John 6:44). "We love because God first loved us," John wrote (I John 4:19). Solomon, in today's first reading, does not first ask God for wisdom; rather God first invites Solomon, "Ask what I shall give you." We are here in this congregation today because God acted first. God invited us, inspired us, made it possible for us to come, to pray, to worship. Any spiritual movement by us is already God's initiative, not ours.

What a difference that realization can make to our prayer! When we are the invited guest, we relate differently to the host than if we are a gatecrasher trying to justify (or conceal) our presence. When we know we are wanted and welcomed, we are much more ready to be there and to be fully present. When we discover, returning home, that our Father, keeping watch for us, runs and embraces us and kisses us (as in the story of the prodigal son in Luke 15:20), we regret that we have waited so long.

Even when we do grasp, however, that our prayer is not our attempt to get God to notice and to love us, but our response to God's love already offered to us, we still struggle with our prayer. What are we to ask for? How do we pray in complex and seemingly hopeless situations? How do we pray for resignation at one of life's seeming inevitabilities, and yet also strength, perhaps still to change it? How do we express our anger at a senseless crime and yet pray for both the victim and the perpetrator? How do we genuinely pray for our enemies and those who have hurt us? How do we ask to forgive them when we do not really want to? That brings us to our final phrase, which is at once beyond our understanding and too good to be true.

"The Spirit himself intercedes for us with sighs too deep for words." Hear that again. "The Spirit himself intercedes for us with sighs too deep for words." In the midst of our confusion and fear and doubt, the God within us connects us to the God without. Rather than leave us isolated under our burden, the Spirit translates our longings and our half-articulated hopes into prayers that transcend words, that unite us with the Lord and Giver of life, with the source of "the peace that passeth all understanding." What else can God do for us? "Glory to God whose power working in us can do infinitely more than we can ask or imagine" (Ephesians 3:20).

The prayer God desires from us is not the most poetic, not the most articulate, not the most talkative. What God asks is a prayer that springs from a heart that is open to the pain of the world, from a spirit that admits our weakness and need, from a soul that allows the Spirit to move, to breathe, to pray deep within us.

We need to move beyond our uncertainty and our fears and even our unbelief. We need to absorb the reality of God's Spirit at work within us. Let us believe that "the Spirit helps us in our weakness" and, even on a daily basis, "intercedes for us with sighs too deep for words."

I Kings 3:5-12
Romans 8:26-34

Five Loaves and Two Fish: Not the Sensible Solution
The Eighth Sunday after Pentecost, Carolina Meadows
August 3, 2014

This Gospel story, which we have heard many times, is central to the Good News of God in Christ. One reason we have heard it so much is that it unusually appears in all four Gospels, even twice in Matthew's Gospel with different numbers involved of loaves and people and baskets! Obviously Jesus' early followers considered this extraordinary event of major importance in communicating and understanding the kingdom of God brought in by Jesus — whatever the numbers of the actual event. It is a multi-layered story with much to teach us and inspire us.

Prior to today's passage, Jesus has just learned that Herod had frivolously killed Jesus' cousin and precursor, John the Baptist. Entranced at a banquet by the dancing of his stepdaughter, this self-indulgent king gave in to her demands for John's head and literally served it to her on a platter. Deeply saddened, Jesus withdrew in a boat "to a lonely place apart" to grieve. Or at least he tried to. Thousands of people, hungry for his presence and his teaching, preceded him on foot and were waiting for him. Despite his grief, Jesus had compassion on them and began to heal the sick and to tell them more about God.

And then even more extraordinary things began to happen. As evening came, the disciples got anxious about how they would feed all these people — "about five thousand men" and presumably a like amount of women and children, 10,000 people or so in all. The disciples came up with the most sensible solution. "Send the crowds away," they urged Jesus, "to go into the villages and buy food for themselves." Overruled by Judge Jesus! "They need not go away," Jesus responded, "you give them something to eat." Stunned, they did a quick inventory and came up with five loaves and two fish, but they could not see how these would help. "Bring them here to me," Jesus told them. Then he took these meager gifts "and blessed, and broke and gave the loaves to the disciples," who gave them to the crowd. "And they all ate and were satisfied." In fact 12 baskets were left over.

The meal, of course, is at the heart of the kingdom. A meal, that is, where everyone is welcome, from which no one is turned away, and where all eat and are satisfied. Notice that Jesus does not first weed out orthodox Jews or liberal Jews or Gentiles or immigrants or Roman sympathizers or those who interpreted scripture differently. Everyone counted; no litmus tests were required. "All ate and were satisfied." What a contrast with Herod's banquet, which was not only exclusive, but also rife with self-indulgence and political intrigue. Jesus, the real king, provides even in a lonely place apart, an experience of God's kingdom in a common but extraordinary meal.

There is something about the very nature of sharing food together, food which nourishes by dying, so to speak, and becoming transformed into human beings, who also are dying in some way to being mere individuals and becoming part of a community larger than themselves, which embodies the reality of the kingdom of God. The Eucharist, of course, is the fullest expression of that in this life, and the evangelists quite intentionally use the same words in this Gospel passage as they do at the last supper, when Jesus took the bread, blessed it, broke it and gave it to them, saying, "This is my Body." The profoundly spiritual nature of an "ordinary" shared meal is transformed even further when the food we share is the very body and blood of Jesus, given for us and broken for us. It points us to the ultimate fullness of the heavenly banquet, where, no longer separated by differences, real and imagined, all are made one with God and with one another, and all will eat and be eternally satisfied. This significant Gospel story then, expresses the universal, life-giving, unifying nature of God's kingdom "on earth [and] as it is [and will be] in heaven."

But it also teaches us about the nature of discipleship. *We* are often faced with situations where there is not enough, where the demands of getting to what could be seem too great, where the most sensible solution seems to be to send everyone away. About 15 years ago at the Chapel of the Cross, we became aware that our facilities at that time would become more and more inadequate to handle the continued local population growth. Growth experts were predicting that 2,000 people a year for 30 years would move into Orange County alone. Some of us said that we needed to start a new congregation to handle the newcomers. Others

224

said, no, we needed to expand our own buildings. Many thought we did not have the means to do either one, let alone both at the same time. That did not seem feasible, and certainly not sensible.

When as human beings, we imitate the first disciples and try to choose the sensible solution, Jesus says two things to us. First, "They need not go away; you give them something to eat;" and then when we lament that we have so few resources, he tells us, "Bring them here to me." "Bring them here to me." If we are to be people of faith, we must joyfully heed Jesus' encouraging invitation. If we would truly place our trust in God and not in ourselves, we must take the risk of rising to the challenges God calls us to and of asking God to bless our limited efforts. If we would help reveal God's kingdom, we must bring whatever it is we have to Jesus and let him do something extraordinary with it. That is what the Chapel of the Cross and Holy Family and St. Matthew's resolved to do; and the amazing result today is that the Church of the Advocate is now worshipping in its own historic building on 15 acres of land, and each of the three sponsoring congregations is also significantly expanding its own facilities for ministry at the same time.

We should all be encouraged and emboldened by that example. When we put our trust in God and not in our meager resources, we help to unleash the power of God in lonely places of our world that so desperately need it. We progress in becoming the disciples of Jesus that God calls us to be. We gather around the banquet table of the Lord and share what God gives us, knowing that there will be more than enough, even basketfuls left over.

Matthew 14:13-21

The Theology of Abundance II
The Ninth Sunday after Pentecost
July 13, 2008

We have all been experiencing shortages lately. While so far there is gasoline to go around, the rapidly accelerating price is making it a more precious commodity and cutting back on our travel plans and our usual ways of doing things. Increased energy costs are rippling through the economy, driving up the price of food and building materials and other commodities, making life and even survival particularly hard for the poor and the disadvantaged. Property values and stock values have fallen, depressing the economy and seriously cutting into people's assets and their education and retirement plans. Even our water supply is not something we can take for granted anymore.

Nor are we Americans the only ones facing such deficits. Despite the weakened dollar, our situation pales in the face of what many around the world are dealing with. Hunger and homelessness and disease remain significant global problems in this 21st Century.

Our temptation in the face of such deprivation is to withdraw into what might be called a theology of scarcity. We begin to assume that there is not enough for everyone to go around and to hoard what we have and to look out for ourselves at the expense of others. That is not necessarily a conscious decision, but our understandable anxiety becomes a powerful force. We easily lose our sense of gratitude and focus on our deficits rather than on appreciating what we do have. We shrink away from challenges, thinking we do not have the wherewithal to handle them. We begin to trust less in God and more in ourselves and in our limited resources. In our theology of scarcity, we become less generous, less cheerful, less trusting that God does and will provide.

But we have a choice! Rather than sink into this theology of scarcity, we can consciously adopt a theology of abundance. We can choose to focus beyond ourselves and beyond our limitations and to concentrate on God, the continuing source of all that is. We can open our eyes to the abundance that is all around us and to God, the very paradigm of overflowing generosity.

Today's Gospel is one of many scriptural places that speaks of God's bountifulness to the point of extravagance. Jesus tells us that God is much more like the farmers of first-century Palestine than the careful gardeners of today. For these contemporaries of Jesus, sowing was the first stage of planting and not the last. After scattering the seed generously over the entire area, the farmers would then plow the ground in order to cover the seed and trigger germination. That seems like a waste of seed to us, since much fell on ground too rocky for the plow or on the paths the farmers walked to have access to their crops or among the thorns that lay nearby. But to them that lavishness was necessary to ensure that all the good soil received enough seed. Generosity equaled abundant crops.

Jesus is telling us that God is like that. God is not stingy or measured. Rather the word of God, the seed of faith, is offered to all lavishly and generously, regardless of suitability or track record. God's ways are not our ways. "He makes his sun rise on the evil and on the good, and sends rain on the just and on the unjust."

In *every* way God is generosity itself, exhibited in the extravagance of creation, from the complexity of genes to the infinity of space. Just consider for a moment our sun, something we take completely for granted. In its universe made up of all the planets, their moons, the stars, and comets, it contains 96 percent to 98 percent of all matter. It is enormous! The sun creates energy by nuclear fusion. Every second of the day and night, 700 million tons of hydrogen are converted into 695 million tons of helium and 5 million tons of energy, which give life to our planet. Every second! The sun is about four and a half billion years old, and it contains enough hydrogen to give off 5 million tons of energy every second for 2 billion more years. So sinner, get ready! Only two billion years left for our small planet!

Or go from the macro to the micro and consider the complexity of the genetic base of matter. The human genome is over "3 billion letters long, and [is] written in a strange and cryptographic four-letter code," according to Francis Collins, who chaired the herculean task in the last decade of mapping the genome. He writes, "Such is the amazing complexity of the information carried within each cell of the human body, that a live reading of that code at a rate of one letter per second would take thirty-one years, even if reading continued day and night"!

These two examples, the incomprehensible vastness and power of the sun and the incredible minute complexity of the genome, along with the depths and the riches of the oceans, the mind-boggling diversity of species of animals and birds and fish and insects, and trees and bushes and flowers, and even the multiplicity of human civilizations and languages and cultures, should help us at least glimpse this God of abundance and pull us out of our tendency toward a myopic theology of scarcity.

Scripture consistently paints this vision of a lavish God. In the free gift of creation, in multiplying Abraham's descendants to number more than the stars in the heavens, in providing daily manna in the desert to the wandering Jews, an abundant God is revealed. In Jesus' multiplying the loaves and fish to feed five thousand with 12 baskets left over, and vastly increasing the wine supply for a wedding, and letting the woman extravagantly anoint his feet with expensive ointment, and encouraging us not to bury our talents in the ground, and to sell all, and, like the widow, to give of our substance, and to forgive others 70 times seven times, and not to be anxious about our life and its necessities, we are showered with images of generosity and impelled toward a theology of abundance.

As God is the extravagant sower, so we who are made in the Divine image are called to be. We are not to let our anxiety about the future control our attitudes and our actions. We are to trust in God that there will be enough, enough to lead happy and productive lives and to help other children of God do the same. We are not to hoard what we have been given, but to share with all as our brothers and sisters. Whether that be our affection or our energy or our commitment or our forgiveness or our hope or our time or our money, perhaps the biggest challenge for us as possessive human beings is that we are to be generous and giving like the God in whose image we are made. No matter what shortages we face, now and in the future, we are called to live a theology of abundance.

Matthew 13:1-9, 18-23

Praying for Peace
The Eleventh Sunday after Pentecost
August 12, 2012

You may have read in Friday's email or in today's bulletin that Bishop Curry has asked us to join with the people and congregations of Wisconsin in making this a day of prayer for those killed and seriously affected in the shooting rampage at a Sikh Temple there. We are to pray for the victims of the violence, "for peace and calm in the midst of heated tensions, for the family members of those who were killed, including the perpetrator" and "for a spirit of respect, that we may honor all people as beloved children of the living God."

We are relieved to do something in response to this tragedy. Such violence horrifies us. We shake our heads in amazement that human beings can turn such deep-seated hatred against one another and destroy so senselessly the fragile and beautiful gift of life. No venue seems safe: workplaces, movie theaters, schools, places of worship. Every week seems to bring another violent tragedy, another mind-numbing scene of the destruction of human life. Add to this the multiple arenas of armed conflict around the world, whether of direct military clashes or of suicide bombings of civilian populations, and we realize our world is saturated to the brim with violence and destruction. Even the inspiring sight of the Olympics, where athletes from all the nations of the world have competed with respect and honor, cannot obscure the continual and awful eruptions of human violence against one another.

This is not a new phenomenon, of course. Today's first reading tells us of a battle between armies of the same homeland in which 20,000 men were slaughtered. And then the writer brings home the excruciating pain of each of these deaths by relating the story of Absalom, who was killed by his father's soldiers, causing David to weep inconsolably at the bitter loss of his son. The one lost his very life, and the other the essence of his life. Such is the price of violence, destroying all that are touched by it.

As it happens, this week we are commemorating on the liturgical calendar Jonathan Myrick Daniels. Jonathan was born in New Hampshire and answered a call to ordained ministry. At seminary in Boston in 1965, he also heard the appeal of Martin Luther King, Jr. to come to Selma to help secure for all citizens there the right to vote. He returned to seminary after the march, but, inspired during Evening Prayer at the chanting of the Magnificat, "He hath put down the mighty from their seat and hath exalted the humble and meek," he asked leave from his classes to work in Selma. After joining a picket line in Haynesville, Alabama, he was jailed and then quickly and unexpectedly released with his companions. The four of them walked to a small store, aware of great danger. As one of the young girls reached the top step of the entrance, a man appeared with a shotgun, cursing her. As Jonathan pulled her from the path of the gun, he was shot by the man and killed.

His letters and papers revealed the depth to which Jonathan was motivated by his Christian beliefs. He wrote, "The faith with which I went to Selma has not changed: it has grown. … I began to know in my bones and sinews that I had been truly baptized into the Lord's death and resurrection … with them, the black men and white men, with all my life, in him whose Name is above all the names that the races and nations shout. … We are indelibly and unspeakably one."

We are not all called to be martyrs for our faith, to give our very lives for another; but we are called to give faithful witness. We are all called to be peacemakers. We are all called to reflect in our attitudes and actions the great underlying realities of our faith, especially our radical unity with God and with all the children of God. We cannot prevent all violence; we cannot stop all tragedies; we cannot rid the human race of its sinfulness and brokenness. Only God can do that. But we can try to be instruments of God's peace. We can aspire to let our faith make a difference in our lives and in the world, as did Jonathan Myrick Daniels. We can aim, in the words of our second reading, to "let all bitterness and wrath and anger and clamor and slander be put away from [us], with all malice, and be kind to one another, tenderhearted, forgiving one another, as God in Christ forgave [us]." We can "be imitators of God, as beloved children."

232

One of the great resources of our Christian faith to help us live that calling is the gift of the Eucharist. And what an extraordinary gift it is! The Bread of Life, as it has for centuries, is made available to all of us, despite our level of faith or virtue. Each of us, just as we are, with all our scars and anger and sinfulness, comes forward to receive this life-giving gift, with no conditions or demands attached to it. All of us together set aside our petty bickering and our disagreements and our real or imagined divisions, and, opening up our hands, we are all blessed with the gift of the self-giving God who calls us beyond our narrow vision and obstinacy to embrace all people as our brothers and sisters. In a ritual that transcends explanation and even moves us beyond our imaginations, we receive the transformed elements of bread and wine and are ourselves transformed into the unified Body of Christ.

In an uncertain world, where violence begets more violence and we feel helpless in the midst of it, let us receive this transforming Divine gift with great gratitude. Let us allow its grace to deepen in us and to enlarge our hearts. Let us pray, as we have been asked, for all those deeply touched by this most recent outburst of violence, and let us pray that the unifying reality that the Eucharist both effects and signifies may draw the whole world into God's saving embrace.

2 Samuel 18:5-9,15,31-33
Ephesians 4:25-5:2
John 6:35, 41-51

Mystery and Music
The Eleventh Sunday after Pentecost
August 14, 1988

A mystery is not that which as yet remains unsolved; a mystery is that which is beyond our comprehension. Who will win the presidential race in November is not a mystery. How to conquer the scourge of cancer is not a mystery. Neither is the question of whether there is life on another planet. These are merely things not yet known.

A mystery cannot be fully understood. It is beyond our grasp; it defies our intellects. It can only be glimpsed, reverenced, believed. God's love is a mystery, and Jesus, and each human person, and the wonder of creation, and the depth and beauty of music, and the Eucharist.

Jesus says something in the Gospel this morning that cannot be comprehended; it does not make sense. "He who eats my flesh and drinks my blood abides in me, and I in him." We are not the only ones to by stymied by those words; the Jews, to whom they were first spoken, were horrified. Drink blood? The Law forbade it. The "nephesh" or "Life-principle" was in the blood. For a human being, also filled with nephesh, to consume the nephesh of beasts was anathema. The blood of slaughtered animals was drained into the ground and covered with earth. Now were they to drink human blood?

William Temple, the former Archbishop of Canterbury, explains that Christians drink the blood of Jesus for the same reason that Jews are forbidden to consume blood: The blood is the life. The blood of Christ is the life of Christ. But that still does not fully illuminate what Jesus is talking about. It still remains obscure.

When we are faced with some aspect of our faith which we cannot understand, our temptation is to dismiss it or to ignore it. But to do so is to reduce our faith to a mere rationalism and to make God into our quite limited image.

In her novel *Wise Blood*, Flannery O'Connor's street-corner evangelist, Onnie Jay Holy, offers the public "The Holy Church of Christ Without Christ." He says of it, "You don't have to believe nothing you don't understand and approve. If you don't understand it, it ain't true, and that's all there is to it." When we exclude from our faith those things which we cannot understand, when we eliminate the mystery from our belief and from our apprehension of God and of our world, we opt for a "Church Without Christ."

How can we resist that temptation? How can we keep ourselves open to, and in awe of, and responsive to, the mystery? I want to list several ways, and then develop one at more length.

First, we must be in frequent contact with scripture. By regular reading and study of the Bible, if we are truly open to it, the mystery of God's activity will become more alive for us. Passages like today's Gospel will confront us and challenge us to believe.

Second, we must become people of passion, that is people who care deeply, people who weep and who laugh. While moderation is a virtue, apathy and numbness do not qualify as the Golden Mean. Without passion in our lives we will find no attraction in mystery.

Third, we must worship regularly — weekly — with the community. The mystery of God is found not only in solitude, as important as that is, but also with one another, and especially when our assembling transcends itself in time and in place and in dimension, as occurs when we join in the worship of the Church.

Finally, to remain in touch with and responsive to the Divine Mystery in our lives, we must cultivate a gift, which in itself is of inexhaustible depth, the gift of music. This pathway to mystery incorporates the other three I have mentioned: scripture, passion, and worship. Music is an integral part of community worship, both when it is played and listened to, in pieces that stir our passions, and when it is sung, especially in hymns based on, or taken from, scripture. As Paul encourages us in today's Epistle, "Be filled with the Spirit, addressing one another in psalms and hymns and spiritual songs; singing and making melody to the Lord with all your heart."

235

Let me show you, in language more elegantly appropriate than I could muster, what some Christian writers of historical note have written about the importance of music.

St. Basil, writing delightfully in the fourth century, emphasizes music as a teaching vehicle, to help us learn from scripture more deeply:

"Whereas the Holy Spirit saw that mankind is unto virtue hardly drawn, and that righteousness is the less accounted of by reason of the proneness of our affections to that which delighteth; it pleased the wisdom of the same Spirit to borrow from melody that pleasure, which mingled with heavenly mysteries, causeth the smoothness and softness of that which toucheth the ear, to convey as it were by stealth the treasure of good things into man's mind. To this purpose were those harmonious tunes of psalms devised for us, that they which are either in years but young, or touching perfection of virtue as not yet grown to ripeness, might when they think they sing, learn. O the wise conceit of that heavenly Teacher, which hath by his skill found out a way, that doing those things wherein we delight, we may also learn that whereby we profit!"

Richard Hooker, the Anglican Divine, wrote convincingly and beautifully of the power of music itself, even without words, to stir us and to connect us with the Divine Mystery:

"Touching musical harmony whether by instrument or by voice, it being but of high and low in sounds a due proportionable disposition, such not withstanding is the force thereof, and so pleasing effects it hath in that very part of man which is most divine, that some have been thereby induced to think that the soul itself by nature is or hath in it harmony. ...

"Although we lay altogether aside the consideration of ditty or matter, the very harmony of sounds being framed in due sort and carried from the ear to the spiritual faculties of our souls, is by a native puissance and efficacy greatly available to bring to a perfect temper whatsoever is there troubled, apt as well to quicken the spirit as allay that which is too eager, sovereign against melancholy and despair, forcible to draw forth tears of devotion if the mind be such as can yield them, able both to move and to moderate all affections." (Laws, Book 5, Chapter 38)

I cannot resist including here, a quote from Dietrich Bonhoeffer, which shows how music and life and the love of God are all intrinsically intertwined. In his *Letters and Papers from Prison*, Bonhoeffer advises his brother-in-law on the nature and role of his love for his new wife:

"God wants us to love him eternally with our whole hearts — not in such a way as to injure or weaken our earthly love, but to provide a kind of 'cantus firmus' to which the other melodies of life provide the counterpoint. One of these contrapuntal themes (which have their own complete independence but are yet related to the 'cantus firmus') is earthly affection. Even in the Bible we have the Song of Songs; and really one can imagine no more ardent, passionate, sensual love than is portrayed there. It's a good thing that the book is in the Bible, in face of all those who believe that the restraint of passion is Christian (where is there such restraint in the Old Testament?). Where the 'cantus firmus' is clear and plain, the counterpoint can be developed to its limits." (III, letter of 20 May 1944)

Finally, as one who recently, when no one was looking, climbed the steps to the pulpit of St. Mary's Church, Oxford, to see what it felt like to stand in the very footsteps of John Wesley as he preached, I offer you Wesley's "Directions for Singing," with which he prefaced his hymnal in 1761. The directions are of a very practical nature, but underlying them one can sense the passion for praise and the love of God that motivated them.

I.   Learn these tunes before you learn any other; afterwards learn as many as you please.

II. Sing them exactly as they are printed here, without altering or mending them at all; and if you have learned to sing them otherwise, unlearn it as soon as you can.

III. Sing all. See that you join with the congregation as frequently as you can. Let not a slight degree of weakness or weariness hinder you. If it is a cross to you, take it up, and you will find it a blessing.

IV.   Sing lustily and with good courage. Beware of singing as if you were half dead, or half asleep; but lift up your voice with strength. Be no more afraid of your voice now, nor more ashamed of its being heard, than when you sung the songs of Satan.

V.   Sing modestly. Do not bawl, so as to be heard above or distinct from the rest of the congregation that you may not destroy the harmony; but strive to unite your voices together, so as to make one clear melodious sound.

VI.   Sing in time. Whatever time is sung be sure to keep with it. Do not run before nor stay behind it; but attend close to the leading voices, and move therewith as exactly as you can; and take care not to sing too slow. This drawling way naturally steals on all who are lazy; and it is high time to drive it out from us, and sing all our tunes just as quick as we did at first.

VII.   Above all sing spiritually. Have an eye to God in every word you sing. Aim at pleasing him more than yourself, or any other creature. In order to do this attend strictly to the sense of what you sing, and see that your heart is not carried away with the sound, but offered to God continually; so shall your singing be such as the Lord will approve here, and reward you when he cometh in the clouds of heaven.

This morning we are here to sing to God, aiming at pleasing God more than ourselves. We are here to hear the scripture read and sung, and to let ourselves be stirred to the love of God by the music. We are here to worship the Lord in the beauty of holiness, and with the whole earth to stand in awe of' him. We are here to eat the flesh of Jesus and to drink his blood, and to abide in him as he does in us. All that is incomprehensible, but not unbelievable. Let us believe. Amen.

Ephesians 5:15-20
John 6:53-59

Fear Not, Little Flock
The Twelfth Sunday after Pentecost
August 11, 2013

"Fear not, little flock, for it is your Father's good pleasure to give you the kingdom." I have always loved that opening line of today's Gospel. "Fear not, little flock." It comes right after Jesus has told his followers not to worry about what to wear or to fret over what they will eat or to "be of anxious mind," but to consider the lilies of the field and the birds of the air and to trust in God. And then, knowing that human beings are not too good at doing that, Jesus gets even more compassionate and affectionate and, as if smiling and putting his arms around us all, he says, "Fear not, little flock, for it is your Father's good pleasure (not "obligation" or "begrudgement") to give you the kingdom." Wow! Isn't that Good News?!

Having just gotten back from a sabbatical trip that included significant time spent in rural parts of Scotland, including Iona, where the sheep are more plentiful than the people, that term "little flock" stirs my heart more than it did before. Sheep are not very smart, of course, and need a lot of guidance, which is probably why Jesus used that metaphor for us so much! Individually and collectively we need shepherding a good part of the time! But Jesus also obviously found sheep endearing, and one incident Betsy and I were privileged to experience helped us to see why.

We had just walked down a small road past a spot where pasture gates were open on either side of the road with some sheep crossing from one to the other. Not much further on we had started up a mountain path that was already giving us some perspective back on the road we had just traveled, when we saw and heard one sheep standing there between those sets of pasture gates baaing loudly and repeatedly. She seemed lost and confused, and we thought she just could not figure out how to proceed into the second pasture with the others. She would not stop her constant and, by then, irritating "Baa, baa."

Finally from a distant corner of the first pasture, we heard a frantic higher bleat, and a lamb who had not noticed the others had moved on, came running full tilt the length of the pasture toward the sound. Finally getting to the road, it practically crashed into its mother and began vigorously nursing as fast as it could! Then together they trotted into the second pasture. So touching — and perhaps that vignette gives us some deeper sense of the affection in Jesus' heart in calling us "little flock." "Fear not, little flock," who get lost and need insistent calling back. Fear not; believe it or not, yours is the kingdom.

But then Jesus goes on to tell us how to access that kingdom, how to walk into that pasture. "Sell your possessions, and give alms; provide yourselves with ... a treasure in the heavens that does not fail. ... For where your treasure is, there will your heart be also." "For where your treasure is, there will your heart be also."

Those are words of life for us. For one thing, the implication of Jesus is that it is of utmost importance where our hearts are, what it is we give our hearts to. Our hearts are at the very core and center of our being; and it is the focus of our hearts which is most significant about us and which is most important to Jesus.

He spoke of this significance constantly: "Love the Lord thy God with all thy heart," (Mark 12:30). "For I am meek and lowly in heart," he characterized himself (Matthew 11:29). "So also my heavenly Father will do to every one of you, if you do not forgive your brother from your heart," (Mark 12:30). "This people honors me with their lips, but their heart is far from me," (Matthew 15:8).

The Good News Jesus proclaims to us does not merely ask from us external conformity to prescribed religious and moral codes. Rather God, in the person of Jesus, invites us into something much deeper and more encompassing: an intimate relationship with God such that our hearts are totally focused on and given to God. God's values become our values; God's will becomes our will.

Because we are created in the image of God, and because we are baptized children of God, we might think that this would be an automatic process, that our hearts would naturally focus on God, almost without choice.

But there is so much that competes for the loyalty of our hearts. Money and all that it brings, power, fame, the esteem of others, our own convenience and comfort — so many things deceive us and promise us ultimate satisfaction. These are strong suitors for our hearts' loyalty, although deep down we know the truth of Augustine's insight, "Our hearts are restless until they rest in thee, O God." How do we actively work against those strong temptations and make choices that steer our hearts toward God?

Jesus, out of that same love and affection with which he calls us "little flock," gives us a simple, if hard to hear, action plan. "Sell your possessions, and give alms; provide yourselves with … a treasure in the heavens that does not fail. … For where your treasure is, there will your heart be also." If our treasure is bound up in the wealth of this world, our hearts will be as well. If we put our treasure at God's disposal, our hearts will be focused on God. "For where your treasure is, there will your heart be also."

We would probably have said it the other way around. "Where your heart is, there will your treasure be also." That makes perfect sense. If our hearts are with a particular cause or political party or educational institution, we will support it with our treasure to the degree that it has captured our hearts. Any fund raiser knows this principle.

But Jesus was not teaching fund raising, but preaching conversion. He reversed it: "Where you put your treasure," he said, "your heart will surely follow." Action precedes belief. Through freely sharing what we have been given, our hearts will come to rest in the Divine.

Over a century ago, Robert Bridges, later Poet Laureate of England, wrote to his friend, Gerard Manley Hopkins, a Jesuit priest who became widely recognized after his death for his intense religious poetry. Bridges, struggling with his faith, asked Hopkins how he, Bridges, could grow to believe. Hopkins wrote him back with only two words, "Give alms." "Give alms."

Perhaps Hopkins was not only familiar with Jesus' Gospel words today, but also realized how profoundly religious almsgiving is. In giving away part of what we have, we acknowledge that all that we have is given to us by the Creator. In using our treasure for others, we do not hoard it for ourselves. In giving to those in need, we give to God, who considers the poor a very special part of the Divine little flock.

That takes courage and trust on our part, of course. We might print on our money, "In God we trust," but we do not really, and we know our creditors don't! Giving away what we may later need is risky, and giving God our hearts is even riskier. Where might all this lead, and what else might I be asked to do? That is where anxiety takes over and fear can block faith. We can be afraid to act, to do what may lead us to faith. That is when we need to turn to God's word and to hear again Jesus' assurance in today's Gospel reading, "Fear not, little flock, for it is your Father's good pleasure to give you the kingdom."

Luke 12:32-40

Oh, It's You Again
The Thirteenth Sunday after Pentecost
August 30, 1998

In a recent interview, the renowned actor, Sir Anthony Hopkins (knighted by the Queen six years ago), now featured in *The Mask of Zorro*, was reflecting on his star status. "When you're young," he said, "you crave power and fame. Now I know it's ... no big deal. I get up and look into the mirror and say, 'Oh, it's you again.'"

I assume he smiles when he says that to himself — I hope he does — with a slight rueful shake of the head that says, "I know who you are: a flawed human being that doesn't deserve all that comes your way, but life is a gift!"

If that is true, what a wonderful model for us: true humility grounded in gratitude and joy, but how difficult for us to imitate! How seriously we take ourselves. How we puff ourselves up or tear ourselves down, both forms of arrogance. How hard it is for us to look in the mirror and neither to frown nor to genuflect, but without pride or condemnation to smile and say, "Oh, it's you again."

"Arrogance is hateful before the Lord," our first reading says, hateful because it is untruth. Arrogance postulates its own reality, creates its own universe centered on itself, denies its limitations. Arrogance lives a lie.

The book of Ecclesiasticus does not want to let us do that. "The king of today will die tomorrow," it says, adding graphically, "he will inherit creeping things and wild beasts and worms." "How can he who is dust and ashes be proud?" Death is one of those limitations, perhaps *the* limitation, that our arrogance tries to deny. It only happens to others. It only happens after a very long life. It will not really happen to me. That is our arrogance speaking, our re-creation of reality, "our grasping for God-like power." It sets us in opposition to the true Creator; it separates us from God. "The beginning of man's pride," Ecclesiasticus declares, "is to depart from the Lord; his heart has forsaken his Maker."

243

Arrogance is a heart disease, as deadly as any other. Its symptoms reveal that our hearts are not centered on God for whom they were created. Instead they are fatally centered on ourselves.

Arrogance is much easier to diagnose in someone else. We can see it, for one prominent example, in our president. He has forgotten that the office which he temporarily holds is a sacred trust, given to him for leadership and service, not for exploitation and self-aggrandizement. That mandate calls for honest truth and genuine repentance, not deception and spin control.

The infection of arrogance however, is much harder to detect in ourselves. Like death itself, we think it is something that happens only to someone else. Certainly the guests at the dinner in today's Gospel thought that, even though they were vying to sit in the places of honor. Jesus encourages them to take themselves less seriously and so allow others to do so. He also urges his host not just to satisfy social obligations and so serve himself, but to show genuine hospitality to those who truly need it. It is more blessed, as he says elsewhere, and less arrogant, to give than to receive.

Jesus can, and does through scripture, address many such exhortations to each of us as an antidote to our arrogance — the ones, for example, in today's reading from Hebrews.

"Let brotherly love continue. Do not neglect to show hospitality to strangers, for thereby some have entertained angels unawares. Remember those who are in prison, as though in prison with them; and those who are ill-treated, since you also are the body. Let marriage be held in honor among all, and let the marriage bed be undefiled. … Keep your life free from love of money, and be content with what you have."

These and other scriptural counsels read easily and sound harmless, but they make great demands on us and are not easily lived. The arrogance in us that constantly urges us to put ourselves at the center of our universe, to view others with suspicion, to use others for our own purposes, causes us to fail frequently. As limited human beings, "sinner" is part of our identity.

When we sin, our arrogance seems to give us two choices: One is to deny it, to smooth things over, to excuse ourselves and so puff ourselves up some more. The other is to punish ourselves for it, to tear ourselves down over it, to use it to continue to take ourselves deadly seriously.

Our Baptismal Covenant gives us a third choice. "Whenever you fall into sin," it asks, will you "repent and return to the Lord?" Rather than continue to focus us on ourselves, genuine repentance will center us back on God. If "the beginning of man's pride is to depart from the Lord," the beginning of man's faith, of man's humility, of man's love, is to return to the Lord. Since "his heart has forsaken his Maker," now it must once again welcome the One for whom it is made.

That is not easy for us to do, especially time after time, day after day. We cannot believe that God is that patient, that understanding, that forgiving; but scripture is full of assurances for our fears. Today's reading from Hebrews declares that God "has said, 'I will never fail you nor forsake you.' Hence we can confidently say, 'The Lord is my helper, I will not be afraid.'" Even beyond God's word in scripture, Jesus is the very incarnation of God's word, of God's forgiveness, of God's love. It is through faith in the crucified, resurrected Jesus that we know and can be assured of God's never-failing love. "I will never fail you nor forsake you."

Each time we need forgiveness, we can smile and say, not only to ourselves, but also, with relief and gratitude and adoration, to God, "Oh, it's you again."

Ecclesiasticus 10:7-18
Hebrews 13:1-8
Luke 14:1,7-14

That Leviathan — Made for the Sport of It!
The First Sunday of the Creation Cycle
The Fourteenth Sunday after Pentecost
September 18, 2011

For the third straight fall, we at the Chapel of the Cross are entering into a four-week liturgical creation cycle. Through our common worship of God, the Creator of heaven and earth, we are focusing the scripture readings, the music, the preaching and the prayers on God's dynamic presence in the gift of that creation. With added wildflowers and with stoles featuring our children's drawings of God's living creatures and other gifts of nature and, two weeks from now, with the lively presence and blessing of our cherished pets, we are reminding ourselves of the lavishness and vitality of God's gift to us of creation and of our role as grateful receivers and stewards of it.

During these four weeks, an adult education series is being offered in the chapel with consecutive presentations on the elements of Water, Air, Sun, and Wind. Generous displays of articles and information on these themes are now available in the dining room. Creative bulletin boards around the building highlight endangered species; a parish tour of the Duke Lemur Center is being offered, with a large enticing display in the parlor; and art with nature and creation themes is being collected for display in October, including Church School class art projects. Even this evening's annual outdoor picnic, now called Fall Feast, has been reshaped to feature local and healthier foods. We can only hope that this first Sunday's theme of Water does not play itself out tonight by additional bountiful gifts from heaven! Everything in its own place and time...

Given today's theme of Water, I want to share with you an experience that Betsy and I had last spring, which embedded even more deeply in our hearts the awesome mystery of the dynamic, creative, giving God, in whom, as Paul says in our second reading, "we live and move and have our being." This was a trip to Maui we were privileged to take for my niece's wedding. Our time there literally brought to life the words of today's psalm, "Yonder is the great and wide sea with its living things too many to number, creatures both small and great. There move the ships, and there is that Leviathan, which you have made for the sport of it."

Besides time spent with family, the unquestioned highlight of our 10-day adventure was our frequent experience of the many humpback whales teeming in the waters around the island. We were delighted to find out that one of the successes of the environmental movement has been the agreement of all but a very few nations to stop hunting and killing humpback whales. As a result, the population has been increasing about eight percent a year. These mammoth creatures, averaging about 50 feet in length and about 40 tons in weight — the heart alone weighs about 430 pounds! — feed in cold polar waters in the summer and then migrate over 3,000 miles, about 1,000 miles a month, to warmer waters for the winter months to have their calves and to mate for the next year's calves.

We were fortunate to visit Maui during that warm water period and to catch numerous sightings of these creatures, often mothers and calves who are never separated from each other for the first year of the calf's life, with hopeful males tagging along. I would guess that we saw about 25 whales a day, on boat tours we took or driving down a coastal road or walking down the beach or even sitting on our deck. Sometimes they would just surface regularly, somewhat like you have seen dolphins do. Sometimes they would lie on their backs and flap their long tails or their enormous white flippers against the water — as many as 50 or 60 times in a row, creating major splashes. And on occasion we got to see them breach. We have all seen the insurance company's commercials of a whale leaping high out of the water and slapping it as it comes down. To see it in person is as awesome and incredible as you might think it is. Nobody knows exactly why they do this. It could be to loosen skin parasites, or it could be connected with mating rituals, or simply be out of playfulness. That is what the psalmist seemed to have in mind when millennia ago he admired God's creation of "that Leviathan" and exclaimed in awe, "which you have made for the sport of it"!

That is one of my favorite lines in all of scripture. The Bible, of course, deals with life's deepest mysteries of life and death and suffering and pain and alienation and reconciliation, and so it frequently takes on an appropriately serious tone. But here is a clear reference to God's sense of humor and playfulness — God having a great time creating and enjoying the whales! Which means we are being Godlike when we enjoy them and do our best to support their existence. God bless all those nations and leaders who have had the courage and the foresight to protect these amazing creatures!

One last anecdote. On one boat tour, the captain turned on a microphone hanging below the boat, and immediately we heard an amazing outpouring of whale singing! It sounded something like elephants trumpeting, but it was a continuous stream of what one web site I consulted calls "long, varied, complex, eerie, and beautiful songs that include recognizable sequences of squeaks, grunts, and other sounds." The captain told us that the song changes every year, but they all sing that season's melody for hours at a time. Only the males sing, and then only in warm waters, perhaps for mating purposes. "In cold waters," the web site says, "they make rougher sounds, scrapes and groans, perhaps used for locating large masses of krill (the tiny crustaceans that they eat)." (That sounds just like us — groaning in the winter and happier to sing in warm weather!)

Hearing that almost other-worldly music drove home to me experientially the mystery that there is so much about life and creation and the spiritual dimension of things that we regularly have no clue about. As we rode along on top of the ocean, we were completely unaware of the multi-faceted world of these whales beneath and around us and their singing to one another until we turned on the microphone.

I hope this creation cycle will in some way turn on a microphone for you. As we give thanks for the numerous dynamic gifts of creation all around us, may they enliven our sense of wonder and joy and gratitude. May they strengthen us to be good stewards of all that we have been given. And may they lead us to a deeper faith in the God from whom all blessings flow. In the words of the collect on the back of your bulletins, "As we probe the mysteries of your creation, [O God, grant that] we may come to know you more truly, and more surely fulfill our role in your eternal purpose; in the name of Jesus Christ our Lord. Amen."

Psalm 104:25-31; Acts 17:22-28

The Mysteries of God's Creation
The First Sunday of the Creation Cycle
The Sixteenth Sunday after Pentecost
September 20, 2009

Wonder or radical amazement is the chief characteristic of the religious man's attitude toward history and nature. ... There is thus only one way to wisdom: awe. Forfeit your sense of awe, let your conceit diminish your ability to revere, and the universe becomes a market place for you. The loss of awe is the great block to insight. (God in Search of Man: A Philosophy of Judaism)

So wrote Rabbi Abraham Joshua Heschel, one of the most distinguished thinkers of the last century, over 50 years ago. He warned even then of the dangers of objectifying the universe. "The Greeks learned in order to comprehend," he asserted. "The Hebrews learned in order to revere. The modern man learns in order to use." That contemporary shift in approach, Heschel instructed, leads the human race away from its real identity, away from its true purpose, away from its Creator, from whom all blessings flow. "Dazzled by the brilliant achievements of the intellect in science and technology," he wrote, "we have not only become convinced that we are the masters of the earth; we have become convinced that our needs and interests are the ultimate standard of what is right and wrong."

Over the next four weeks, we at the Chapel of the Cross want to restore some balance to that skewed approach to life. We want to focus again on God as the center and source of the wonders of the universe. We want to acknowledge that we are stewards, not masters, of the gift of the earth. We want to rediscover, in Heschel's words, our wonder and radical amazement and sense of awe at our Creator. As the collect on the back of your bulletins asks of this almighty and everlasting God, "Grant that, as we probe the mysteries of your creation, we may come to know you more truly, and more surely fulfill our role in your eternal purpose."

The portion of Psalm 104 that we recited together gives us a place to start. The Psalmist, in Heschel's definition, is certainly a religious person, captivated by wonder and radical amazement. As David Frazelle told the 7:30 congregation this morning, "the psalmist finds God in every element of the created order — fire, water, air and earth; beasts of the field and birds of the air; wild animals and monsters of the sea; sun and moon, wind and thunder, bread and wine, and daily labor." Yet despite this broad recitation of so many aspects of creation, as David noted, "its subject and object is God. In the 24 verses we read, God is mentioned 22 times. '*You* wrap yourself in light as with a cloak.' '*You* send the springs into the valleys.' '*You* make grass grow for flocks and herds.' 'O Lord my God, how excellent is your greatness! You are clothed with majesty and splendor!'" The psalmist's experience of the vibrancy and the complexity and the abundance of creation leads him into losing himself in awe and the praise of God. It prompts him, as we sang in our opening hymn, to "worship the King, all glorious above," to "gratefully sing his power and his love!"

Living as we do, less close to nature, in the protective environments of our houses and our offices and our air-conditioned cars, we do not have as much chance as this long-ago Israelite to encounter God so directly in the mysteries of creation. For the most part, we are unaffected by storms, unfamiliar with the forest and the jungle and the desert, untouched by the intricacies and patterns of ageless nature. But every once in a while we bump into the surprising majesty of the Creator: We are overwhelmed by a summer sunset; we marvel at unspeakably beautiful blossoms; we feel small in gazing at a starry night.

Betsy and I had just such a gift last month in spending a week at Emerald Isle and enjoying once again the ageless pounding of the ocean surf; the long, silent, graceful lines of pelicans gliding overhead or just above the water's surface; the smooth, rhythmic undulations of the dolphins swimming slowly together down the beach; and this time even a large manta ray somersaulting in the air to shake off barnacles and splashing loudly back down into the hidden depths. But the highlight of the week and the most overt epiphany of the divine presence was a vigil we kept each night at a loggerhead sea turtle's nest.

Sixteen nests had been discovered over the course of the early summer by the hundreds of volunteers who walk the beach each morning, not only picking up the litter, but watching for the telltale deep furrows of the 300-pound-plus mother turtle who has dragged herself well up onto the beach during the night to lay a laboriously prepared nest of 100 or more ping pong ball-sized eggs. A few feet below the surface, the embryos develop over several months until the determined baby turtles break through the rubbery egg surface and finally one night erupt up through the sand in what is rightly called a boil of tiny, struggling baby turtles to eventually make their way down to the water's edge to be swept out into the immense sea.

This was nest number 11 and was due to hatch just around the time Hurricane Bill was causing unusually high tides on the Carolina coast. Fearing that the nest would be inundated at its most vulnerable point and the fledgling turtles drowned before they ever got started, volunteers moved the nest higher up the beach, next to the first dune. In digging it up, they found some baby turtles all ready to go out on their own, and they released them to the sea. Some others had hatched, but were still covered with the yolk of the egg, which they needed to absorb into their bodies for a day or so, in order to provide their first several weeks of nourishment as they learned how to survive in the ocean.

These the volunteers kept in a tub of sand, releasing them the next day. Other eggs were still unhatched, and it was these that were buried higher up the beach and became the object each night of a vigil of anywhere between 10 and 40 of us on a given night. Perhaps because the nest had been disturbed and the timing thrown off, no boil occurred; but each of four straight nights, one or two or a few more would finally poke up their heads through the sand. Sometimes immediately and sometimes after regaining their strength for an hour or two, they would follow the light provided by the volunteers and head down the long, smooth sand chute prepared for them to loose themselves in the vast ocean. The final night, the last 11 made the 15-minute journey, stopping periodically to lift their little heads, as if listening for the surf from which their mother had come, and thrilling us with their determination and ultimate success.

We knew that some of them were probably eaten by crabs or other predators only minutes into their young lives, adding in their own way to the richness of ocean life. Others will survive for longer periods, but very few will make it to the age of 20 or 30 necessary to help generate future nests of eggs on the same beach where they were born. That is the reason for the large number of eggs and the extraordinary determination built into these turtles: to provide for the continuation of the species.

What an extraordinary experience that was to come so close to one small yet powerful manifestation of the dynamism of the earth and the life cycle! With our hearts we could look at the almost imperceptible movement of the sand indicating the mysterious bursting of life beneath it and think, "In that tiny microcosm is all that you need to know about the dynamic, life-giving, lavish God." With our minds we could realize that this ageless process was far beyond human cause and control and simply stand in awe. But we also grasped that sometimes human cooperation is needed to assist the process; in this case many dedicated volunteers spent time and energy ensuring that this nest of sea turtles had every chance to continue the presence of loggerheads among God's creation.

That is where our role as stewards of God's creation comes in. We did not create life; we cannot control it. We are not the masters of the earth. But we are its stewards, and in grateful and awe-filled response to our Creator, we are to take care of it. Rabbi Heschel went on to say, "It is not a feeling for the mystery of living, or a sense of awe, wonder, or fear, which is the root of religion; but rather the question of *what to do* with the feeling for the mystery of living, what to do with the awe, wonder, or fear. … Wonder," he concludes, "is the state of our being asked."

Let us pray together from the back of your bulletins: *Almighty and everlasting God, you made the universe with all its marvelous order, its atoms, worlds, and galaxies, and the infinite complexity of living creatures: Grant that, as we probe the mysteries of your creation, we may come to know you more truly, and more surely fulfill our role in your eternal purpose; in the name of Jesus Christ our Lord. Amen,*

Psalm 104:1-24

Our Use of Money
The Nineteenth Sunday after Pentecost
October 15, 2006

Today's scripture readings focus on a topic that we do not easily talk about: our use of money. Let's say that phrase together: "Our use of money." Again with more energy: "Our use of money." See? Already we are getting more comfortable talking about it!

Amos, the prophet most known among us for his thunderous call, "Let justice roll down like waters, and righteousness like an ever-rolling stream," a few verses before those words, in today's first lesson strongly condemns those who acquire and retain money by trampling upon the poor and turning aside the needy. "You ... turn justice to wormwood," he warns, "and cast down righteousness to the earth!" "Hate evil and love good," he exhorts, "and establish justice in the gate," i.e. where commerce is done and where the poor come, looking for help. Justice and compassion, Amos implies, are of God and ought to be of more concern to us than our personal financial gain.

In a country and in a world where the gap between the haves and the have nots continues to widen, that ought to concern us. It should grab our attention not just because poverty leads to social and political instability and so to aggression and destruction, but because God created all people to share the resources of the earth and to establish justice by respecting and loving one another. From at least the time of Amos forward, nearly 3,000 years, we human beings have not done that well. Just Thursday night, I was at a fundraising dinner for St. Paul AME honoring Rebecca Clark on her 91st birthday. I first met Mrs. Clark in the 1990s when she traveled with us to Costa Rica for rugged church-building mission trips when she was 82 and again when she was 84! At the banquet, after many well-deserved tributes to this remarkable person, she gave thanks for her full life, while reminiscing about some of the harder times. She worked, for example, as a young adult at the Carolina Inn seven days a week, with only Sunday mornings and Thursday afternoons off (never a full day), week in and week out, for $7 a week. Amos would not have been happy.

Thankfully, many working conditions have improved dramatically over the decades, but far short of leading us to satisfied complacency. The number of Americans living below the poverty line, for example, and without health insurance, and without much hope in the future, is staggering, if most often invisible. Global figures are even worse. In fact throughout the Episcopal Church today, we are encouraged to pray for an end to global poverty and instability and to use the Collect for Peace that you find on the back of your bulletins. Our concern for justice and our compassion for those in need are to arise out of our identity as people of faith and as followers of Jesus.

Jesus also talks about money in our Gospel reading. We, like his disciples, might be amazed at his words, but he has much to teach us. A young man eagerly runs up to Jesus and asks for guidance. Jesus tells him to be honest and treat others justly. When he apparently truthfully declares he is already "there," Jesus looks on him with love and invites him on a deeper journey. "Sell what you have, give to the poor … and come, follow me." But the young man could not, for as Mark tells us, "He had great possessions." That is when Jesus amazes his followers by pointing out how easily our riches get in our way and keep us from following God. His listeners regarded wealth as a sign of God's favor, and we do too, if we think about it. When we prosper, we unconsciously assume we must be doing something right and so be pleasing God. The logical conclusion to that line of thinking, of course, is that the richer we are, the closer to God.

But Jesus taught that the sun shines and the rain falls on the just and the unjust. Wealth in that sense is not a sign of divine favor or disfavor. But our possessions, he warns, can be a stumbling block. The more we have, the more we want, and the more our attention focuses us away from God to ourselves. A reporter once asked J. Paul Getty how much was enough. The billionaire replied, "Enough is always a little more than I've already got." That is human nature for all of us, no matter how little or how much we have. We get pulled along, often at the expense of others and of our own souls.

But Jesus invites us to freedom. Come follow me, he says. Do not be so focused on what you will eat or what you will wear. Follow me on the adventure of a spiritual journey. Do not be content with even the security of just following the rules. Follow me in relationship, letting other things be secondary. The rich young man could not do that. He was too satisfied to move further.

I came across an image that may be helpful here, from the personal writings of Leo Tolstoy. See if it speaks to you. A man who is satisfied simply following the law, he wrote, "is like someone standing in the light of a lantern fixed to a post. It is light all around him, but there is nowhere further for him to walk." But a man trying to follow Christ, he declared, "is like a man carrying a lantern before him on a long, or not so long, pole: the light is in front of him, always lighting up fresh ground and always encouraging him to walk further." That is what Jesus calls the rich young man to; that is the adventurous journey to which Jesus invites us. Do not be satisfied with the safety of accumulating and securing your space around the pole, he urges. Be generous with what you have been given and be concerned for others and come follow me on the way.

That call is not simply to each of us individually, of course, but to all of us as a parish, as the Church. Our ministry is to be outward, especially to those to whom Amos calls our attention. The Heifer Project and Project 5000 and our hospitality to our Burmese refugee families are current manifestations of that focus, as is our work on the budget for next year. This year through our fruitful Annual Giving Campaign, we were able to increase the percentage of money going beyond the parish from 18.5 percent to 21.5 percent, or an increase of about $80,000. When each of us responds generously to Jesus' invitation to freedom through commitment, we can all respond more faithfully and more effectively together.

Today we begin our Annual Giving Campaign for 2007. As participants at the Chapel of the Cross, each of us is asked and expected to pledge for next year an increasing percentage of our income to God through the ministry of the parish, stretching toward the tithe as a goal. If you have not received a packet in the mail, more are available on the back table. On November 26, the Sunday after Thanksgiving, Ingathering Sunday, we will offer all the pledges received at the altar. I commend to you this opportunity for each of us as individuals and all of us as a parish to grow in sharing what we have been given, in showing our concern for others in need, and to walk further in following Jesus on the way.

Amos 5:6-7, 10-15; Mark 10:17-31

Baptism with The Rt. Rev. Michael Curry,
bishop of the Diocese of North Carolina

Ascribe to the Lord
The Fourth Sunday of the Creation Cycle
The Twentieth Sunday after Pentecost
October 10, 2010

*Ascribe to the Lord the honor due his Name; bring offerings and
come into his courts.*

For the second consecutive year this fall, we have been engaging in a
liturgical creation cycle, reminding ourselves of the abundance of God's
dynamic and freely given creation and of our response to this lavish,
loving giving. In our scripture readings and our music and our prayers,
we have been acknowledging the God who made us and bestowed upon
us all good things, and we have been asking for the grace to be good
and grateful stewards of all that God has entrusted to us. As we prayed
last week, "For the beauty and wonder of your creation, in earth and
sky and sea, we thank you, Lord. ... For our daily food and drink, our
homes and families, and our friends, we thank you, Lord. For minds
to think, and hearts to love, and hands to serve, we thank you, Lord"
(p.837).

Jesus teaches us the importance of this gratitude in today's Gospel
reading. Ten human beings, but not really treated as human beings by
society, banded together in their misery and in their despair. As lepers,
they were required to live apart and even to warn others away who
might unwittingly stray too close to them. It was an alienating and
seemingly Godforsaken existence for them. Even in the extremely rare
instance of a cure, lepers had to be inspected and certified by the priests
before reentering society and assuming their longed-for normal life.

When these desperate outcasts pleaded with Jesus for help, he sent them
to the priests to begin this process. To their credit, they set out on this
faith journey, knowing they were not healed but unsure of what might
happen. When the scourge that had turned their lives upside down
was miraculously lifted from them on their way, their understandable
preoccupation was to continue on to the priests and reclaim their

former lives — their families, their homes, their work, their friends. They all ignored the *source* of their new life and health and rushed on single-mindedly — all, that is, except one.

One of the foreigners among them, a Samaritan — an immigrant, if you will — could not ignore the gratitude he felt welling up in him. He "turned back, praising God with a loud voice; and he fell on his face at Jesus' feet, giving him thanks." Jesus admired his grateful spirit, and he sent him on his way saying, "Your faith has made you well." There is no implication in these words that the other nine were not permanently made well, that they suffered for their ingratitude by being re-inflicted with leprosy. They were all healed, and God's gifts are not given so capriciously or conditionally. Jesus is simply stating here that in listening to his soul, this child of God was restored to health not only in body but also in his spirit. "Your faith has made you (fully) well."

If we listen to that same prompting of the Spirit within us, our faith will also make us well. If we allow that welling up of gratitude for all that God daily bestows upon us to express itself in our lives, we will also come to that spiritual wholeness. If we recognize ourselves to be the receivers of all that we have and are and make room in our lives for expressing our praise and gratitude to God, we will be filled with even more of God's life-giving grace and love. That is the model Jesus holds up to us in this once-pitiful leprous foreigner, whose life was completely transformed by his encounter with Jesus and who has been remembered by countless generations as a model of faith and gratitude.

Most of you are aware through mailings and announcements and emails that we have begun this fall not only our annual financial stewardship campaign, but also a long-planned, much needed capital campaign called "A Light on the Hill: Building to Serve." In thinking about this sermon today, I had thought of ways to lay out the need, to make the case for the urgency both of fully funding our expanding annual budget and of adding to and upgrading our aging and increasingly inadequate buildings. I could do that with complete conviction and passionate sincerity. I am fully committed to the ministry of this parish, and I am completely convinced of the wisdom and necessity both of our anticipated annual budget and of our long and carefully worked-out vision for transforming the facilities needed for our present and future ministry. In fact, I and others have already articulated that urgent case in information both sent to you and available on the web site: two letters, an informative brochure, reprints of articles, even a powerful video vividly portraying where we are and where we need to be. I hope and trust that you are digesting all of this and reflecting thoughtfully on what your participation can and should be.

So for today then, in the context of our creation cycle and of our assigned scripture, rather than repeat the case, let me simply make these five observations, which are the spiritual basis of what we are doing together:

An essential part of our spiritual journey with God to wholeness and the full life Jesus came to bring us is gratitude. Like the leper, we are to realize that everything is God's gracious gift to us, and we are to turn back, before all our other preoccupations and responsibilities, and give great thanks to God.

A key opportunity for us to give genuine expression to that gratitude is to give back to God a generous portion of all that we have received. "Ascribe to the Lord," our psalm instructs us, "the honor due his Name; bring offerings and come into his courts."

As members of this worshipping community called the Chapel of the Cross, together we have a significant opportunity to pool our grateful giving, not only to support our many vital ministries in the coming year, but also to strengthen and ensure those ministries for generations to come.

Both for our spiritual health and wholeness then, and for the sake of our common ministries, which flow from our worship of God here in the beauty of holiness, each of us and all of us should participate in this joint annual/capital campaign, pledging to give back to God according to the means with which God has blessed us.

If all of us do our part, we will not only move powerfully forward in utilizing the resources needed to carry out the historic and dynamic ministry of the Chapel of the Cross, but we will in fact become that grateful, generous community that can be a light on this hill to others. The spiritual health we grow into together will radiate well beyond these walls, and God's grace will work in mysterious ways undreamed of by us.

Glory to God whose power, working in us, can do infinitely more than we can ask or imagine: Glory to him from generation to generation in the Church, and in Christ Jesus for ever and ever. Amen.

Psalm 96; Luke 17:11-19

A Theology of Money
The Twentieth Sunday after Pentecost
October 25, 1987

The big news of this week has been the wild fluctuations in the stock market. The plunging, then seesawing Dow Jones industrial average has caused major ripples around the world: affecting countries' relationships with one another, changing the fortunes of various political candidates, and no doubt causing great anxiety for Every Member Canvass chairmen everywhere!

We do not have to look further than this present trauma (and perhaps how it has affected us personally) to realize how central money is to our lives, how utterly we depend on it, and how thoroughly preoccupied with it we are. I do not say this as a matter of judgment, but simply as a statement of fact. There is nothing which occupies our consciousness more, nothing which comes closer to "where we really live," than money and what it will bring us.

To some extent, that is only how it should be. Most of us are or will be responsible for ourselves and perhaps others. The struggle for financial security, a reasonable share of this world's goods and all that implies of plain survival, status, comfort, and the ability to do some of the things we want to do, are all legitimate human concerns and worthy of our best efforts.

However, connected with all this, if we are honest enough to admit it to ourselves, is also a great deal of anxiety and tension and fear. Trying to hold onto or increase what we have becomes a kind of web, imprisoning us and severely limiting our perspective, enslaving us. Jesus has told us "You cannot serve God and mammon."

Instinctively, we know that is true; but existentially, we find ourselves paying more attention to mammon. How can we find a way out of this burdensome contradiction? How can we truly serve God without exempting ourselves from our financial responsibilities?

Perhaps an old Peanuts cartoon strip can give us a clue: Linus and Lucy are in the house looking out the window in a heavy rain storm. Lucy says, "Boy, look at it rain. What if it floods the whole world?" To which Linus replies, "It will never do that. In the ninth chapter of Genesis, God promised Noah that would never happen again, and the sign of the promise is the rainbow." Lucy is reassured and smiles, saying, "You've taken a great load off my mind." To which Linus replies, "Sound theology has a way of doing that."

Sound theology does indeed have a way of doing that, and I would suggest that most of our anxiety and tension that focus on our finances, stems from the lack of a sound theology concerning money. What I propose to help us develop this morning is a theology of money.

What is it about money that makes it such a powerful force? Ever since money was developed in some form, where it could be saved, the accumulation of money has been a strong interest for most people and a consuming hunger in others.

Money brings with it many things. It not only defines our ability to buy goods and services, and therefore our capacity to shape our lives in the way that we want, but it also touches very deeply on primary elements of personality. Money seems to have the power to confer upon us a sense of self worth, or to deprive us of it. The difference between the standing of different individuals in the community may be entirely based on their money. Money, or the lack of it, can give us or deny us a sense of personal power or a sense of power over other people.

Indeed, money has a great influence over personal relationships. How many times have we heard these sentiments, learned from experience, ruefully expressed, "Never borrow money from (or lend money to) a friend, or you will lose a friend"?

It may or may not be surprising to you, that Jesus understood, as well as anyone who ever lived, the complex relationship of a person with his or her money and its powerful potential for good or ill. In fact, he was so convinced of the significance of the relationship between a person and his or her material possessions for deepening or destroying one's relationship with God and one's neighbor that, as the New Testament records it, he spoke more about that one subject than any other. Fully one-sixth of all the words of Jesus in the New Testament, and over one-third of all Jesus' parables are devoted to it. That comes as a shock to most of us, but consider just these few well known examples: the parable of Lazarus and the rich man who was blind to Lazarus' need (Luke 16:19-31); the parable of the rich farmer who could think of nothing else to do with his wealth than to tear down his old barns and build bigger ones (Luke 12:15-21); the teaching of Jesus about not being anxious concerning our food and our clothes (Matthew 6:19-34); the story of the widow's mite (Mark 12:41-44).

The perception that the manner in which a person uses his or her money and possessions touches centrally on one's relationship to God did not originate with Jesus. It is a common theme in the Old Testament as well. The prophet Amos, for example, speaks of how God's judgment will fall on those who selfishly earn and spend money and allow it to be valued ahead of their worship and before God (Amos 8:4-8). In our Old Testament reading today, from the book of Exodus, a creditor is reminded that, even if he takes another's garment in pledge of payment for a debt, he is to return it to him every evening that he may sleep warmly. (Exodus 22:21-27)

In fact, the very first sentence of the Bible lays down the principle upon which a Judaeo-Christian theology of money is to be based: "In the beginning God created the heavens and the earth." The theme of God's ownership (through creating) of all that is, and of human trusteeship (through receiving it all from God) is a strong, recurring biblical theme. The writer of the book of Deuteronomy, in a passage always read in our liturgy at Thanksgiving, picks up this theme. After listing many human accomplishments, such as building houses, raising herds and flocks, and accumulating money, he then warns his readers, "Beware lest you say in your heart, 'My power, and the might of my hand has given me this wealth.' You shall remember the Lord your God, for it is he who gives you power to get wealth." (8:18)

The first book of the Chronicles powerfully illustrates the same truth. David, near the end of his reign, proclaimed a day of offering for the

Temple of God. The text describes at length how first David and then the head of every household came forward and made their offerings. When all had been given, David addressed this prayer to God: "But who am I, and what is my people, that we should be able thus to offer willingly? For all things come from thee, and of thy own have we given thee. ... O Lord our God, all this abundance that we have provided for building thee a house for thy holy name comes from thy hand and is thy own." (29:1-16)

Jesus develops this same theme in a number of parables. One we heard read as the Gospel some weeks ago is the parable of the laborers in the vineyard (Matthew 20:1-16), the one in which those who worked only the last hour were paid the same as those who worked all day. This story illustrates that God is a giver of gifts far beyond our capacity to earn them. The householder's words, "Am I not allowed to do what I choose with what belongs to me?" proclaim not only God's ownership, but also God's desire to give to us freely and lovingly.

Another parable we heard recently, the parable of the tenants (Mark 12:1-12), who rejected and killed those sent by the owner to collect the fruit, also suggests that whatever human beings have, they have because it has been given to them at the hand of God. And from the gift, a return is expected.

A third parable, which we will hear proclaimed in a few weeks, is even more explicit. In the parable of the talents in which three individuals either use the talents they have been given to earn more or bury them (Matthew 25:14-30), Jesus is saying that whatever we possess (whether money, skills, opportunities, education, or life itself), we possess because it has been given to us by God. We have nothing that was not given to us. Out of a sense of justice, and indeed from a sense of gratitude, we are to give God a return on his gift.

The idea that we have nothing that was not given to us is one that we can perhaps accept intellectually, since scripture is so clear about it. But truly acknowledging it in our hearts, so that our gratitude to God is authentic, is another step. After all, we have worked hard and earned what we have. How can we feel grateful for what is rightfully ours? Perhaps the following illustrations will help.

Not many years ago, an agricultural school in Iowa undertook a study which showed that the production of 100 bushels of corn from one acre of land, in addition to the many hours of the farmer's labor, required 4,000,000 pounds of water, 6,800 pounds of oxygen, 5,200 pounds of carbon, 60 pounds of nitrogen, 125 pounds of potassium, 75 pounds of yellow sulphur, and other elements too numerous to mention. In addition, rain and sunshine at the right times were critical. It was estimated that only 5 percent of the produce of a farm can be attributed to human efforts.

That example can serve as a metaphor for any other human endeavor. In getting an education, for example, it takes the ideas of those who have gone before us, textbooks and teachers and buildings and all the institutional components necessary, good health and time to reflect and study, the support of family and friends, etc., in addition to our 5 percent human effort. That is not to say that our 5 percent is not essential or not something to be proud of. Quite the contrary. But it is to say that any "Look what I have done" statement is incomplete until it becomes "Look what I have done with what God has given me and with God's help."

A final illustration makes the point in another way. Some years ago, a Louisiana law firm was asked to undertake a title search for some property in New Orleans. They successfully traced the title back to the Louisiana Purchase in 1803. But their clients were not satisfied with that. So, the search went on. Finally, the law firm sent the following letter to their clients:

Gentlemen: Please be advised that in the year 1803, the United States of America acquired the territory of Louisiana from the Republic of France, by purchase. The Republic of France, in turn, acquired title from the Spanish Crown by conquest; the Spanish Crown having obtained it by virtue of the discoveries of one Christopher Columbus, who had been authorized to undertake his voyage by Isabella, Queen of Spain, who obtained sanction for the journey from the Pope, the Vicar of Christ, who is the Son and Heir of Almighty God, who made Louisiana.

What we are accustomed to call our own is not really ours; it is God's. What we do is hold it for a time, use it, give God a return on it, and then pass it on. Any other perception is self-deceiving. What then have we developed in the way of a theology of money? It can be summarized in four points:

Money, the earning of it and the spending of it, has always been one of the major preoccupations of people in all ages, including our own.

Jesus, and the prophets before him, understood the implications of this better than we do and, over and over again, spoke to the potential spiritual good or ill that rises out of our relationship to our money.

The message of both Old and New Testaments about our money is the powerful but simple reminder that God is the owner and the bountiful giver of all that we have and are, and we are recipients of these great gifts.

In the recognition and acceptance of this basic fact, we can understand and come into a relationship with this generous God of love through our giving, motivated by our thanksgiving for these unearned gifts from God's hands.

Those of you who are on the mailing list should have received by now the information for the Every Member Canvass, along with an invitation to an area gathering and a request to return your pledge card at one of the services three weeks from today, on November 15. I intend to say more about this whole matter — not next Sunday, which is All Saints' Day, but two weeks from today, November 8, I will preach on the question, "Why Should I Give to God Through the Church?" On Ingathering Sunday itself, November 15, I will preach on "The Joy of Giving."

But sufficient for the day is the sound theology thereof ...

Let us pray. Open, O Lord, the eyes of all people to behold thy gracious hand in all thy works, that, rejoicing in thy whole creation, they may honor thee with their substance, and be faithful stewards of thy bounty. Amen.

One Communion and One Fellowship
All Saints Day
November 1, 2002

When you came to the church this evening, you passed by the yard in front of the chapel where ashes of parishioners are buried. In the nearly 25 years we have been committing "earth to earth, ashes to ashes, dust to dust" here on our grounds, we have done so now for over 200 people. Their spirits are not confined here, of course, only their physical remains, along with their names, preserved in stone on the church wall. But I often feel their presence and their witness and their beckoning us forward on our spiritual paths. They serve as reminders of our destination and fulfillment, of our final incorporation into the communion of saints, into the "great multitude which no man could number, from every nation, from all tribes and peoples and tongues," who stand before the throne of God "lost in wonder, love, and praise."

In a society where individualism is so highly prized, the communion of saints reminds us that we are created for union. In her novel *My Antonia*, Willa Cather says through one of her characters, "That is happiness; to be dissolved into something complete and great." Death is that final dissolution, that being "knit together," as today's collect puts it, "in one communion and fellowship in the mystical body ... of Christ our Lord." At death, as in birth, we both gain and lose; but in the process we become what God creates us to be: first an individual, and then knit together, dissolved, into something complete and great.

We do not have to wait until death, however, to be connected to that one communion and fellowship, which we celebrate on All Saints Day. Through our baptism we are already part of the Body of Christ; we are already being dissolved into something complete and great. We are already dying to the old self and rising to the new self. We are already decreasing that Christ may increase. We are already losing our life that we might find it. We are already gathering before the throne of God and falling on our faces and worshipping God, saying, "AMEN! Blessing and glory and wisdom and thanksgiving and honor and power and might be to our God for ever and ever! Amen."

That being caught up into and surrounded and supported by "this fellowship of love and prayer" is not an awareness we regularly maintain in our consciousness. The limitations of this life and our individual finitude block our vision of this mystery and present to us the apparent reality that we are alone, disconnected, isolated. Do not believe it. Darkness obscures our perception of reality; it does not change that reality. It is the infrequent lightning flash of illumination or the sometime steady stream of the sunshine of God's grace that reveals our true connectedness.

An occasion such as this glorious feast of All Saints can act like a bolt of lightning in our dark night of belief. The scripture, the music, the attentive congregation, the dignity of the liturgy, the communion, may suddenly reveal to us the awesome reality of the great cloud of witnesses and our deep relationship to that mystery. But outside in the darkness again, it may all seem like fantasy. Believe what is shown to you in the light. Accept the mystery God's grace reveals.

As you come forward for Holy Communion this evening, that age-old sacramental rite in which God is dissolved into us so that we might further be dissolved into something complete and great, receive it thankfully as a present grace and as a promise of union to come. As you depart the church tonight and are sent forth in the name of Christ, be supported and strengthened not only by the more than 200 souls whose ashes are buried there, but by the whole cloud of witnesses throughout the centuries. While "we feebly struggle, they in glory shine; yet all are one in thee [O God], for all are thine." Let the God who longs for your surrender enfold you and shelter you with his presence and give you strength for your path ahead. Not only in your words but in your lives, fall down before God and proclaim with one voice, "AMEN! Blessing and glory and wisdom and thanksgiving and honor and power and might be to our God for ever and ever! Amen."

Entrusted with Great Wealth
The Twenty-Third Sunday after Pentecost
November 16, 2014

On these last few Sundays of the liturgical year, the Gospel readings each proclaim a parable of Jesus, i.e. a contrived story that makes a central point. Not surprisingly, since the end of the liturgical year focuses on the end of time and Jesus' second coming (as you heard in the other readings), these parables speak to us about those end times.

Next week's well-known story of the separation of the sheep and the goats suggests a final accountability for all human beings and declares the criterion of that accountability to be the acts of mercy we do or do not do to "one of the least" of our King's brethren.

The story today, the parable of the talents, also stresses the final accounting "that we must all one day give." It indicates, however, a slightly different criterion: Depending on how we use what we have been given, we will either "enter into the joy of [our] master," i.e., enjoy intimacy with God — the fulfillment of that longing created deep within us, or forever weep and gnash our teeth.

That is pretty strong stuff and very puzzling. How does that radical abyss between sheer ecstasy or abject misery make any sense? Why should the man with one talent, who after all does not steal from his master but returns his property safe to him, deserve such a consequence? What are the theological assumptions of the parable that make that a legitimate conclusion of Jesus' story? I suggest there are three such principles, all very important to living out a truly Christian life.

The first tenet of the parable is that the master, i.e., God, gives to his servants everything they have. He "entrusted to them his [not their] property." It starts out God's and it ends up God's. In between, others use this divine property, but it is only on loan.

As Harold Bosley, an American Methodist preacher, put it, "The whole earth belongs to God. Life belongs to God. The use we make of our life as we live from day to day is a use that is paraded as on a stage before God Himself. Our bodies, our minds, our spirits, our relationships, everything we are pleased in a moment of absent-mindedness to call our own actually belongs to God."

It belongs to God, but God generously gives it to us — all of what we see and experience. God does not give it equally to all — to one he gives five talents and to another two and to another one — but, and here is the second theological assumption, God gives something of enormous worth to each one of us. The talent, a coin purposely utilized in the parable, was of great value — about 6,000 denarii, or 15 years' wages to a laborer! By today's standards, one talent would approach a half a million dollars. The point is that the life with which God entrusts us, and our ability to do and to create and to love, are staggering gifts that should surprise us into utilizing them boldly.

Leslie Weatherhead, a gifted English preacher, in commenting on this parable, said, "If I tried in the language of today to express one of the great truths of the parable in a sentence, it would be this: Your ability is God's treasure. It was his in the beginning. We sometimes say such ability is a gift. It is, in a sense. In a truer sense, it is an investment. God has invested in you. And, like all investors, he looks for a return. What dividend does he get from you? His wealth is anything that furthers his kingdom. Therefore, all those gifts that you have — and there is no one without talents, and there are many with more than they dreamed — are to further his kingdom and increase his wealth by a faithful employment of them all."

That is the third theological teaching of the Gospel story: that God invests enormously in us, expecting a return. Not a return of exactly what we have been given, unused and unharmed; but with our boldly utilizing what has been entrusted to us, a return of it to God increased in value.

That is our challenge as servants. That is what Jesus, through telling the parable, would have us do. That is why the one servant did not fare so well in his reckoning with his master: he refused to respond to that challenge. He chose instead to bury his treasure in the ground, and in so doing he buried himself.

We face the same temptation. Like the man who received one talent, we can undervalue the enormous wealth that is entrusted to us, comparing it to that of others. Phillips Brooks, the eloquent Episcopal preacher of the 19th century, characterized those who do so as "crushed and enfeebled by a sense of their own [in]significance [so] ... that any attainment really worth attaining is totally out of their reach."

He goes on to give this example: "A man is deeply conscious of the misery that is in this world. He tries to help it, but when he sees how little he can do, how big the bulk of wretchedness is against which his poor effort at relief is found, it seems to him so utterly not worth his while that he lets it all go, and sinks back into the prudent merchant or the self-indulgent philosopher, looking on at woes that he no longer tries to help."

How many times have we done the same? How often have we failed to say the encouraging word or the thoughtful reflection that someone needed to hear because we underestimated the difference we might make? How frequently have we refrained from volunteering for a task because we thought another more qualified should step forward? How many times have we held back from trying something significant because of our fear of failure? How often have we not joined in a communal effort to help those in need because we thought our small part did not make any difference? How often have we been held back from giving generously of our resources because we were afraid we might run out?

"Too many times," we can all respond. Like the servant in the parable, we confess to God, "I was afraid, and I went and hid your talent in the ground."

But Jesus' story urges us beyond that fear. He encourages us to think of all that we have and are as God's gift, God's investment. He urges us to recognize that it is the wish of the donor that we *risk* our valuable treasure — our selves, our lives, our abilities, our financial resources

— for the short time that we have it, by using it for the good of our master, its real owner.

In so doing, we will fulfill our true roles as servants. By refusing to devalue what we have been given, we will appropriately live out our gratitude. By courageously developing and sharing our God-given resources, we will give back as we have been given. In boldly utilizing what has been entrusted to us, we will hear God say, "Well done, good and faithful servant. … Enter into the joy of your master."

Matthew 25:14-30

Much Obliged, Dear Lord
Thanksgiving Day Ecumenical Service, Chapel Hill Bible Church
November 23, 1989

Today's second lesson, acted out for us in dramatic fashion, is a story about ostracism and healing and gratitude.

The 10 lepers, who stood at a distance and lifted up their voices asking Jesus' mercy, are the ostracized ones. This separation was the practice of the day. Leviticus 13:45-6 says, "The leper who has the disease shall wear torn clothes and let the hair of his head hang loose, and he shall cover his upper lip and cry, 'Unclean, unclean.' He shall remain unclean as long as he has the disease; he shall dwell alone in the habitation outside the camp."

That may not be shocking to us, happening so long ago. I was astonished, however, to read recently that there is still one leper colony left in the world, in Carville, Louisiana. The ostracism from society has been so complete over the years that tombstones there carry only numbers, or for some special people, first names. One woman, now 82, was left there at the age of 21 by her father, whom she never saw again. The letters she sent him, begging to see him again before she went blind, were sterilized and went unanswered.

If present-day lepers still seem a distant image of ostracism, we have only to think of those who today suffer from AIDS. Our fears about this disease and the moral implications attached to it serve to effectively isolate those who suffer from it, in physical and psychological ways. Each of us has read horror stories about the mistreatment of even children afflicted with this fatal disease. The recent failure to establish an AIDS House in a local neighborhood, one of a series of "not in my backyard" episodes in our community, points to this ostracism.

It is this same kind of painful situation, where outcasts are reduced to standing at a distance and pleading for help, into which Jesus walked in today's lesson. He told the 10 lepers to go show themselves to the priests, who according to law had to purify former lepers and declare them clean that they might re-enter society (Lev. 14:2-32). Even though the 10 were still leprous, and so had no reason to show themselves to the priests, they went; and on their 'faith journey' they were cleansed.

What a moment that must have been for them! To feel the disease which had plagued them and made them outcasts lose its hold on them and disappear. To see their source of shame vanish. To feel whole and fully alive again.

All of them were cured and, no doubt, all were overcome with joy. But only one was healed; only one returned "praising God with a loud voice, and [he] fell on his face at Jesus' feet, giving him thanks." Only one went beyond the amazing gift, to the even more amazing Giver. What is it that allowed this response? On this Thanksgiving Day, let us look at what characterizes those who give thanks.

The essence of those who are grateful is that they realize their own unworthiness. They see all things as given to them despite their having done nothing to deserve it. They claim nothing for themselves, but receive everything as gift with joyful and thankful hearts.

The human tendency is just the opposite. We are convinced of our worthiness. We think of things as ours, earned and deserved by us. We are sure that we have earned our money, our reputation, our place in society, our families; that we deserve our food, our friends, our health. We are like the bartender in the "Eek and Meek" comic strip who, when asked by one of his customers, "How is life treating you?" responded cryptically, "It's not. I pay my way."

The truth, of course, is that everything we have to "pay with" has been given to us. We came into this world (by benevolent invitation) with nothing; we go out taking nothing with us; and in between we use all that has been freely given us. In the reading from Deuteronomy this morning, we heard those very striking words, "Beware lest you say in your heart, 'My power and the might of my hand have gotten me this wealth.' You shall remember the Lord your God, for it is he who gives you power to get wealth." Even our capability to use well the gifts God has given us, the talent and the resources and the opportunities to make the most of our abilities, is God's gift to us.

Thus it is the grateful person who is, in the deepest sense of the word, religious, who can see the Divine in all things, who worships God in spirit and in truth.

J.B. Mozley, Regius Professor of Divinity at Oxford over a century ago, in preaching on gratitude, declared, "The grateful spirit alone believes, because it alone acknowledges the source of its life and being. The grateful spirit alone finds out God; to it alone God reveals himself. It alone discovers its gracious Maker in its own faculties, its own perceptions, its own capacities of happiness: and with the grateful one out of ten, it falls down before Him, giving Him thanks."

Fulton Ousler told a true story that I would like to share with you, of an old woman he had known, who had been born into slavery on the Eastern Shore of Maryland. Her former master had thought it a great joke to christen her Anna Maria Cecily Sophia Virginia Avalon Thessalonians.

Ousler remembered eating with Anna as she sat in his home with her hard old black hands folded, praying, "Much obliged, dear Lord, for my vittles."

"But Anna," he pointed out, "you'd get your vittles whether you thanked the Lord or not."

"Sure," she responded, "but it makes everything taste better to be thankful.

"You know," she went on, "it's a funny thing about being thankful; it's a game an old preacher taught me to play. It's looking for things to be thankful for. You don't know how many of them you pass right by, unless you go looking for them. Take this morning for instance. I wake up and I lay there wondering what I got to be thankful for now. With my husband dead and having to work every day I can't think of anything. What must the good Lord think of me, His child? But the honest truth is I just can't think of a thing to thank him for. And then what do you think? My daughter comes and opens the bedroom door, so from the kitchen comes the smell of coffee. Much obliged, dear Lord, for the coffee and a daughter to have it ready for an old woman when she wakes up.

"Now for a while I have to do housework. It's hard to find anything to thank God for in housework. But when I come to the mantelpiece to dust, there is Little Boy Blue. I've had that little china boy for many years. I was a slave when I got it as my one Christmas present. I love that little boy. Much obliged, dear Lord, for Little Boy Blue.

"And almost everything I dust reminds me of something. Even the pictures that hang on our cracked, unpainted wall. It's like a visit with my family who have all left this world. They look at me and I look at them and there are so many happy things to remember. Much obliged, dear Lord, for my memory. And then I go for a walk down town to buy a loaf of bread and cheese for our dinner. I look in all the windows, so many pretty things."

Fulton Ousler broke in, "But Anna, you can't buy them, you have no money."

"Oh, but I can play — play dolls. I think of your ma and sister how they would look in those dresses and I have a lot of fun. Much obliged dear Lord for playing in my mind, it's a kind of happiness.

"Just like once I got caught in the rain," she said. "It was fun for me. I've always heard about people's shower baths; I've never had one, but now I have one. You know God is just giving heaven away to people all day long. I've been to the park and seen the gardens but you know what I like? The old bush in my back yard by the railroad track, but better. One rose will fill you with all the sweetness you can stand."

Ousler ended his story with these words. "The soul of long dead Anna was a big soul, big enough to see God everywhere and she taught me a great deal about life; for I will never forget when word came to me from the dingy street where she lived, that Anna was dying. I remember driving in a cab and standing by her bedside; she was in deep pain and her hard old hands were knotted together in a desperate clutch. Poor old woman, what had she to be thankful for now? She opened her eyes and looked at me. 'Much obliged, dear Lord, for such fine friends.' She never spoke again, except in my heart but she speaks to me every day there and I'm obliged, dear Lord, for that."

That is much more than a powerful "Pollyanna story." Anna was not simply an optimist, who, no matter what, could look on the bright side of things. She was, in Ousler's words, "a big soul, big enough to see God everywhere." She was a grateful spirit, one who had a deep sense of all of life as God's gift to us. Demanding nothing as her due, she received gratefully all that she was given, and, like the one of the 10 lepers, "praised God with a loud voice … giving him thanks."

We are called to be grateful people. No less than the 10 lepers, we have received life and healing and freedom from God. No less than Anna, God is giving heaven away to us all day long. No less than our ancestors in the faith who first heard the words of Deuteronomy, we are to bless the Lord our God for all that he has given us.

And if our gratitude is sincere, it will express itself, not only in our prayers and in our worship, but also in our continual generosity with others, in our compassion for those who are in need, and in our intolerance for injustice and any form of ostracism of any of God's children. We will see our money not as something to accumulate and store up for ourselves, but as an invaluable opportunity to share with those in need. We will look on our time not as something to be used merely personally, but as a means to serve those who need us. We will regard our neighborhoods not simply as areas to be protected, but as places where we can welcome all our fellow receivers.

On this Thanksgiving Day, when we emphasize in a special way the attitude and the posture that is to characterize us as we live out each day of the lives that are given to us, let us ask God for one more gift: the gift of grateful hearts. As we pray and sing together, and as we share our Thanksgiving meal with friends and family, let us petition God to open our hearts to see the gift in all that surrounds us. Let us pray that we might always say, both with our lips and in our lives, "Much obliged, dear Lord, for all that you give us." Amen.

*Peter, Stephen and Tyler sing "Brown Eyed Girl" to
Betsy at the Sweet Potato Ball, 2015*

III

The Chances and
Changes of This Life

God At Work in Our Lives
The Sixth Sunday after Pentecost
July 3, 1988

The readings for this morning have had special meaning for me for some years now. You know that our lectionary assigns specific readings for each Sunday on a three-year cycle. These are the ones for Year B, Proper 9, "The Sunday closest to July 6." Six years ago, when they were read on July 4, 1982, that happened to be the first Sunday that I had ever been to the Chapel of the Cross. Betsy and I had flown in from Seattle for some vacation with her parents in Durham, and for me to interview for the vacant associate for parish ministry position here. In preparation for that interview, to see what the Chapel of the Cross was like, we came, incognito, to the 10 o'clock service and heard these readings.

When the readings came up again, it was July 7, 1985, my first opportunity to preach as your rector. I tried very hard at that time to refute any providential inference that I, too, might be a prophet without honor in his own country; and I certainly refused making any connection between the Chapel of the Cross and those to whom Ezekiel was sent in the first reading, whom the Lord characterized as an "impudent and stubborn" people!

But these readings are important to me, not only because of the special historical circumstances surrounding their proclamation, but also because of the very contents themselves.

A number of important theological themes emerge from these readings, deep truths about God and us upon which we must reflect and to which we should assent in faith.

The first is that God speaks to us. Ezekiel says, "The Lord said to me, 'Son of man, stand upon your feet, and I will speak with you.' And when he spoke to me, the Spirit entered into me and set me upon my feet; and I heard him speaking to me."

Paul says in the second reading, "I know a man in Christ who fourteen years ago was caught up to the third heaven — whether in the body or out of the body I do not know, God knows ... and he heard things that cannot be told, which man may not utter."

Both Ezekiel and Paul had direct encounters with God; they heard God speaking to them in some way. While their experiences of God were unique, I do not believe they are uncommon. I believe that God speaks to all of us, to each of us, with some frequency. For the most part, however, we are only prepared to believe that God spoke to exceptional people in Biblical times, and we do not hear him. I can attest to you that God has spoken to me in my life, about which I want to share more with you in a moment.

Another profound truth that emerges from today's lessons is that God guides us in our lives. He sent Ezekiel to the people of Israel to be a prophet to them. He was to speak God's word to them whether they heard or refused to hear. Our own callings may seem less dramatic or less clear-cut. But God works out his purpose with us just the same. Sometimes in obvious ways and sometimes in less obvious, God guides us and guides our lives.

A third theme proclaimed to us by today's readings is that God is the real strength of our lives and not we ourselves. We struggle with our weaknesses, we hide them or deny them, we let them discourage us and drag us down, as if they are what really matter. Even Paul did not understand. Three times he besought the Lord to rid him of his weakness, but God said to him, "My grace is sufficient for you, for my power is made perfect in weakness." In some real way, our strength, our performance, is not what counts, or is even what is real. Rather, it is God who labors in us, who at the very point of our failures, meets us and lifts us up and strengthens us.

These mysteries, these deep theological truths, are not mere abstractions for me, but powerful expressions of the God at work in our lives. They are scriptural confirmation and articulation of God's presence and activity as I have experienced it in my own life.

Ten days ago, I was spending some time with my good friend and long-time parishioner, Dr. Jimmy Taylor, in his hospital room the night before his surgery. He was asking me how I came to be in the Episcopal Church and how I had come to the Chapel of the Cross. As I was telling him the story, I began to realize that, with the exception of interviews with the Vestry and some conversations with individuals, in six years I had never really shared my story with the parish as a whole. That incident and the timing of this week's readings, special both for their circumstantial connections and for their contents, have led me to think that it would be appropriate to do so now. I certainly do not believe that God works any more in my life than in yours. But perhaps hearing my story will help you to recognize God in your own.

Many of you know that I was ordained a Roman Catholic priest, a Jesuit, in the mid-1970s. I was basically happy, living and ministering in Seattle, although I had begun to realize that I had never embraced or truly chosen the celibacy that went along with priesthood, but had merely endured it as a mandatory obligation. That realization was dramatically sharpened when I met Betsy Elkins, and after a time I was faced with the dilemma of two seemingly contradictory calls from God: One to priesthood and one to married life. I, we, agonized over that for a while, and finally through the gift of several powerful prayer experiences, not unlike what Paul described in today's Epistle, I came to complete peace and joy in the conviction that God was calling us to be married. In an unexplainable but undeniable way, God simply removed all the guilt, uncertainty, and fear of the future that I felt, and said, "Go."

After I resigned from active priestly ministry in 1978, we responded to a classified ad in the newspaper for a youth minister, and found that it was for an Episcopal church. We were employed there on a half-time basis as the youth ministers for a grand salary of $500 a month!

Within a few months, I was hired on full time to replace the assistant, who had moved on. I was licensed to preach by the Bishop, and we taught the Youth Confirmation Class, even though we did not become Episcopalians until we were confirmed with our second class!

At that point, I applied to be received as an Episcopal priest, and after two years of interviews and red tape, but thankfully not having to go back to seminary, I was officially received as a priest in late May of 1982.

Shortly thereafter, we heard about the need of an associate at the Chapel of the Cross in Chapel Hill, in the heart of North Carolina, which after six years away from home, Betsy was beginning to miss very much. I found out that the rector was a man named Peter Lee, and I called him up without much hope in my heart, since I had absolutely no connections whatever in the Episcopal Church in the South. As we talked, however, we discovered that the rector who had originally hired me in Seattle had been at a parish adjoining Peter's in Washington, D.C., and that my current rector was the son of the bishop who had ordained Peter. I suddenly began to feel as if this process was out of my control.

I mentioned earlier that we came here on our vacation in July of 1982 to interview. I was subsequently offered and accepted the job; We bought a house the next week, 10 minutes down the road from Betsy's family, and moved here two months later.

Most of you know the rest of the story. After I was associate here for a year and a half, Peter Lee was elected bishop coadjutor of the Diocese of Virginia, where he is now bishop, and after a year's search, I was elected rector, a position I officially began on July 1, 1985. Unless God has some other funny ideas, I hope to be able to stay here a good long while and raise my children, who are approaching 7 and 4, here in Chapel Hill.

You all could tell similar stories, some more dramatic, some less so, because God works differently in each of our lives. But the point is that God does work in our lives, does guide our lives, does speak to us, does invite us into prayer, into an intimate relationship, and does prevail and strengthen us despite our weaknesses, our blindness, our lack of vision.

The one thing God asks of us is faith — not even the heroic faith of martyrs willing to die for their belief nor even necessarily of missionaries who give up all that is familiar to go to a different part of the world to spread the faith. God asks a faith that lets God act, that can see God in the ordinary events of our lives, that believes beyond one's self.

In today's Gospel story, Jesus "could do no mighty work" in his own country, because of the people's lack of faith. They could not see God in Jesus, whom they already knew. They handcuffed God because they demanded that God meet their expectations. The people of Israel responded to Ezekiel in the same way, with a lack of openness and faith. Not to be manipulated, God instructed Ezekiel to persist in speaking God's word.

The people of Israel, the people of Jesus' "own country," and we, are all called by God to have faith, to be open to God, to let God speak to us, to guide us, to strengthen us. God does and will do that, if we but have the faith to allow God to work in our lives — if we but believe. Let us believe. Amen.

Ezekiel 2:1-7
II Corinthians 12:2-10
Mark 6:1-6

The Marriage of Barbara Tolin and Larry Rowan
September 10, 1994

A fact that I dare say none of you in this room know about me is that 33 years ago, I played the part of the Mock Turtle in a summer presentation of the play, "Alice in Wonderland"! The reason that I mention that is not to suggest that Larry and Barbara's marriage has any "Through the Looking Glass" quality to it, but merely to explain the source of a refrain that has been running through my mind these past few days in thinking about this relationship.

I sang the refrain as the Mock Turtle while dancing the Lobster-Quadrille with Alice and the Gryphon. It occurred after each verse and in fact ended the song, and it went, "Will you, won't you, will you, won't you, will you join the dance?" Isn't it amazing what the subconscious will bring up after so many years?

The obvious reason it occurred to me is that dance is so important for Larry and Barbara. They met as dance partners. A great part of their social and "aerobic" life is built around dance. At the Parish Barbecue a few weeks ago, they were the first ones, after the preschool set, to give in to the music and start dancing together!

That is what I think this marriage is about for you, Larry and Barbara, giving in to the music God has been playing for you and joining the dance.

Marriage is very much like a dance. Two people move together, sometimes in time-honored steps, sometimes in spontaneous initiative. At one part of the dance they may move in the same direction; at another point they may move apart going in different directions, but always coming back together. The music they hear and respond to may elicit exuberant joy or it may call forth slow, mournful movement. But at all times the two people are in relationship, listening and responding together.

That is the dance which you as a couple are yielding to and joining today, the holy dance of married life. But let none of us think that that has been an easy surrender. There have been reasons to resist. You have both been married before, so you know the pains and the problems that can arise. There is a significant age difference between you, which can be problematic not only now, but especially later. I know that you have struggled with these things and have worked to discern the answer to the invitation, "Will you, won't you, will you, won't you, will you join the dance?"

Today you have answered that question in the presence of God, the "Master Caller," and of your fellow dancers. You have each said, "I will," and in support of you, we have also promised, "We will."

Our prayer for you is that you will be faithful to your partner and to the music, which is God's grace, that, in the words of our reading, you may "let the peace of Christ rule in your hearts, to which indeed you were called in the one body," and that above all, you "put on love, which binds everything together in perfect harmony." May God, who has begun this good work in you, give you the grace to fulfill it.

The Marriage of Mary Friday and Jon Leadbetter
June 3, 2000

Our joyous ceremony this evening, both in its elements and in all of you, the participants, reflects the unusual reality that our principals, Jon Leadbetter and Mary Friday, have a foot firmly planted in each of two countries. They travel back and forth from the United States to England, from New York to London, at least monthly, and they count many friends, including those of you here tonight, from both countries. Jon was born in England and Mary here in the colonies, but both feel at home in the other's country and they are truly an international couple, as attested also by the presence tonight of those of you from many other countries.

Their bond of unity is evidenced by the fact that Mary was recently baptized in the Episcopal Church, which of course derived from the Church of England, of which Jon is a member. The hymn we just sang is practically a national anthem for England. To put it in terms we Americans can understand, it is similar in role, I suppose, to Kate Smith's singing "God Bless America," although the English version is much more poetic, theological, and beautiful!

One bit of English culture that is missing tonight is a limerick, that wonderful verse form that has made use of so many lyrical geographical names. Having noticed that our groom was born in Hitchin, Herfordshire, I could not resist offering you the following:

An Englishman, Jon, born in Hitchin,
Developed a powerful itchin'
To be married to Mary,
Who is not contrary
And does rather well in the kitchen!

I would hasten to add that Mary does rather well also in the boardroom and at the theater, but that would have spoiled the rhyme scheme!

So here is this couple who in this sacramental union are transcending not only their individualities and their families but also their nationalities to become one flesh. As our second reading proclaimed, "This mystery is a profound one." It reminds us that even though we are born into this world as individuals with specific identities and cultures, we are always called beyond our own particularities into closer union with others. It points us below the surface of our everyday lives to the awesome reality that we human beings are more alike than different. It confronts our petty rivalries and declares to us the fundamental reality at the heart of creation that we are all children of God.

Jon and Mary, we are grateful to you for your faithful witness, for your courage and energy and generosity of spirit in sharing your lives with each other and so with us. "You are the salt of the earth," as our Gospel reading declared. "You are the light of the world." A city [or a country or a family] on a hill cannot be hid." Salt and light do not exist for themselves but to enhance and to make visible other realities. Your marriage is not just for you but also for all of us. Your life together is to be, as we will pray in a moment, "a sign of Christ's love to this sinful and broken world, that unity may overcome estrangement, forgiveness heal guilt, and joy conquer despair."

We have promised you our support in this new phase of your journey. Together we can faithfully and fruitfully move beyond ourselves to our deeper identities and fulfillment in God. As you join yourselves to one another this evening, coming from particular families and countries and cultures, know that ultimately we are all of one family with God as our Father, all of one city, one country, the new Jerusalem.

Let Your Light So Shine
The Ordination of Joshua Varner as Priest
St. Luke's Episcopal Church, Durham, N.C.
May 18, 2002

It is a great joy to be with you at St. Luke's this afternoon. This parish is after all the grandchild of the Chapel of the Cross! In the late 1870s, Joseph Blount Cheshire, Jr., later longtime Bishop of this diocese, but then at the Chapel of the Cross in Chapel Hill on his first clergy assignment, would hop a ride on the mail hack to Durham, which he characterized in his privately published autobiography as "a very busy town of perhaps two or three thousand inhabitants ... beginning to be of importance for the manufacture of smoking tobacco." With these trips he began the congregation of St. Philip's, which some 75 years later started St. Luke's. It is in part, then, because of these historical faith connections that as the rector of the Chapel of the Cross, I find it a great joy to be with you and preaching in this pulpit.

The other source of joy, of course, is this occasion, the ordaining of Joshua Harris Varner as priest. Joshua has been a lifelong member of the Chapel of the Cross. Twenty years ago this fall, when I first came to the parish, Joshua was just starting second grade. It will come as a surprise to any of you children that Joshua was ever that young — or that small! Believe it or not, at one point he could not see over the pew either! But he grew quickly — in more than height. My first few years of playing guitar and leading singing for Vacation Church School, Joshua sang along with the other children from the pews in the chapel where Bishop Cheshire began preaching: "This little light of mine, I'm gonna let it shine." And he certainly did! After he spent a few years in the junior choir, we started calling it Joshua Varner and his Back-up Singers! He has never managed to be inconspicuous! By high school, he was playing guitar and helping me lead Vacation Church School singing. We have sung countless verses of "This little light of mine" together! In fact it is wonderful that next month, when I am on sabbatical, Joshua will come to the Chapel of the Cross first thing every morning for the week of Vacation Church School and lead the children in exuberant singing.

"This little light of mine…" After four years at Sewanee and two at Harvard Divinity School and two more at Virginia Seminary and one here as deacon at St. Luke's, Joshua is now ready to let his light shine in a new way: through serving as a priest in Christ's one, holy, catholic, and apostolic Church. That is not the only way to let one's light shine, of course; in fact it is not the usual way. Most of us will never be ordained. But Jesus' words, "Let your light so shine…" which we will hear as today's Offertory Sentence, are for all of us. Our lives as followers of Jesus can never be simply private and singular. Where would we be if Bishop Cheshire or the founders of St. Luke's or Joshua's family or others from whom he has caught the faith, lived like that? Certainly not gathered in this house of worship this afternoon, being strengthened and empowered to live out our lives of faith and service and witness.

Joshua is not the only one or even one of a few charged with preaching the Gospel. He is uniquely prepared to do so and charged to do so by the traditional laying on of hands by the Bishop. Ordinarily it is clergy who proclaim the Gospel within the liturgy. But at our Baptism, we all are charged to "proclaim by word and example the Good News of God in Christ." "The Good News (capitalized) of God in Christ," of course, is another way to talk about the Gospel, and not just the written down Gospel versions, but the whole Good News of the Jesus event, of Jesus dwelling among us. We are charged, privileged, to let our light shine by proclaiming "by word and example" this Good News.

In other words, the faith we are given, like any other gift from God, is not given just for each of us to enjoy and be nourished by. Every gift from God — there's a redundancy, since all gifts come from God, "from whom all blessings flow" — every gift is in a real sense a communal gift. It may be a specific gift, like God's call to Joshua to be a priest or a look of delight on a child's face that only you are privileged to see or the opportunity to encourage a friend that another is not given. But it is not a private gift only for you to survive another step on your singular path through the world. All gifts are meant to strengthen us and strengthen others, to build up the whole Body of Christ. As one Eucharistic Prayer puts it, "Deliver us from the presumption of coming to this Table for solace only, and not for strength; for pardon only, and not for renewal." We are all to share our faith, that precious gift, by example and by word —not forcing it on others of course, but letting it be caught. We are all to let our light shine — to let the light of Christ that God has given us shine before others to warm and encourage and illuminate and strengthen them.

Those of you who have participated in an Episcopal ordination before know that it is customary for the preacher, at the conclusion of the sermon, to ask the ordinand to stand to receive a charge. I do not favor that custom. Not only is there more than enough charge in the liturgy itself for any one individual to respond to, but focusing in on the prospective priest in such a personal way disturbs, it seems to me, the already delicate balance in the ordination liturgy between one person's ministry and the ministry of the whole Church. I do think it is appropriate, however, to ask all of you at this point, including Joshua, to stand up.

You are all loved, forgiven, empowered, and sent children of God. Although like the apostles, Jesus no longer calls you servants, but friends, he does call you to serve others and to be his witnesses to them. Listen to that call. Yield to the God who loves you more than you love yourself. Listen obediently, as did Jesus, for the will of his Father. "I have come," he tells us in today's Gospel, "not to do my own will, but the will of him who sent me." Support and serve one another as you seek to do God's will. Especially support your clergy, including Joshua, that they respond obediently and let the light of Christ shine through them for all to see.

You have many resources to help you respond to God's call: the Word of God in scripture, the Eucharist, the gift of one another, the whole Church, the challenges and even failures that call you to serve, the beauty of creation, music, even Vacation Church School songs (!), a mind to think and a heart to love. Most of all you have the constant presence of the Father, Son, and Holy Spirit along the way. Listen for that Divine presence. Yield to the call to love and serve others. Let your light so shine that others may hear your words and see your example and glorify your Father who is in heaven. Amen.

The Funeral of Ida Elizabeth Friday
July 19, 2002

Just over two years ago, many of us joined in this same sacred space with the Friday family to celebrate the joyous occasion of Mary's marriage to Jon. It was a memorable gathering — of people far beyond simply the Friday relatives — and a transcendent experience. The palpable outpouring of love, the powerful presence of integrity and commitment, the deep sense of worship all served to transport us beyond ourselves into the mystery of God's active presence and of the real bonds that unite us and of the truth of those deeper realities that daily life most often hides from our eyes.

Today we gather again but for a much sadder occasion, the commending into the hands of Almighty God of our sister, our friend, our aunt, our daughter, Betsy. We come with much heavier hearts, weighed down by our ache and loss, by our disbelief that this could have happened to one so young and vibrant, by our anger and confusion and doubt. Rather than being transported beyond ourselves into faith and love and hope, we are pushed further into ourselves by alternating numbness and emotions we tend to avoid. Death is that final, that wrenching, that isolating.

Yet we still profess our faith. "The Lord is my shepherd," we reassure ourselves in the 23rd Psalm, "I shall not want. ... Yea, though I walk through the valley of the shadow of death, I will fear no evil; for thou art with me," O God. Even hemmed in by this narrow valley of death's inescapable consequences, we can believe in something larger than ourselves, the faithful and strengthening and life-giving God.

It was, of course, this generous God who blessed us with Ida Elizabeth Friday, known to us as Betsy, in the first place. Made in God's image, she reflected the Divine creativity with her interest in and flair for music and dance and drama. As a child in school, and as an adult, she devoted her time and energy to these creative arts. Her list of credits runs long.

But Betsy was much more than a performer, a choreographer, an organizer. First and foremost she relished life, radiating a certain sparkle, which drew others to her with great affection and admiration. She not only loved her family and her many friends, but her acts of kindness to others were legion, whether to a colleague or one of her doctors or her hairdresser. To the end, Betsy did things for others.

She never hid behind passivity but took an active role in all that she was involved in, including her illness and medical care. When faced with the risks either of a bone marrow transplant or of hoping for continued remission from her leukemia based on occasional bouts of chemotherapy, Betsy declared, "It's not my style not to face things head on." Earlier this year she sent out a card informing us of her impending bone marrow infusion. This little multi-page booklet, in rhyming verse and illustrated by clever, colorful drawings, reflected Betsy's creativity and joy and hope and affection. On the front, a cartoon showed her having risen from her hospital bed to confront some surprised doctors huddled in consultation. Arms folded matter-of-factly in her hospital gown and IV at work, Betsy informed them, "Yes, *I am* part of the medical team. Without me, you have nothing!"

That last line now becomes ironic for us. The more we loved her, the more we may now feel that without her we have nothing. That is not true, of course, despite how we may feel. We have not only the gift of having known and loved and been influenced by Betsy, but also the spiritual union that we now enjoy with all those who have gone before us (called by the Church the communion of saints), and the prospect of future, more fuller union than time and space at present allow. "Eye has not seen," Paul tells us, "nor ear heard what God has prepared for those who love him."

We also have each other, the family and friends and companions we have been given to strengthen and challenge us and to call us beyond ourselves. Our very presence here today strengthens and reminds us of our unseen bonds.

And most of all we have the loving God who creates and redeems and sustains us. Against this God death is powerless, and like Betsy, we shall never be abandoned. With her and with all those with whom she is now united, we profess our hope in the age-old words of scripture drawn on by countless generations: "Surely goodness and mercy shall follow [us] all the days of [our lives], and [we] will dwell in the house of the Lord forever."

The Funeral of Shirley Wilkerson Elkins
March 10, 2004

When I go to prepare a place for you, I will come again and will
take you to myself, that where I am you may be also (John 14:3)
– Jesus' words to his first disciples and to us

One of the deepest desires and needs within us as human beings is to
be at home. We all relate to the world through our ingrained sense of
home. Home is where we are assured that we do belong, where we learn
our identity, where we know we are loved. We can handle the many
changes and chances of this life to the extent that we feel at home.
Home is what the many immigrants of the world are searching for, what
soldiers long to return to, what parents try to provide for their children.

One person who instinctively grasped the deep importance of home to
us as human beings was Shirley Wilkerson Elkins. She lived in Durham
her entire life, but she knew that home is much more than geographical
location. She realized that home is created by loving attention, by time
spent together, by appreciating and affirming the gifts and contributions
of others, by generous celebrations, by gracious hospitality. She spent
her nearly 60 years of married life fashioning that sense of home for
her husband, her daughters, her sons-in-law, her grandsons and more
recently, her granddaughters-in-law. Whether that "at-homeness" was
centered on the family residence at Nottaway Road or at a lake house or
at the beach cottage, her family and extended family have known what
it is to be at home, to be welcomed, to feel the inviting warmth of her
contagious attentiveness.

Nor has that been limited to her family. All of you here in one way
or another have felt her welcoming embrace, have experienced her
hospitality, have been more comfortable in your lives because of Shirley
Elkins. She helped us all to feel at home.

Let me give you a personal example. Over 25 years ago, Shirley found
out what must have been stunning news that her younger daughter,

Betsy, doing post-baccalaureate volunteer service 3,000 miles away in Seattle, intended to marry and settle down there. Not only that, but her husband-to-be (namely me!) was not only an "older man," but a former Roman Catholic priest with no job prospects! Undaunted and apparently undismayed, Shirley invited us to fly out and join the expanding Elkins family the next month for several weeks of summer vacation at their new home-away-from-home at Emerald Isle. Never having even visited the South before and not knowing what to expect, I was surprised and deeply touched to receive a pre-vacation package the next week in the mail from my future mother-in-law, whom I was yet to meet — a bathing suit to welcome me to the beach and to make me feel at home. You could all tell numerous similar stories, and I hope you have and will. When I became rector here at The Chapel of the Cross, for example, in 1985, Shirley needle-pointed this stole for me for the bishop to use in investing me. Each stitch was sewn with love, which continues to be shared with the numerous couples who have been married so far under its symbolic witness.

One area of her life where Shirley never found quite the right home was church. She grew up Baptist, then midway through life joined the Methodist Church; but she frequently told me, perhaps to make *me* feel good, "I should have been an Episcopalian." She did tell her Methodist pastor not too long ago that she wanted an Episcopal funeral, and she told him, "I don't want my name mentioned"! I understand that self-effacing desire, but if she had said that to me, I would have said, "Shirley, you surely know that I cannot promise that — as surely as you were born!" We cannot have all our wishes.

Christians believe, of course, that we are never completely at home on this earth and in this life. As scripture tells us, "Here we have no lasting city, but we seek the city which is to come" (Hebrews 31:14). For several reasons then, it was not surprising during the last precipitous and tumultuous three weeks of her life for Shirley to struggle to sit up in her hospital bed and plead with some poignancy and conviction, "I want to go home." On one level her plaintive cry expressed how deeply that human desire runs in us to be home and to be at home in this changing, uncertain world. On another level, her words revealed Shirley's and our true destination, the Divine and eternal home where we shall be forever loved and welcomed and, in Paul's words, "fully understood." It was on this level that Shirley repeated several times, "I am ready to go."

"When I go to prepare a place for you, I will come again and will take you to myself, that where I am you may be also." That is our true home: to be with Jesus where he has prepared for us to be. We believe that is now the lasting home of Shirley Wilkerson Elkins. Just as she made a home for so many, so does God make a home for her. "The Lord bless her and keep her, the Lord make his face to shine upon her and be gracious to her, the Lord lift up his countenance upon her and give her peace." Amen.

The Funeral of Agnes Mary Williams
St. Anthony's Parish, Missoula, Montana
July 9, 2004

It is a daunting task to preach at your mother's funeral and frequently an unwise challenge to take on. I heard one unfortunate minister who began by saying that since he was preaching the homily at his mother's service, he wanted us all to think of it as his "momily." It went downhill from there.

I will attempt not to do that, not to turn these few moments into a saccharine eulogy more suited to private conversation with friends, but to make it a public proclamation appropriate within the community of faith. I decided to accept this unusual challenge because, having experienced a good deal of my mother's life and now her death, I want to hold up for us the fitting Christian response of gratitude. In fact I was delighted when my sister and I were ordering these roses for today — which Mom loved to cultivate, in various shades of her favorite color, pink — to see the florist's sign declaring that the meaning associated with dark pink roses is gratefulness. Gratefulness then is our theme for today, gratefulness, and the meaning ascribed to light pink roses: grace and joy.

Perhaps no one can be more grateful for the gift of another person than one to whom she has quite literally given the gift of life, her beholden child. While I certainly have found myself experiencing deep grief at my mother's death, especially in that hospital room at St. Patrick's where she painfully struggled with yielding the last ounces of breath within her, the predominant response in me since then has been one of gratitude.

I am grateful for the unique personhood of Agnes Mary Cope Williams. No one has been or will be created in the image of God in just the same way. I am grateful for her long life. Living to the age of 89, she was given to us as support and stability and affection for much longer than we had a right to expect.

I am grateful for her adventurousness. She not only set up household for my father and our family in many different locations in many different states until we finally settled permanently in Missoula in 1957; she later traveled extensively throughout the world to all the continents except Antarctica, first with Dad and then on her own. At the age of 57, after 32 happy years of marriage, she courageously faced the challenges of widowhood, vigorously living yet another 32 years. Among other adjustments, she learned and got rather good at golf, bowling, and cross-country skiing (as you see there in the picture). After her stroke five years ago, she made an amazing comeback and managed quite well with the support of assisted living. Even though in her final years her adventurousness grew dormant, she claimed, along with one of her sisters, to have been in the early 1930s the first young women in their hometown, Coeur d'Alene, Idaho, ever to wear pants downtown! An early blow for women's liberation.

I am grateful for Mom's devotion to baking! Not only throughout our childhood, but even during our college years and for many subsequent Christmases, she kept us children and later her grandchildren well supplied with generous amounts of her nurturing, affection-filled, great tasting cookies. Her care packages were always dependable and always welcomed!

Most of all I am grateful for her nurturing in us, her children, the gift of faith. Faith in God was the highest value for her and through her personal example and faithful participation in the Church, she imparted that spark to us. The collect used toward the beginning of our service certainly applies to her, Lord "look kindly upon a mother, Agnes, who sought to bind her children to you." Her mother's rosary and our family bible present here today symbolize that deep faith.

All of us who gather around this altar this morning have come to give thanks to God. Those of us who are Agnes' family and extended family know that our lives have been dramatically affected by God's gift to us of her. For some of us, our very lives or the existence of our spouses or parents have been dependent on her. For all of us, our values and our approach to life's mystery have been in part shaped and influenced by her life, even in ways that we do not realize. We are most grateful.

We also give thanks for our friends who are here and for those of you who came here this morning for the regular Friday morning mass. Even if you did not know of my mother, we are grateful to be able to commend her into the hands of Almighty God surrounded by the Church, the community of the faithful, and to do so in the context of the Eucharist, which of course means "thanksgiving." We are also grateful on returning to St. Anthony's to find Fr. John Miller, who knew Agnes when she could be active in the parish, still here after 14 years! He may not reach the record tenure of 44 years of Monsignor Dennis P. Meade — who encouraged me 40 years ago to go to seminary — but we wish him much more fruitful ministry here in Missoula.

Most of all we are all grateful for the gift of renewed life that God constantly gives us. No matter what the losses and the pains and the separations we are suffering, God's generous grace is larger. "The favors of the Lord are not exhausted," we heard in the first reading from Lamentations. "His mercies are not spent. They are renewed each morning, so great is his faithfulness."

"Who shall separate us from the love of Christ?" Paul wrote in our second reading to those suffering in Rome and to all of us. Nothing, he proclaimed unequivocally "will be able to separate us from the love of God." That is true for us and for Agnes, even in death. Nothing separates us from God. Jesus promised in our Gospel reading, "I am indeed going to prepare a place for you, and then come back to take you with me, that where I am you also may be." Today we gather to declare our faith in that promise and to give thanks to our bountiful God, who blessed us with Agnes Mary Williams.

The Lord bless her and keep her; the Lord make his face to shine upon her and be gracious to her; the Lord lift up his countenance upon her and give her peace.

Lamentations 3: 17-26; Romans 8: 31-35, 37-39; John 14:1-6

With his predecessor at the Chapel of the Cross, The Rev. Peter Lee

The Funeral of Walter Royal Davis
May 23, 2008

From our first reading from *The Book of Ecclesiasticus* from the Apocrypha:

There are some of them who have left a name, so that men declare their praise. And there are some who have no memorial, who have perished as though they had not lived.

Can any of us here have any doubt which of these categories Walter Davis fit into?! Look around you. Not many of us, if we are fortunate to live beyond our 88th birthday, will be able to have this kind of sendoff! Without many contemporaries there or unless we are the oldest child of a very large family, each member of whom has also raised extraordinarily big families, most of us will not come close to this kind of attendance at our funerals! The numbers here alone, including so many in positions of leadership, not to mention the press coverage this week, tell us that Walter Royal Davis definitely left a name, so that men declare his praise.

But that was not Walter's motivation. While he sought to make the best use of his influence and to have a positive impact on society, as much as humanly possible he did so, not for the sake of power, but for the sake of people. He genuinely wanted to help others and to make life better for them. Having come out of poverty himself, Walter repeatedly used money he accumulated to help others in need. Having been denied a college education himself, he assisted many a young person in getting a solid start in life by underwriting their academic studies. Grateful for having received important guidance and mentoring from adults in his life, he poured energy and time into those in whom he saw great promise. His intention was not so much to create a name for himself or to impress others with his generosity. In fact often, if he could not help anonymously, he would look elsewhere to be of assistance. And he never gave to others in a way that demeaned them. He respected others of all walks of life, and he wanted to do what he could for them and for society. As his wife, JoAnn, told me, his fondest wish and greatest

305

sense of satisfaction was to be able to say with sincerity and conviction, "I did the best I could."

Through JoAnn and others, I have learned a great deal about Walter Davis the last few days. I had only met him briefly two times before. The first was four years ago at the funeral here of his stepdaughter, Helen, who very sadly for her family and for many of us died at a relatively young age of cancer. The second was a few months later when one of my energetic sons hit an errant golf ball into the Davis' rose garden near the fourth green of the Chapel Hill Country Club! JoAnn was outside gardening and invited us in for a chat with Walter. He was always interested in human conversation. (I hope none of you were in the foursome waiting behind us!)

I have also enjoyed reading about Walter. His biography is still in production, but I noticed with admiration the creative understatement of his obituary, which states about his early life that "His parents enrolled him in the military disciplinary regimen at Hargrave [Military Academy] because of his independence and high level of youthful energy"! The fuller details beyond that statement came out in a front-page article about his death and his life in the Raleigh *News and Observer*. "As a boy," it reads, "he butted heads with his father over pre-dawn chores that included milking the cows and feeding chickens, hogs and 22 mules. He walked three miles to school and was kicked out the first day, he recalled in 1982, for slugging the principal"! I would definitely call that "independence and high level of youthful energy!" Joann acknowledged that he was "a rough and tumble" guy, although with a wonderful gentleness, and that despite his many passions and convictions he used very little profanity. At heart he was humbly grateful for any kindness received. That was particularly noticeable in his weakened state the last few weeks of his life when, with caregivers and family and the many who came by, a high percentage of his vocabulary consisted of "Please" and "Thank you."

JoAnn and Mary Anne, his stepdaughter who lives locally, described an amazing vignette during Walter's last days. Several days before he died, he had not been saying much. He had not even been able to move or sit up or hold anything or help himself in any way. JoAnn was sitting holding his hand when he began to speak in a low voice. "Dear God," he breathed, "I hope I have been worthy of the life you have given me. I hope that I have done everything that I could for those who needed it." As he spoke, he lifted up his arms in prayer in what is sometimes called the *orans* position. This went on in this vein for five minutes or so. I do not know how he ended, but I imagine it was something like, "I hope, O God, that you think I did the best I could." The next day, he repeated a very similar prayer, lifting up his arms to God, and then he never spoke again. He died a day or so later.

Despite our personal loss today and despite the loss to our state and to our educational institutions and to our public conversation about the common good of this visionary and generous and humble man, Walter made it known numerous times that he wanted his departure to be the occasion of a last big party! He desired no dirges, no wallowing. He was a man of faith and believed in celebrating the new life that awaited him. We have tried to do that with this service, with powerful scripture readings, with exuberant hymns, with the soaring trumpet and expansive organ. We have tried to do that with the catered reception, festooned with flowers, which follows this service and with the gathering after that at the Davis home, to which you are all invited. All of this Walter would have enjoyed and approved of and said "thank you" for. I hope he would not have found anything missing or think that we made too big a fuss over him because, Walter, if you are listening, I am sure you know, like you, "We did the best we could."

The Marriage of Returi Priti Rao and Stephen Tyler Elkins-Williams
Fearrington Village, N.C.
September 18, 2010

As a veteran of almost 32 years of marriage, I have come over that time to a deep appreciation for the mystery of this sacred vocation. To be called to share your total self and life with another until death is a deeply joyful, wrenching, transformational experience. Not only in its noble concept, but especially in its often mundane day-to-day lived-out existence, truly sharing your life with another for better for worse, for richer for poorer, in sickness and in health, changes you from the inside out. Slowly, sometimes dramatically, marriage transforms you from mere individuals focused on meeting your own needs into a couple who are capable, if not always successful, of putting the needs of the other first and together of nurturing into life the children you may be blessed to raise into adulthood.

My appreciation for the sacred vocation of marriage has become even deeper over the last few years as Betsy and I have been privileged to be part of Tyler and Priti's flourishing relationship, now to be elevated to the level of this lifelong union. We have watched them grow from two individuals who shared common friends and background and vocational interest, to those who wanted to spend more and more time together, to those who began to plan their futures together, to those who are now ready to enter into the holy covenant of marriage.

In the process of their sharing more of their lives together, I have come to understand in an even deeper way what the marriage journey, if you will, is really about. In fact, in the very story of their meeting and their first conversation, I found in retrospect a paradigm of the call to married life. Some of you know the story. Tyler and Priti were, by chance or by grace, introduced to each other by a mutual friend at a local food and beverage establishment! Tyler was there at a stag party for the groom of a wedding to be held a few days later. He was not sure, however, he confided to Priti, that he would really enjoy that happy occasion since he would be attending by himself. And here is the grace part. "I will go with you," Priti was prompted to say. And after some discussion, grace prompted Tyler to accept!

Some weeks later, Betsy was out of town, and I invited myself over to his townhouse to watch the Duke lacrosse team play in the final four, not knowing he would already have company! But he graciously welcomed me and introduced me to Priti. After a very exciting game, I mentioned to Tyler that the next day was Pentecost, the 25th anniversary of his baptism, and it would be good for him to come to church! "But Mom will not be there," he said, "and you will be up in front. I would be by myself." You can already guess what Priti said at that point: "I will go with you." And since going to church with someone is a pretty big deal, especially with the minister's son, that was no small step to take!

"I will go with you." That is what the vocation of marriage is about — committing yourself to accompany the other wherever that may be. "I will go with you." Today, Tyler and Priti, you say that to each other in a much more comprehensive way. Now you are promising to accompany each other, not just to a specific event, but wherever your life journey takes you literally and metaphorically. For better or worse, I will go with you. For richer or poorer, I will go with you. In sickness and in health, I will go with you. Whatever happens, I will be there with you.

You have some real role models who have lived this out before you. Your grandfather is here, Tyler, who has always been an example for you. Coolidge and Shirley, for almost 60 years were always there for each other, perhaps most notably in their later years during their mutual debilitating bouts with cancer. Your grandfather is here too, Priti. Bhaska and Sarada were married for 50 years and persevered until her death in traveling unforeseen roads together. Your parents also, Arun and Nadene, undaunted by different nationalities and cultures and faiths, courageously committed to go with each other, although their life journey together was tragically far too short. Your parents, Tyler, were another unlikely combination! But together with God's grace Betsy and I have accompanied each other through (among others) denominational and vocational and geographic journeys.

And now it is your turn and your opportunity. Through God's grace and providence, you have been given the gift of each other and the extraordinary privilege and challenge of sharing your life's journey together. Friends and family from all phases of your lives thus far are here to celebrate with you and to promise their continued support and encouragement. Like those who have come before you, you are now called to the sacred vocation of marriage, which through its good times and bad will change you and transform you into more than you can possibly be on your own. As you make your vows to one another, as you hear the other promise, in so many words, to go with you wherever life takes you, know that you are not just on your own. Divine grace continues to operate. God also says to both of you, "I will go with you."

The Funeral of Augustus Coolidge Elkins
Epworth United Methodist Church, Durham, N.C.
December 22, 2012

*I have fought the good fight, I have finished the race, I have kept
the faith* (2 Timothy 4:7)
– words from our second reading

Certainly these words of Paul toward the end of his life characterize
the final struggle of Coolidge Elkins at the end of his. The metaphor of
a fight is not too strong an image to characterize his slow and painful
decline in health, particularly over the last year or two, but especially
this past month or so. He could not eat, he could not move his legs,
he could barely sip water and keep connection with the devoted nurses
and sitters at the Forest at Duke and with those of us who maintained
a round the clock vigil with him. But with courage and graciousness he
fought that good fight, and he finished the race as the man of faith and
warmth and generosity that we were all privileged to know and love
over the years of his life's journey.

In fact, Paul's words can be expanded to form the framework of all
of Coolidge's life, not that it was a fight or a race in the sense of a
difficult and tragedy-filled life; it was not. He lived a very fulfilled
and happy life in this community, with a supportive family, many
friends, and a remarkable record of significant and productive service
to others. But a major dimension of his life was continually dealing
with the unexpected. So much of Coolidge's life turned out different
than he thought it would! If life is what happens when you are planning
something else, Augustus Coolidge Elkins lived a very full life indeed.

Some things did not surprise him, of course, especially his long and
happy marriage with Shirley Wilkerson, his childhood sweetheart. You
see them on the cover of your bulletin there on their honeymoon in San
Francisco, where Coolidge was waiting to ship out to Guam. When he
returned, they did live their whole lives in Durham and their daughters,
grandchildren, and great-grandchildren have lived nearby. He relished

being their Big Daddy. He also maintained lifelong friendships with so many people, which gave continuity and fullness to his life.

But consider that Coolidge wanted to be an engineer and seemed born for it. His quick and logical mind got him into Duke a year earlier than his peers, and he then graduated in engineering in three years with highest honors, tutoring and bringing along many classmates as he went. When he returned from the Navy, he wanted to go on in postgraduate studies and was, in his words to me, "ready to go"; but his father asked him to help establish the dealership's participation in a new Chrysler distribution system, and he agreed. Not so long after that his father died of a sudden heart attack, leaving Coolidge and his brother Ted to pick up the reins of the family business. Ted's debilitating accident some years later increased Coolidge's oversight responsibilities, which he maintained for another 40 years.

Although Coolidge had to forgo his dreams of being an engineer, he made a wonderful businessman and a demanding but fair-minded boss, who actively looked out for the welfare of all under his supervision. I accompanied Coolidge to a funeral of a former employee a year or so ago, and many of his former workers were thrilled to see him and made sure to impress upon me their heartfelt conviction that he was the best boss they had ever worked for. His reputation was equally strong with his many customers, who experienced him as a man of integrity, generosity and competency, and he built up a thriving business.

His leadership expanded well beyond the dealership. He led the local board of Wachovia Bank, the Durham YMCA board, and the North Carolina Automobile Dealers Association, besides participating in many civic organizations. But perhaps his most lasting contribution was on the board of the Raleigh-Durham Airport, in helping this vital part of our local and state economy to flourish into what it has become. His friend Dillard Teer wrote in testimony a decade ago, "The best day in the history of the RDU Airport Authority was the day I recruited Coolidge to come on board. His contribution for 27 years was phenomenal." His best friend from boyhood, Kenan Rand, echoed that sentiment: "Your outstanding contribution to RDU has been beneficial to the growth of RTI and has provided economic opportunities and a better quality of life to thousands."

Even though he was not able to pursue his dream of becoming an engineer, Coolidge's way of running the race and fighting the good fight was to pour himself into many avenues of service to others, drawing upon all the many gifts that God had blessed him with. He spent his life helping to build strong institutions for the betterment of the community. He was so engaged in it all that he did not retire until the age of 74, when he finally looked forward to more time with Shirley and the golden years when he could enjoy the fruits of all his labor.

Again, of course, life turned out differently. Although, much to his and everyone else's amazement, he had been able to defeat far advanced cancer through an experimental treatment, Shirley suddenly died of cancer only five years after his retirement. He never expected to outlive his cherished and supportive wife, especially by almost nine years, and that was a major adjustment, to say the least. Then Chrysler went bankrupt, and the dealership went vacant. Even his trusted Wachovia Bank crumbled and disappeared. And in the midst of all that disappointment, Coolidge struggled with the increasing ravaging of his body that both the disease of Myasthenia Gravis and the medicine used to treat it relentlessly imposed upon him.

Yet through it all, Coolidge persevered. He continued to maintain his interest in so many areas of life, he looked out for his family and his friends, he lived his faith. Although it turned out to be further away than he had expected, he planned for this day. Every few years he would come in and revise his final wishes. He did not want a lot of fuss about himself, in fact you should have seen the brief, dry obituary he proposed (which we later overruled)! But he wanted the prelude music of the familiar Methodist hymns of his childhood. He wanted us to read together the Prayer of St. Francis, which articulates so much of what he believed and stood for. He wanted us to sing "Amazing Grace" and to be grateful for God's continuing and faithful presence in our lives, even, and perhaps especially, when things do not go as we expect. He did not think to ask for an inspiring rendition of "O Holy Night," but since he had requested it for Shirley's funeral as a comfort for him in a time of a great need, we honor him and the God who sustained him by including it today as well.

As we commend Augustus Coolidge Elkins into the arms of his most merciful Savior, we do so with great gratitude for all that he has been to us over many years. He has fought the good fight, he has finished the race, he has kept the faith in a way that inspires us all and gives great glory to God. "The Lord bless him and keep him; the Lord make his face to shine upon him and be gracious unto him; the Lord lift up his countenance upon him and give him peace." Amen.

The Marriage of Jeffrey Beame and Stanley Finch
May 9, 2015

What a day of thanksgiving and celebration this is! What a joy for all of us to be here this morning, and especially for you, Jeffrey and Stan! It has been a long road getting here, many years of faithful commitment, much unsatisfied hope of ever being able to stand before God and before the Church community to profess your lifelong union to each other, and to receive the blessing of God and the public support of the Church in living out that deep commitment.

But at last that day is here! What a gift it is finally to gather here in this treasured and historic chapel in the midst of those closest to you and with full sanction of both the Church and the state to seal the covenant you made to one another 35 years ago. Thanks be to God for this immeasurable gift. Thanks be to God from whom all blessings do flow. Thanks be to God for this dramatic demonstration that indeed, all things are possible with God!

And while we are being grateful, I think I would be remiss not to thank our state legislature! Had they not overreached and insisted on Amendment One, we would surely not have gotten here nearly so quickly! God works in mysterious ways!

But our gratitude this morning is focused not only on the present and on the past. It also looks to the future. For your recognized commitment, Stan and Jeffrey, is a gift not only for you, but also for the whole community. Your blessed companionship is not merely to console you, but to strengthen you in the days ahead as together you continue to love and serve the Lord by loving and serving others. You are not just to breathe a sigh of relief and fade off into your dotage! You are both very outward-looking and giving people, and the gift of this day calls forth in you an even greater blossoming of your love and service to others.

As you come before us now to renew your covenant, our prayer is one of great gratitude for the two of you, for the role you play in our lives and for your inspiring example. We pray that the epiphany of today may strengthen you for the road ahead and for all the good works God has prepared for you to walk in. Thank you for bringing us all, literally and metaphorically, to this joyful place. May God who had begun this good work in you so many years ago, give you the grace to continue to fulfill it.

The Funeral of William Wallace Guthridge
May 25, 2015

Bill Guthridge was usually a man of few words, and those he spoke were weighed carefully. Unlike many of us, he had no desire for the spotlight or to impress others with his knowledge and insights. Betsy and I had the privilege of going with Bill and Leesie to an exciting Tar Heel game a few years ago — a come-from-behind victory. As we were leaving, a fan spotted him and ran up excitedly. "Coach, what did you think?" "Well," he smiled, "we won!"

He did not particularly relish interviews, and no doubt that is one of the reasons he enjoyed his partnership with Dean Smith for so many years. Although these two friends were so similar in their outlooks, in their values, even in their faith, Bill was very happy to let his truth-seeking doppelganger do the public talking. I think he would have readily endorsed a perhaps surprising comment Coach Smith made in an interview in *Sports Illustrated* in 1998, not long after he retired. In response to a question about the connection between his Christian faith and giving up control, he said:

> "Churchill had to give a speech once, and he didn't know what to say; so he got up and said, 'Never, never, never, never, never, never quit.' Seven words. So I got up [at the commencement at Eastern College in Pennsylvania] and said, 'Always, always, always, always, always, always quit.'"

> He went on, "I think we're most happy and free when there is a creator … in charge of our lives. I said 'happy and free,'" he concluded. "And that's where I struggle because I want to take over constantly."

"Always, always, always, always, always, always quit." All of us familiar with Carolina basketball know that those unusual words cannot mean, "Do not keep trying for as long as you can." These two mentors drilled into countless players the lifelong habit of never giving up. They cannot mean, "Do not work as hard as possible." Their preparation was meticulous and their effort untiring. What, then?

I think these words are an intriguing expression of Jesus' words, "Whoever seeks to gain his life will lose it, but whoever loses his life will preserve it." (Luke 17:33) "Always quit." Always let go. Never substitute yourself for God. Accept reality and let God transform it. When things do not go the way we want — "when" not "if" — we are to surrender and quit our misconceived notion of what was to be. Clinging to our disappointments does not bring us life or freedom. Only the truth shall make us free. Even when things do go our way, we are not to regard our success as all flowing from us. We are to quit our claim of control.

"Always, always quit." That is a difficult lesson to learn in the abstract, but much easier to grasp when we see it lived out in a human life like that of Bill Guthridge. Alongside his strong competitive passion and his commitment to succeed, there was a remarkable humility, a gentleness, a recognition that we are not the Creator of life in all of its glorious aspects. We are not the ones in charge, not the ones around which the universe revolves.

Bill was a true and grateful child of God, and his death is a great loss for us. Its coming so quickly after that of his longtime colleague and friend and spokesman is a double blow and difficult to accept and understand. We have trouble quitting our desire still to have him part of our lives and gently letting him go. Death has robbed us of such a cherished gift.

But listen to the words of Teilhard de Chardin, the Jesuit anthropologist and theologian, who opens up for us an expansive perspective on death and on life in the midst of it.

> We must overcome death by finding God in it. In itself, death is an incurable weakness of corporeal beings, complicated in our world by the influence of an original fall. It is the sum and type of all the forces that diminish us, and against which we must fight without being able to hope for a personal, direct and immediate victory. Now the great victory of the Creator and Redeemer in the Christian vision is to have transformed what is

in itself a universal power of diminishment and extinction into an essentially life-giving factor. God must, in some way or other, make room for himself, hollowing us out and emptying us, if he is to finally penetrate into us. And in order to assimilate us in him, he must break the molecules of our being as to re-cast and re-model us. The function of death is to provide the necessary entrance into our inmost selves. It will make us undergo the required dissociation. It will put us into the state organically needed if the divine fire is to descend upon us. And in that way its fatal power to decompose and dissolve will be harnessed to the most sublime operations of life. What was by nature empty and void, a return to bits and pieces, can, in any human existence, become fullness and unity in God. (The Divine Milieu)

"God must, in some way or other, make room for himself, hollowing us out and emptying us, if he is to finally penetrate into us." We certainly experienced that in the life of William Wallace Guthridge, as he worked at letting go of control and at always quitting being in charge. We saw that even more clearly in the disease that slowly emptied him out, eventually bringing him to his final death. God made room for himself in Bill Guthridge.

But these words are also true for us. Our mourning and loss are part of a progressive hollowing out of all of us to make room for the Divine presence. Our pain is part of our need to quit being in charge, of our need to lose our life in order to preserve it. There is not merely privation here, not only death, but life and grace and fullness, not only for Bill but for us.

Today we give great thanks for the full and fruitful life of Bill Guthridge. We quit any further claim we might have on his life and earthly presence among us. And we gently commend him into the compassionate hands of his loving Creator and Redeemer, with whom he has now found, in the words of Chardin, "fullness and unity in God."

The Lord bless him and keep him. The Lord make his face to shine upon him and be gracious unto him. The Lord lift up his countenance upon him and give him peace. Amen.

Epilogue

Reflections on Ministry at the Chapel of the Cross, 1982-2015
Vestry Retreat
May 1, 2015

I had only been an official Episcopal priest for four months when, in the fall of 1982, Peter James Lee hired me to be the Associate for Parish Ministry at the Chapel of the Cross. I was received from the Roman Catholic Church in May of that year. I came from the parish staff of a congregation in Seattle founded in the 1940s to this one, which had been operating since the 1840s. I discovered that 100 more years of history, especially as strong a history as the Chapel of the Cross has had, made for a deeper sense of identity and of purpose. The Vestry had a clear sense of connection with the University, with the town, and with the Diocese of North Carolina.

While this was not yet the era of mission statements and there were no strategic plans, the lay leadership knew who the Chapel of the Cross was and what it stood for — a poor but prominent university-based congregation, faithful to the tradition of the Episcopal Church, but progressive in its social views, particularly notable in a South only beginning to be changed by the influx of Northerners brought in by the flourishing Research Triangle Park, the prominent universities and hospitals, and the eventual burgeoning of retirement centers.

Our two inspirational and, at the time of their construction, spacious worship spaces are jewels which proclaim that the worship of God is clearly at the heart of who we are and what we do — and that all are welcome. But an even more specific glimpse of what God calls us to can be found in the scriptural scenes portrayed in the stained glass windows over the altar in the church. On the left is a portrayal of Peter in the forbidden house of the Roman centurion, Cornelius. Both of them have had divine visions, which has led Peter to realize that "God is no respecter of persons."

The inclusion of 12 women's names on the articles of incorporation in 1842 (along with the canonically required 12 men's names); the rector's willingness in 1865 to wade into scandal by marrying the daughter of the president of the University and former governor of the state to the commanding general of the dreaded occupying Yankee troops; the rector's racially integrating the parish in 1952, two years before Brown vs. Board of Education; as well as the quiet, steady integration of gay men and women into parish life in the 1970s and 80s and beyond, and our eventual blessing of gay unions and now of gay marriages, are examples of enfleshing that identity and that mission.

The window on the right shows Paul speaking in the square to the men of Athens, the heart of the educated world at that time, about "the unknown God" inscribed on the only pedestal there without a statue on it. Paul tells them that that unknown God is Jesus of Nazareth, who died for us all and rose again from the dead. This scene speaks profoundly of our mission to preach the Gospel on the campus and in the community of our nation's oldest public university.

The Vestry and the elders also knew what the Chapel of the Cross was not: not a country club church, not one that "spent money on ourselves," but one that tended to balance the budget on staff vacancies and to pay as minimal salaries and program costs as possible, one that deferred maintenance and took pride in facilities some people liked to refer to as "chicly shabby." This austere mindset was a strength — for example, from the beginning the ABC Sale gave away every dollar raised. It also was an inhibitor of flourishing ministry — a gift of $25,000 to air condition the church in the 1950s was turned down by the rector because the parish could not raise an equal amount to give away; the result was that 30 years later we finally air conditioned the church for $125,000!

Money was certainly not plentiful in those days — as if any current leadership ever thinks it is! The annual giving campaign for 1984 was just a bit over $300,000, well more than a million dollars less than more recent years. With the exception of the Cobb Fund, a $100,000 principle whose interest could be used only for any extraordinary building expense, there were no special funds, endowments or otherwise. This apparent lack of resources along with this mindset of austerity made it significantly easier to operate in a survival mentality and more difficult to move into a full "focused mission" mode.

On the other side of the balance, the Chapel of the Cross has a strong history and a clear sense of identity and mission. There are moments of incredible boldness by its leadership, like the building of the imaginative chapel in the 1840s, unlike anything in the village at that time, which took five years to complete due to lack of money; and the quantum leap of the building of a remarkably different church in the 1920s, far bigger than was then needed, along with a parish house whose debt took 17 years to pay off. I rank our recent decision to move ahead with the recent visionary and sorely needed renovations right up there with those two turning points in the life and ministry of the Chapel of the Cross. But a significant dimension of our history, including the last three decades, has been the limits put on its mission by a lack of financial resources, both actual and perceived, and the leadership style that developed out of those limits, both actual and perceived.

The number one identified need that emerged during the rector search of 1984-85 was growth in financial stewardship. The leadership realized the limitations we were operating under and set about to correct it. I am not sure how much that desire influenced the search, however, since I was eventually chosen rector and I had no stewardship experience whatever!

But I did take that identified need seriously and proceeded to attend diocesan workshops on stewardship and to establish a stewardship committee. I also began to preach more intentionally and often about financial stewardship. A proud but painful moment was when a parishioner stood up and left the service during the sermon when she realized I was intruding upon this unmentionable subject! I also pushed for an inclusion of an outreach line item in the budget, and I pushed to increase the percentage of our outreach giving each year. If the parish cannot be perceived as mission–minded and generous by its members, how can we expect them to be in their individual giving to the parish?

Partly due to the increasing and flourishing population of the area and partly due, I hope, to our intentional stewardship efforts, we began to grow the financial resources available to us — not only in annual giving but in communal outreach giving and in establishing additional funds outside the budget. We also managed to grow the staff. The addition of a fourth clergy person, establishing positions for Christian formation and youth ministry, increasing the organist/choirmaster position to full time, and significantly upgrading our level of administration and maintenance positions were all significant steps forward.

As part of all that effort, we began to be more intentional about articulating the mission of the parish, influenced in large part by what became known in the national church and in the diocese as SWEEPS — an acronym that stood for service, worship, education, evangelism, pastoral care and stewardship — all dimensions of congregational ministry. In 1998 the wardens and I recommended to the Vestry a mission statement that articulated those aspects of our ministry. Eventually we felt that that articulation needed energizing and streamlining, and so in January of 2010 a small committee took a fresh look and proposed our current mission statement to the Vestry, who adopted it.

Several years later in 2012, a strategic planning committee charged by the rector explored the role of the Church in today's society, identifying the challenges facing the Chapel of the Cross in light of that changing perception, and putting together a strategic plan to chart the way forward. They did not rework the mission statement but suggested that that happen in a parish-wide discernment process, likely to be done now in connection with the new rector search.

I will list the five areas of engagement or components of our parish's ministry they identified: 1) Shaping Christian lives through worship, music, education and healing compassion; 2) Creating a living embodiment of Christian community with a sense of belonging, fellowship, support and engagement; 3) Inviting, welcoming and engaging all who come to the Chapel of the Cross, encouraging diversity and practicing inclusiveness and hospitality; 4) Sharing our faith, values and voice with the community, University, diocese and beyond, and translating them into faith-in-action projects; and 5) Sustaining our church by being responsible stewards of our people and staff, facilities and financial resources as we grow and evolve.

Those five areas encompass the variety and depth of the ministry God calls us to at the Chapel of the Cross. In many ways, they are not much different from what previous vestries have grasped as essential to the work of our congregation, but perhaps they are made fuller by our having been blessed in recent years with more resources to work with.

A lot has changed in 33 years. We are no longer a poor academic parish living a hand-to-mouth existence. We no longer rotate Vestry leadership among 15 to 18 individuals. We have a much wider range of leaders. We no longer defer maintenance or balance budgets on staff vacancies. Our numerous committees are now much more organized in a commission system. We finally have the building space to think much bigger in terms of possible programming and support of our many partners and other worthwhile ministries.

But a lot has also stayed the same. Jesus Christ, as scripture reminds us, "is the same, yesterday, today, and forever." We still proclaim that faith handed on to us by those who have preceded us. We still worship God in the beauty of holiness. We still seek and serve Christ in all persons and respect the dignity of every human being. Everything you do going forward must embody this balance of continuity with creative change.

I have been thinking of our new building as a model for us, an icon, if you will, of this balance. It is new, it is inspirational, it is effective, and it opens up so many new possibilities. But it also blends in with our treasured worship spaces and our other well-trod buildings. It even fits in well to the campus and surrounding environs!

When I ask people new to the area if they have seen our new building, they say, "What new building?!" It inspires, it proclaims the divine dimension, and it has a great impact on people, but it does so in context and as part of a greater whole. My hope and charge is that the creatively changing but continuous ministry of the Chapel of the Cross going forward will do the same.

In keeping with that analogy, I want to close with an address from one of our former bishops. Ascension Day, May 14, was the 90th anniversary of the dedication of our church building. These are the comments Bishop Edwin Penick made about a year earlier at the laying of the cornerstone of what was then called "the new Chapel of the Cross." I think you will hear elements of both change and continuity in it, and I hope its oratory about the continuous ministry here at the Chapel of the Cross will inspire you.

For the parishioners of the Chapel of the Cross, this service, I venture to believe, is an occasion of gratitude. For they see in this new structure not only the outward sign of growth and progress, but the expansion of their facilities for spiritual ministration to the life of the University. The happy design of the architect in incorporating the beautiful and hallowed old church building with the new in harmonious grouping typifies the desire of this congregation that in laying the cornerstone for future service, nothing whatever shall be lost from the honored traditions of the past. The Chapel of the Cross shall soon be "bringing forth out of its treasury things both new and old."

I think of the students who will worship here. For them this structure is more like home than any building on the campus. Here they will share in the precious things of family life. Here they will feel the invisible presence of loved ones, especially in the mystical fellowship of the Holy Communion. Here they will join in the refrain of favorite hymns or lift their hearts in prayer on the rich cadences of a scriptural liturgy. Under the roof that will shelter this spot they will hear echoes of boyhood and girlhood days when the voices of parents and children mingled in family devotion around the fireside altar. We stand on the spot where students will make their life decisions and dedicate themselves to idealistic service. Already, in anticipation of the crises of youth that this new church will look upon, we feel that we stand on holy ground.

Members of the University faculty will worship here. I doubt if any more earnest prayers will ascend in this house than those which rise from the hearts of these keenly sensitive, intelligent, responsible men. A sense of dependence upon God is characteristic of true leadership. Self-sufficiency belongs to shallow souls. The burden of a commission to mould the future of impressionable youth is heavy enough to crush any superficial mind that dares to teach without dependence upon that wisdom of which the fear of God is just the beginning. Scientists, historians and philosophers will kneel in humility here like the wise men of old who fell down and worshipped the infant Christ.

Finally, the Word of God will be preached in this place. And I pray that this Word may always be "rightly divided." Let it be proclaimed to every generation of students that Scripture speaks with the authority of Truth, and that the Church, her divinely commissioned interpreter, welcomes reverent investigation of her teachings from any source. Let it be said to self-conscious, inquiring dispositions that in the family of God mental and temperamental differences are tolerantly and sympathetically allowed. May the pulpit of this Church shout in the ears of thinking men and women that Truth can never be arrayed against Truth any more than a God of Holiness can contradict his own character. There is no real enmity between true science with its characteristic humility and the Christian Church with her unpretentious open mindedness. They walk together hand in hand in the joyous arduous search for Truth. I say again and again that here no essential antagonism is so much as known. Friendly, therefore, towards her neighboring lecture halls, eager to seize upon material discovery and to show its harmony with spiritual truth, quick to sympathize with honest doubt and slow, exceeding slow, to denounce or condemn, standing as a witness on this campus to the supernatural background and foreground of all life, testifying to the presence of God in creation, in history and in the hearts of men today, and certifying to all the neighborly duties involved in man's relationship to God — upon this "law of liberty," which is the spirit of Christ, as upon a cornerstone may this church be built.

Stephen Elkins-Williams grew up in a devout Roman Catholic family. At age 20, he joined the Society of Jesus and earned a degree in philosophy at Gonzaga University; he followed with a Master of Divinity degree at Regis College in Toronto. His education kindled a keen interest in Ignatian Spirituality, and he was ordained a Catholic priest in 1975.

While working in campus ministry at Seattle University, he met a young volunteer, Betsy Elkins, of Durham, North Carolina. Their friendship deepened, and after a year of discernment — exploring the possibility that God's purposes for his life were changing — Stephen left the Jesuits, and he and Betsy were married in 1978. They joined the staff of St. Stephen's, Seattle as youth ministers, and Stephen was received as an Episcopal priest in 1982. That same year, he arrived at the Chapel of the Cross in Chapel Hill, North Carolina as associate for parish ministry. In 1985, he was chosen rector from a pool of more than 100 applicants.

Chanting the *Exultet* from the altar or leading "This Little Light of Mine" with guitar for Vacation Church School, Stephen has embodied the contrasts that best characterize the Chapel of the Cross: traditional and progressive, inclusive and discerning, reverent and approachable. He has retired after 30 years, the parish's longest-serving rector.

Printed in the United States
By Bookmasters